Manchester Medieval Sources Series

series advisers Rosemary Horrox and .

This series aims to meet a growing need among students and teachers of medieval history for translations of key sources that are directly usable in students' own work. It provides texts central to medieval studies courses and focuses upon the diverse cultural and social as well as political conditions that affected the functioning of all levels of medieval society. The basic premise of the series is that translations must be accompanied by sufficient introductory and explanatory material, and each volume, therefore, includes a comprehensive guide to the sources' interpretation, including discussion of critical linguistic problems and an assessment of the most recent research on the topics being covered.

already published in the series

THE ENGLISH MANOR
c. 1200–*c.* 1500

MANCHESTER
UNIVERSITY PRESS

Medieval Sources*online*

Complementing the printed editions of the Medieval Sources series, Manchester University Press has developed a web-based learning resource which is now available on a yearly subscription basis.

Medieval Sources*online* brings quality history source material to the desktops of students and teachers and allows them open and unrestricted access throughout the entire college or university campus. Designed to be fully integrated with academic courses, this is a one-stop answer for many medieval history students, academics and researchers keeping thousands of pages of source material 'in print' over the Internet for research and teaching.

titles available now at Medieval Sourcesonline *include*

John Edwards *The Jews in Western Europe 1400–1600*

Paul Fouracre and Richard A. Gerberding *Late Merovingian France: History and hagiography 640–720*

Chris Given-Wilson *Chronicles of the Revolution 1397–1400: The reign of Richard II*

P. J. P. Goldberg *Women in England c. 1275–1525*

Janet Hamilton and Bernard Hamilton *Christian dualist heresies in the Byzantine world c. 650–c. 1450*

Rosemary Horrox *The Black Death*

Graham A. Loud and Thomas Wiedemann *The history of the tyrants of Sicily by 'Hugo Falcandus' 1153–69*

Janet L. Nelson *The Annals of St-Bertin: Ninth-century histories, volume I*

Timothy Reuter *The Annals of Fulda: Ninth-century histories, volume II*

R. N. Swanson *Catholic England: faith, religion and observance before the Reformation*

Jennifer Ward *Women of the English nobility and gentry 1066–1500*

visit the site at *www.medievalsources.co.uk* for further information and subscription prices

THE ENGLISH MANOR
c. 1200–*c.* 1500

selected sources translated and annotated by Mark Bailey

Manchester University Press
Manchester and New York

distributed exclusively in the USA by Palgrave

Published by Manchester University Press
Oxford Road, Manchester M13 9NR, UK
and Room 400, 175 Fifth Avenue, New York, NY 10010, USA
http://www.manchesteruniversitypress.co.uk

Distributed exclusively in the USA by
Palgrave, 175 Fifth Avenue, New York, NY 10010, USA

Distributed exclusively in Canada by
UBC Press, University of British Columbia, 2029 West Mall, Vancouver, BC, Canada V6T 1Z2

British Library Cataloguing-in-Publication Data
A catalogue record for this book is available from the British Library

Library of Congress Cataloging-in-Publication Data applied for

ISBN 0 7190 5228 9 *hardback*
    0 7190 5229 7 *paperback*

First published 2002

10 09 08 07 06 05 04 03 02   10 9 8 7 6 5 4 3 2 1

Typeset in Monotype Bell
by Koinonia Ltd, Manchester
Printed in Great Britain
by Bell & Bain Ltd, Glasgow

For my children, Katie and Harry

without whom this book would have been completed five years ago

CONTENTS

PREFACE AND ACKNOWLEDGEMENTS

The aim of this book is to provide a broad introduction to the structure and composition of the English manor between c. 1200 and c. 1500 and to serve as a user's guide to its principal records. Such a volume is long overdue for two main reasons. First, all standard treatments of the rural economy and society of medieval England draw extensively upon manorial sources, but offer limited information about the documents themselves. Second, manorial records survive in abundance, and are readily accessible at repositories across the country, but their structure and terminology can appear daunting and arcane to the student or local historian who approaches them for the first, and often the second and third, time. Two brief and extremely useful pamphlets on manorial records already exist,[1] but this book goes further by offering both a detailed commentary on the form, structure and evolution of these sources in the Middle Ages and, in particular, translations of selected documents to illustrate their main features.

The book proceeds from the assumption that manorial records are best understood and utilised as an historical source by placing them firmly within their institutional context. It therefore begins with a brief discussion of the nature and composition of the manor, its variety and flexibility, and its origins and development through the Middle Ages. The reader is then introduced to the most common and important categories of manorial documents: surveys, extents, inventories, rentals, custumals, leases, accounts and court rolls. Each category of document is considered in turn, beginning with a broad discussion of its layout, form, usage, administrative context, changes over time and its potential as an historical source. Two or three full examples of each category of document are then provided in translation, followed by shorter extracts which have been selected either to illustrate particular historical themes or to exemplify certain interesting, commonly occurring, or complex features.

The sheer abundance of surviving manorial sources has inevitably created some difficulty in selecting material for inclusion. As a rule of thumb, this volume draws largely upon records that emanated from the seigneurial administration of manors, and makes little use of royal records, such as the Hundred Rolls of the 1270s and the *Quo Warranto* proceedings of the 1280s, which contain much manorial information. An attempt has also been made to select documents from a wide geographical area: only the extreme south- and

---

1 P. D. A. Harvey, *Manorial records*, British Records Association, 5 2nd edn (2000), and M. Ellis, *Using manorial records*, Public Record Office, London, Guide to Sources, 6 (1994). More detailed discussion (in a less accessible volume) is provided in P. D. A. Harvey, ed., *Manorial records of Cuxham, Oxfordshire, c. 1200–1359*, Oxfordshire Record Society, 50 (1976), pp. 72–8.

north-western areas of England are not represented. I have also included some documents that already exist in print, not least because this policy permits the reader to consult the original Latin and to discover more about the local administrative context of the document. Not surprisingly, the choice of unpublished sources is influenced by my own teaching and research interests.

By concentrating on the written documents generated by a particular institution, this book self-consciously adopts a sources-and-themes approach to its subject. It had been my intention from the outset to include many extracts from each type of document in order to illuminate and explore the manifold historical themes that emerge from manorial sources, but it quickly became apparent that such an approach would require an opus of three or four volumes. The book's focus is consciously maintained upon presenting, illustrating and explaining the basic range of manorial documents rather than upon the many varied and interesting historical themes that they elucidate. The latter are highlighted wherever possible through the provision of an extended preamble to each edited and translated document, and through a select bibliography.

The translations of manorial documents that appear in this book are largely my own, so that I have tried wherever possible to recheck the original Latin when working from documents already published and translated into English. Wherever an entry confused or defeated me, I have offered both a translation and the offending Latin bracketed and in italics. Obscure Middle English and medieval Latin words are also presented in italics. The spelling of place names has been modernised where their identification is secure, including locative surnames, although field names and localities have been left in the original Middle English. Identifiable occupational surnames have also been modernised.

Square brackets [ ] in the text indicate an editorial insertion designed to clarify or explain an original entry. The omission of text for editorial purposes is signified by bracketed spaced dots [...], and a damaged or illegible manuscript by spaced ... dots. Where dates in the original documents are given in feast days and regnal years, I have provided a conversion to the modern calendar in square brackets. The only feast days exempted from this rule are Christmas (25 December) and moveable feasts in an unknown year. Hence, 'he must plough the land every Easter' passes without editorial comment, but 'he received expenses for attending at Easter in the fourth year of the reign of Edward III' is followed by [8 April 1330].

A detailed glossary has been provided at the rear of the book. It includes words that will be unfamiliar to the modern reader, but which recur in medieval manorial records. Any obscure Middle English words appearing in italics in the text are not included in the glossary. Where possible, they are explained either in the introductory sections to the various categories of document or in footnotes to the text, as are unusual technical terms.

The coinage used in medieval England was pounds (£), shillings (s.) and pennies (d.): there were 12 pennies to a shilling and 20 shillings to a pound. Ten shillings is therefore equivalent to 50 pence, although price inflation since the medieval centuries renders such comparisons meaningless: for example, an unskilled labourer received about 10d. for a five-day week in the fourteenth century. The most common unit of area was the acre (0.4 hectare), comprising four roods. The rood itself comprised 40 perches. These terms appear in the glossary.

My awareness of the need for a book of this kind was raised in the early 1980s, when as a Ph.D. student I grappled with manorial records with youthful exuberance and ignorance. That awareness was heightened in the early 1990s when, as a lecturer in local history, I recognised that the enthusiasm of students for medieval studies was frustrated by their unfamiliarity with the format, content and changing nature of the source material. If this book meets its objective in providing an accessible and detailed guide to the form and structure of manorial documents, its success can be largely attributed to the contribution of numerous students who, over the past ten years, have endured various courses on the subject. In particular, the archivists drawn together by the Hertfordshire Record Office, local historians studying with the University of Cambridge's Board of Continuing Education, the Medieval Studies Summer School at Cambridge University, and postgraduates on the university's M.Phil. in Medieval History. Their disquieting questions and comments have shaped and structured this book more than they might imagine.

I first encountered manorial sources in 1981, when Dick Lomas of Durham University ran weekly undergraduate classes on medieval rural England. I recall those sessions with a sureness and clarity that is curiously lacking with my other undergraduate activities. This early fascination quickly developed into a deeper understanding through the wisdom and expertise of the remarkable Dorothy Owen of Cambridge University, who seemed to understand my shortcomings as well as she understood the documents. The research for my Ph.D. thesis drew exclusively upon manorial records, and my competence in using them increased through the guidance of David Dymond, John Hatcher and Margaret Statham, who smiled patiently and offered sound advice whenever (frequently) I pestered them with another query.

Suggestions or transcripts of documents for inclusion in this book were presented by Richard Allnutt, Paul Harvey, Rosemary Hoppitt, Ray Lock, Richard Smith and David Stone. The idea behind Figure 1 (p. xiv) was first developed by David Dymond, who also offered comments on early drafts of each chapter. I have learned much from his deep knowledge of manorial sources across an unusually broad chronological span, and he has consistently, but not too persistently, encouraged me to undertake and complete this work. My ambition to write it may never have been fulfilled but for Rosemary Horrox's suggestion that the project was appropriate for the *Manchester Medieval Sources* series, and her editorial interventions have been characteristically tactful, shrewd and beneficial. Indeed, her meticulous and wide scholarship has saved me from a number of petty errors and inconsistencies. Duncan Bythell and David Stone have also contributed valuable improvements to the text, together with Paul Harvey, whose own work on manorial records is seminal and hugely influential (an influence which is readily apparent in the following pages). To all of these, I am extremely grateful and indebted, although they are not responsible for my subsequent actions.

I am also very grateful to the following public bodies and societies for their permission to use documents either in their possession or from their publications: Bedfordshire and Luton Archives and Records Service; the Public Record Office, Kew; the British Library; Essex Record Office; Hertfordshire Archives and Local Studies; the Keeper of the Ely Diocesan Records, Cambridge University Library; the Keeper of the Muniments, Westminster Abbey; Suffolk Record Office, Bury St Edmunds branch; Suffolk Record Office, Ipswich branch; Bedfordshire Historical Record Society; the Dugdale Society; Lancashire and Cheshire Antiquarian Society; Northamptonshire Record Society; the Selden Society; Suffolk Records Society; the Surtees Society; Sussex Record Society; and Yorkshire Archaeological Society. Any failure to acknowledge or acquire due permission will be happily rectified in the second edition of this volume. In my previous existence as a professional historian, the Board of Continuing Education, University of Cambridge; Gonville and Caius College, Cambridge, and Corpus Christi College, Cambridge, all provided me with the time and resources to undertake this work.

This book has taken five years longer to complete than anticipated, during which time my mind has broadened almost as much as my body. It spans two career shifts and the birth of as many children, Katie and Harry. In our busy and changing lives, Julie, my wife, has accepted stoically my unconventional and periodic desire to disappear into the world of manorial records, while Katie and Harry have been blissfully unaware that their compulsory day trips to castles, abbeys, and obscure landscapes signify an obsessive father who moonlights as a medieval historian. The dedication of this book is sincere, and I would not want it any other way.

Leeds Grammar School

THE MEDIEVAL MANOR
An institutional and topographical analysis

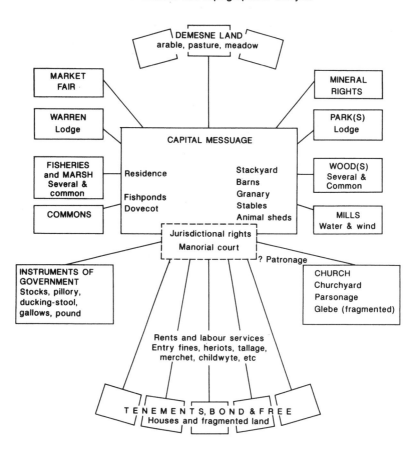

with acknowledgements to David Dymond

Figure 1

I: THE COMPOSITION AND ORIGINS
OF THE MANOR

Introduction

In 1383 at Newton Aycliffe (Co. Durham) William Colson, John de
Redworth and five other men were singled out in the manor court to
explain why they had not provided the authorities with the names of
those who had continued to stage football games, in direct contravention of a recent warning that any participation in this activity
would incur a fine of 20 shillings. At first they refused, and during the
tense stand off Alicia de Redworth, John's wife, repeatedly disrupted
the proceedings by heckling the steward of the court. Reluctantly,
Colson and de Redworth then named eighteen footballers: although
too old to play themselves, some of the players were members of their
households. On being identified as a participant, Thomas Tailor
offered the court his blunt opinion of the whole business, and refused
to shut up when so ordered by the steward.[1]

An official of another manor in County Durham, responsible for the
tenants of Ricknall, was threatened with dismissal in 1355 if he failed
to distrain those who had simply left their holdings in the wake of the
Black Death to occupy other lands elsewhere in the county. The
troubled official had reported earlier in the year that many tenants of
Ricknall were leaving because a local troublemaker named William
Standupryght was so argumentative and malicious that no one would
live near him: a medieval neighbour-from-hell. The landlord obviously
regarded this as a feeble excuse from his official, although by 1356
William had left Ricknall, perhaps because there was no one left with
whom to quarrel.[2]

At the risk of depicting County Durham as an unruly place, these two
examples provide some sense of the potential of manorial sources to
the medieval historian. They illustrate that the manor touched and
influenced the lives of common people in the Middle Ages, probably

1 W. H. Longstaffe, ed., *Halmota prioratus Dunelmensis: containing extracts from the halmote
court of the prior and convent of Durham 1296–1384*, Surtees Society, 82 (1889), p. 180.

2 R. H. Britnell, 'Feudal reaction after the Black Death in the Palatinate of Durham',
Past and Present, 128 (1990), 40.

more than any other secular institution. Thus an understanding of the structure and workings of the manor is essential to studying the economic, social and cultural history of late-medieval England. As an institution, it was central to the organisation of agrarian life in the Middle Ages and beyond. Through the manor, land tenures, rents and many land transactions were administered and recorded, and a wide range of agricultural resources was controlled and exploited. As the medium through which lordship was exercised on the ground, it was also central to the organisation of social relations in the Middle Ages. Through the manor, the personal ties, services and obligations which bound a medieval peasant to a lord were defined and enforced, communal by-laws were agreed and implemented, and many economic and social dealings with neighbours and family were regulated and formalised.

The importance of the manor in English local administration explains its significance to medieval historians, and is further enhanced by the survival of a vast corpus of manorial documents. Only a few manorial sources date from the eleventh and twelfth centuries, but thousands have survived from the period c. 1250 to c. 1500. The richness, detail and uniformity of late-medieval English manorial documents are extraordinary, and are unparalleled for this period anywhere in the world. Their quality was regarded with awe by one seventeenth-century commentator, who remarked that the material contained therein 'is so exact ... that it cannot but give us cause almost of wonder'.[3] Thousands of these local documents have survived, and most are readily accessible in record offices and university libraries throughout the country.[4]

The characteristics of the medieval manor

Providing a watertight definition of 'the manor' between c. 1200 and c. 1500 is almost impossible, because its form was fluid and its characteristics were varied: in the words of Barbara Harvey, the manor is a genus with many species.[5] The word derives from the Latin *manerium*,

3 Quoted from C. Dyer, 'Documentary evidence', in G. Astill and A. Grant, eds, *The countryside of medieval England* (Oxford, 1988), p. 13. Z. Razi and R. M. Smith, eds, *Medieval society and the manor court* (Oxford, 1996), p. 38.

4 The Historical Manuscripts Commission holds a register of all known manorial documents at its office in Quality Court, Chancery Lane, London, WC2A 1HP. Web site: http://www.hmc.gov.uk

5 B. F. Harvey, 'The life of the manor', in A. Williams and R. Erskine, eds, *Domesday Book Studies* (1987), p. 39.

meaning a residence, but the medieval manor was more than just a seigneurial dwelling.[6] The manor was essentially a territorial unit of lordship which also served as the basic unit of seigneurial estate administration. Some of the land on the manor, known as the demesne, was allocated for the lord's own use, which could either be leased by the lord to a willing tenant for an annual rent or directly exploited as a 'home farm' to provision the lord's household or to produce crops for sale. Other land was allocated to a dependent peasantry, who rendered various rents and services to the lord for the privilege. The manor also comprised other economic resources, which might include fisheries, mills and mineral rights.

It would be wrong, however, to assume that the manor was simply a territorial unit comprised of manor house, land and other economic resources. A lord also enjoyed a 'package' of customary and legal rights over the manorial land and resources. Hence the manorial peasantry was bound to the manor and its lord by a range of personal ties and obligations, and not merely by the basic rent rendered for its land. Similarly, an economic resource such as the manorial mill was also linked to a seigneurial privilege that compelled certain peasants to grind their corn there. These manorial rights could ultimately be defended in the central law courts of medieval England, but were most commonly articulated and exercised in the lord's own, private, 'manor' court.

A summary of the possible range of economic and legal components of the manor between c. 1200 and 1500 is depicted schematically in Figure 1 (p. xiv), whose purpose is to convey the internal structures of the manor clearly and effectively. Inevitably, this can only be achieved by over-simplification: it hardly needs emphasising that not every manor contained all the rights and resources identified here, and that the extent of, and balance between, the individual components varied enormously from manor to manor.

As indicated in Figure 1, the capital messuage comprised an enclosed area containing the seigneurial residential complex, gardens, stables and the various agricultural outbuildings necessary to run the demesne as a working farm. It was unlikely to be larger than a few acres. In the 1330s the capital messuage of Glastonbury abbey's manor of Shapwick

6 F. W. Maitland, *Domesday Book and beyond: three essays in the early history of England* (Cambridge, 1897), pp. 107–10. For other introductions to the manor, see F. Pollock and F. W. Maitland, *The history of English law before the time of Edward I*, 2nd edn (Cambridge, 1911), pp. 594–633; P. Vinogradoff, *The growth of the manor* (1911).

(Somerset) covered 7½ acres of land, and included a hall, pantry, buttery, larder, abbot's room, monks' room, clerk's room, wine and ale cellars, a large garden, a small garden, two dovecotes, a byre, barn and granary, and was designed to serve as the abbey's administrative centre for a small group of proximate manors. The capital messuage at High Ercall (Shropshire) in 1424 was moated and contained a three-storey gatehouse, a defensive stone tower, and various residential and agricultural buildings.[7]

The appearance and layout of the manor house itself varied, depending on the status of the lord to whom it belonged and whether the lord was resident. Many manor houses were rebuilt in the twelfth and thirteenth centuries, with greater emphasis placed on display. The majority served as primary residences to lords of relatively humble status, and thus many were rather modest buildings constructed to uniform plans. On the estate of a great lord, the manor house might have been a substantial fortified residence, regularly used by the seigneurial household. Yet many of the manors held by wealthier lords were non-residential, and so the manor house was often a functional building used as temporary accommodation by the lord's administrators, as at Shapwick.

Most of the other manorial components identified in Figure 1 are considered in greater detail elsewhere in this book. Only three features merit particular comment at this stage. First, the physical layout of the demesne and peasant arable lands varied according to the layout of local field systems. For example, both demesne and peasant lands were scattered in small, unenclosed, parcels throughout an open, commonfield, system in many parts of midland England, whereas the demesne arable often lay in contiguous, consolidated and enclosed parcels in central areas of East Anglia, where enclosures were not uncommonly interspersed with open fields. Similarly, large areas of demesne land in parts of northern England lay in detached blocks called berewicks.[8]

Second, the point that the medieval manor comprised both physical and jurisdictional elements is nicely illustrated by the example of the 'warren', which was both an agricultural resource and a legal right. A

7 M. G. Thompson, 'The Polden hill manors of Glastonbury abbey: land and people *c.* 1260–1351' (Ph.D. thesis, University of Leicester, 1997), p. 42; *Victoria County History* [hereafter *VCH*] *of Shropshire, vol.* 4 (London, 1989), p. 85.

8 Maitland, *Domesday Book*, p. 115.

rabbit warren was a place for breeding and exploiting rabbits for profit, but 'warren' also refers to the right of free warren, a legal franchise granted by the Crown which bestowed upon the holder the monopolistic right to kill small game within a defined local territory. Medieval peasants did not own or exploit rabbit warrens, except illegally, and the warren was therefore a status symbol and privilege as well as an economic resource.

Third, many parish churches had originated as the private churches of local lords, so that 'church and manor kept company from the start'.[9] Elements of this early association are still discernible on some late-medieval manors where the right to appoint the rector of the parish church (known as the patronage or advowson) was still enjoyed by some manorial lords, and the exercise of this right could carry important consequences for the running of both the parish church and manor. Where an ecclesiastical institution was lord of the manor, it might appoint itself as the rector of the church and then hire a vicar to perform the necessary pastoral duties within the parish on its behalf. This process of 'appropriation' enabled the ecclesiastical body to acquire the rectorial income of the parish church for its own use, which included the potentially lucrative glebe lands and tithes. Hence Bury St Edmunds abbey appointed itself rector after it had been granted the former royal manor of Mildenhall, which carried the patronage of the parish church. The abbey's manorial records for Mildenhall (Suffolk) subsequently include income from the lease of the glebe land and receipts from tithes. In contrast, Westminster abbey often removed the distinction between Church and manorial lands by absorbing the glebe of impropriated rectories into its demesne lands.[10] Some parish churches were so handsomely endowed with land, including numerous tenants, that their rectories were effectively run as small manors [23].

The size and composition of medieval manors

It is popularly assumed that the 'classic' medieval manor was largely conterminous with the village, possessed a large demesne (say, in excess of 400 arable acres), and contained a high proportion of unfree

9 R. Morris, *Churches in the landscape* (1989), p. 249.

10 British Museum, Add. Rolls 53116, 53134; B. F. Harvey, *Westminster abbey and its estates in the Middle Ages* (Oxford, 1977), p. 127 n. 2.

peasants rendering heavy labour-services. For example, the abbot of Bury St Edmunds possessed a classic manor at Coney Weston (Suffolk), comprising in 1279 a capital messuage, 340 acres of demesne arable, 58 acres of demesne pasture, 1 acre of demesne meadow, 8 acres of demesne woodland, 2 acres of turbary (marsh with rights to cut peat), a windmill, the advowson of the church and various other rights. His unfree peasants held 430 acres of arable land, 40 acres of heath, 5 acres of marsh, and greatly outnumbered the freemen who held 69 acres of arable and 2 roods of marsh.[11]

Classic manors such as Coney Weston are identifiable across late-medieval England, but they were nowhere near as commonplace as popularly believed. In reality, there was much variation in the form, size and composition of manors. Compare Coney Weston with the manor of Hillhall in Holkham (Norfolk), which comprised a capital messuage and 14 acres of demesne arable, a windmill, 3 foldcourses (the right to keep sheep over designated land), a market, a fair, and 143 acres held by unfree tenants and 179 acres held by free tenants; or the manor of Hacun, in the same vill, which had simply a messuage and 30 acres of demesne, a foldcourse, 20 acres held by unfree peasants and 115 acres by free.[12] Some manorial holdings in northern England possessed satellite territories, which were physically detached from the manorial core, held by free peasants who were linked to the manor by relatively weak jurisdictional ties.[13]

The large, classic, manor is decidedly atypical of late-medieval manorial forms, and the majority of manors were small to medium-sized properties covering less than six square miles. E. A. Kosminsky's analysis of the Hundred Rolls (compiled in the late 1270s) reveals that 65 per cent of documented manors possessed less than a combined total of 500 acres of demesne and tenant arable land.[14] It follows from this revelation that most villages embraced a number of manors, so that few medieval villages, parishes or vills were conterminous with

---

11 F. W. Hervey, ed., *The Pinchbeck Register*, 2 vols (Brighton, 1925), II, pp. 211–3.

12 W. Hassall and J. Beauroy, eds, *Lordship and landscape in Norfolk 1250–1350: the early records of Holkham* (Oxford, 1993), pp. 31, 36.

13 See E. Miller and J. Hatcher, *Medieval England: rural society and economic change 1086–1348* (1978), pp. 21, 187.

14 E. A. Kosminsky, *Studies in the agrarian history of England in the thirteenth century* (Oxford, 1956), pp. 68–151, for a comprehensive discussion of manorial variations in late thirteenth-century England. See also Miller and Hatcher, *Medieval England*, pp. 9–22 and 184–8.

one manor of the same name.[15] Of course, it is possible to find some vills which were almost entirely dominated by one large manor, particularly in the central midlands, but they were uncommon. In many parts of England each village contained more than one manor, and Kosminsky reckoned that at least 90 per cent of the Cambridgeshire villages covered by extant Hundred Rolls fell into this category.[16] The situation was different again in many areas of northern England, where it was common for a number of sizeable and separate settlements to lie within one vast manor. The manor of Wakefield (Yorkshire) covered 150 square miles and contained settlements such as Sandal, Osset, Holne, Stanley and Sourby, while the manor of Chester (Co. Durham) contained Chester (le-Street) itself, Ryton, Whickham, Whitburn, Cleadon, Newton, Plawsworth, Bolden, Urpeth, Gateshead and Framwellgate.[17]

Further variations were found in the composition of the three core manorial components of demesne land, free land and unfree land. Many Shropshire manors contained demesnes with little or no arable land, but considerable quantities of pasture and highly valued meadow. No unfree land was attached to Nicholas de Gedding's manor in Brockley (Suffolk) in the 1270s, which comprised merely a messuage, 20 acres of demesne arable and seven freemen.[18] In sum, it is possible to find manors with little or no demesne land, with few or no unfree peasants, with exclusively freemen, and so on.[19] Such variations had significant implications for the social relations between lord and peasants on the manor: a powerful lord with a large number of unfree peasants

15 The broad differences between the manor, vill, village and parish are worth sketching at this point. The parish is the basic unit of ecclesiastical administration, the vill is the basic unit of civil administration, the manor the basic unit of estate administration, and 'village' refers to a particular form of settlement (as opposed to, say, 'hamlet'). For example, the name Rushden (Hertfordshire) was given to a medieval parish, a medieval vill, a medieval settlement and a medieval manor. It is convenient to use the terms 'village', 'vill', 'manor' and 'parish' interchangeably under such circumstances, but strictly speaking this is incorrect: as we have seen, these labels relate to different areas of jurisdiction, and their physical boundaries were often different. Thus, although the boundaries of the medieval parish and vill of Rushden were exactly conterminous, a number of other manors and settlements, with different names, lay within them.

16 Kosminsky, *Studies in agrarian history*, p. 73.

17 Longstaffe, *Halmota*, p. viii.

18 *VCH Shropshire*, 4, p. 86.

19 Maitland, *Domesday Book*, pp. 111–19; S. R. Rigby, *English society in the later Middle Ages: class, status and gender* (1995), pp. 34–44.

generally meant a more onerous manorial regime than a lower-status lord with a high proportion of free peasants.

Although the manor was infinitely varied in medieval England, it is possible for historians to identify broad regional and sub-regional distinctions in manorial characteristics. A key element in determining the local character of manorial organisation is the type of lordship, and the demands it made upon the peasantry. The king possessed many large manors but was a relatively undemanding lord, whereas the older ecclesiastical institutions held large manors and maintained a firm grip over a predominantly servile peasantry. Lay lords, especially the gentry, tended to hold smaller manors and made fewer demands on their peasants.[20] Hence historians dub those areas where large, classic, manors predominated as 'heavily manorialised': for example, many regions of southern-central and midland England, where estates held by the greater and more conservative landlords, such as Benedictine monasteries, predominated. In contrast, 'lightly manorialised' areas are those where smaller manors, associated with gentry lordship and a mainly free peasantry, prevailed: for example, in many areas of south-western and eastern England, and in the north where many manors covered vast territory, but whose tenantry was relatively free of servile burdens.

The explanations for these variations in manorialism remain elusive. However, it is apparent that regional differences in demographic pressure, patterns of colonisation, the nature of local lordship and commercial opportunities were strong influences. Manorial structure tended to be highly complex and fluid in places where colonisation occurred later, population pressure was high or rising rapidly, commercial pressures were greatest, and lordship was relatively weak or low-status.[21] In contrast, areas that had been long settled by c. 1100, and dominated by powerful and conservative lordship, tended to be characterised by a less fluid and fragmented manorial structure. Of particular interest to historians are the implications of these varied manorial structures for the economic and social characteristics of such places. In heavily manorialised areas, settlement patterns tended to be nucleated, farming arrangements were strongly dictated by communal

20 C. Lewis, C. C. Dyer and P. Mitchell-Fox, *Village, hamlet and field: changing medieval settlements in central England* (Manchester, 1997), pp. 185–90.

21 See B. M. S. Campbell, 'The complexity of manorial structure in medieval Norfolk: a case study', *Norfolk Archaeology*, 39 (1986), 225–52.

regulations, and social relations were, perhaps, more controlled, deferential and community-centred. In areas of weak lordship and manorialism, communal controls over agriculture were minimal, settlement patterns dispersed, and social relations perhaps more egalitarian and individualistic. Identifying and explaining such trends represents a formidable challenge.

The marked variety in manorial size and composition in the later Middle Ages, and the importance of location and lordship in influencing such variations, means that manors should not be regarded as static and immutable entities. They could change in size and composition over time, and it is common to discover large manors being broken up into smaller, but still discrete, manorial units, and not uncommon to find other manors being consolidated or enlarged. For example, the Domesday Book (1086) records three manors in the vill of Hanbury (Worcestershire), one of which was a classic manor held by the bishop of Worcester. Yet by 1300 nine manors existed there, carved out of previously under-exploited areas of woodland within the original manor by colonising freemen and enterprising lesser gentry.[22] The royal manor of Havering (Essex), which covered 16,000 acres, also suffered gradual fragmentation. In the mid-twelfth century a new manor was carved out with royal permission for Hornchurch priory, but around twenty more manors were created without formal approval. In the absence of direct and firm control by the Crown, the relatively free and autonomous peasantry of Havering enjoyed the freedom to participate in an active land market, which enabled a few individuals to construct holdings well in excess of 100 acres and to run them as separate manors.[23]

The fusion of manorial units can also be readily illustrated, and, indeed, F. W. Maitland reminds us that the Normans tried to simplify and consolidate manorial holdings in the period between the Conquest and the compilation of the Domesday Book.[24] The greater medieval landlords had always been prepared to make piecemeal additions to

22 C. C. Dyer, *Hanbury. Settlement and society in a wooded landscape*, Leicester Occasional Papers in English Local History, 4th series, 4 (1991), pp. 6–8 and 28–9.

23 M. K. McIntosh, *Autonomy and community: the royal manor of Havering 1200–1550* (Cambridge, 1986), pp. 145–6. See also Miller and Hatcher, *Medieval England*, p. 209.

24 Maitland, *Domesday Book*, p. 149; Lewis *et al.*, *Village, hamlet and field*, pp. 108–11. R. Faith, *The English peasantry and the growth of lordship* (Leicester, 1997), pp. 199–200, considers the reorganisation of demesnes around the time of the Norman Conquest.

their main manors if it suited them, such as when the bishop of Worcester enlarged his manor at Alveston (Warwickshire) by the absorption of tenant land.[25] Elsewhere, opportunist landlords sometimes sought to purchase contiguous manors and then run them as a single unit. The Lestrange family had acquired three of the four manors in Hunstanton (Norfolk) by the end of the fifteenth century and absorbed them into one unit, and in 1539 the lay lord of Easthall manor in Culford (Suffolk) bought the main manor upon the dissolution of Bury St Edmunds abbey.[26]

The example of Havering demonstrates graphically that the pressure to fragment manorial units came from below as well as above. This pressure was often so sustained that it seems large manors only remained intact if their landlord was sufficiently committed and powerful to ensure their survival. On occasion, major landlords carved out smaller manors from bigger units as a deliberate act of estate policy, but for the most part fragmentation occurred as a consequence of piecemeal fission. Of course, sufficient land had to be available in order to achieve this, either through a highly active land market or reserves of colonisable land, and – crucially – the established lord had to 'sanction' such activities in the sense of not preventing them. Havering had all the necessary ingredients: land for colonisation, an active land market, a free tenantry and a non-resident lord with a light touch. Under such circumstances, a few enterprising freemen could nibble away at pieces of demesne land and acquire other tenant land to create, de facto, a new manorial holding. Richard Neel acquired a smallholding in Holkham (Norfolk) and then extended it between 1314 and 1345 by the aggressive purchase of 112 pieces of land to create a new manor in the vill.[27] Some of the many isolated 'halls' occupying moated sites in Essex, Norfolk and Suffolk originated as the capital messuages of small medieval manors, and are monuments to the acquisitive efforts of dozens of Richard Neels.

25 C. C. Dyer, *Lords and peasants in a changing society: the estates of the bishopric of Worcester 680–1500* (Cambridge, 1980), p. 45.

26 C. Oestman, *Lordship and community: the Lestrange family and the village of Hunstanton, Norfolk, in the first half of the sixteenth century* (Woodbridge, 1994), p. 29; M. Bailey, *A marginal economy? East Anglian Breckland in the later Middle Ages* (Cambridge, 1989), p. 52.

27 Hassell and Beauroy, *Holkham*, pp. 12, 44–6.

Origins and development of the manor

So far, our concern has been to sketch the main features of the medieval manor between *c.* 1200 and *c.* 1500, but in this section we consider briefly its origins before 1200 and its evolution thereafter. The word *manerium* first appears in common usage during the eleventh century, although units of lordship which we would recognise as manors are evident at least two centuries earlier.[28] The origins of the manor are obscure, because they date from the mid- to late Anglo-Saxon period when documentary evidence is slight. This obscurity fanned the flames of a famous debate on the subject at the end of the nineteenth century between Maitland and Vinogradoff.[29] Modern scholarship, however, is much closer to a consensus on the general processes behind the emergence of the manor than those pioneering historical heavyweights.

Prior to the eighth century, land was essentially held as a series of large unbroken territories in 'chiefdoms' or by tribal leaders.[30] At this time no proper concept of the private ownership of land existed. However, during the eighth and ninth centuries these substantial territories were either handed over intact to major churches or gradually broken up into small blocks as grants to nobles. This process had the dual benefit of cementing allegiances and loyalty, and enabling the emerging military and ecclesiastical aristocracy to sustain itself in an appropriate lifestyle. Land was thus increasingly 'used in the negotiation and maintenance of the relationships whereby men achieved or sustained eminence'.[31] In effect, a new landholding group of superior lords was being created which enjoyed increasingly secure rights over its land. However, the kings of the various Anglo-Saxon kingdoms still retained some important rights over the alienated land, such as the right to charge certain dues when the lands passed to heirs and the right to demand certain military and public services.

---

28 Harvey, 'Life of the manor', p. 39.

29 Usefully summarised in H. R. Loyn, *Anglo-Saxon England and the Norman Conquest* (1962), pp. 163–7; and T. H. Aston, 'The origins of the manor in England', and 'A Postscript', in Aston, P. R. Coss, C. Dyer, and J. Thirsk, eds, *Social relations and ideas: essays in honour of R. H. Hilton* (Cambridge, 1983), pp. 1–43.

30 P. Stafford, *The East Midlands* (Leicester, 1985), pp. 29–39; Faith, *English peasantry*, pp. 11–4.

31 J. Hudson, *The formation of the English common law* (Harlow, 1996), p. 87.

The fragmentation of larger territories and estates into smaller land-holding units accelerated after the ninth century. One reason for this continuing process of fission was the changing nature of both political power and notions of land ownership. Because the emerging aristo-cratic elite owed military allegiance to the king, its members required the support of a group of lesser warriors (effectively thegns or knights) in order to serve that allegiance and assert their own status. One option was to maintain a large, permanent and itinerant household of dependent thegns, but the preferred option for aristocrats was to take chunks of their own lands and grant them to these lesser lords: once again, this process cemented the bond of dependency and loyalty between the aristocrat and the lesser lord, and provided the latter with independent means.[32] Hence in the ninth and tenth centuries successive bishops of Worcester systematically broke down parts of their compact estates in the west Midlands to create smaller units of between one to six hides for the use of the bishopric's thegns. Initially these landed grants were intended as long-term leases, but the thegns and their families soon acquired permanent rights to inherit and alienate the land.[33] Similarly, an estate at Fawsley (Northamptonshire) was split into four smaller units between 944 and 1023, of which two became further fragmented by 1086.[34]

Other influences in the tenth and eleventh centuries further accelerated the breakup of the old 'multiple' estates and the creation of an expanding group of landholding lords below the level of the aristocracy. Population growth swelled the number of peasants, who in turn were able to support more units of lordship; the development of the cash nexus and commodity exchange encouraged the sale, purchase and transfer of land; and the forces of inheritance divided and split estates. The outcome of these processes was known as *subinfeudation*, and was accompanied by the development of clearer notions of the private ownership of land. The old territories 'seem often to have fragmented along natural fault lines, giving each of their component parts a rough balance of resources', and as the process intensified so boundaries were defined with increasing precision. The emergence of land charters in the late Anglo-Saxon period reflects the desire both to record bounds more carefully and to protect the private

32 Loyn, *Anglo-Saxon England*, pp. 195–9; Faith, *English peasantry*, pp. 155–9.
33 Dyer, *Lords and peasants*, pp. 12–21.
34 Stafford, *East Midlands*, pp. 34–9.

ownership of acquired (as opposed to inherited) land.[35] By the early twelfth century such land had acquired security of tenure, heritability and alienability.[36]

Between the eighth and the twelfth centuries, therefore, the forces of fission produced both a more complex seigneurial landholding structure and a preponderance of localised lordships. The process of fragmentation was especially evident in the east of England, where a lively land market existed based on cash exchange: 'vills were divided between several lords in dizzying confusion ... in this fluid and fissiparous society'.[37] These lesser lords – the 'gentry' of Anglo-Saxon England – resided on their local lordships as early as the ninth century, building a defensive site and church as a mark of their status. Indeed, 'without his defensible seigneurial centre, with its hall large enough to house under its roof his household and his followers, we could not recognise the medieval seigneur, and he certainly would not have been able to recognise himself'.[38] Thus the old 'estates' structure of the mid-Anglo-Saxon period was gradually broken into many small pieces, and these pieces came to be known as manors. Historians now recognise this move to local lordship between the ninth and thirteenth centuries as a profound development in the social and economic history of England because it is strongly associated with the emergence of fundamental elements in religious and agrarian life: parish churches, nucleated villages and common-field systems.

The Domesday Book photographs in 1086 the emergence of manifold localised lordships, and reveals a large number of manorial holdings of different sizes grouped into scattered estates under different ownership. For example, the archbishop of Canterbury held in excess of twenty large demesne manors spread across five counties, which were held and exploited directly, and many other smaller holdings and manors across south-east England held from him by subinfeudated lords and sub-tenants on a variety of terms and tenures.[39] At the other end of the seigneurial landholding scale, a humble lord named Berard

---

35 Faith, *English peasantry*, pp. 154, 159–61.

36 Hudson, *Common law*, p. 91.

37 Quoted from Faith, *English peasantry*, p. 155; T. Williamson, *The origins of Norfolk* (Manchester, 1995), pp. 121–5.

38 Faith, *English peasantry*, pp. 163–4.

39 F. R. H. Du Boulay, *The lordship of Canterbury: an essay on medieval society* (1966), map 3.

held and resided on one small manor in Whatfield (Suffolk).[40] The
seigneurial landholding structure had now acquired a kaleidoscopic
complexity, in which the outlines of the original pattern of large estate
territories are difficult to discern.

One consequence of the Norman Conquest of England was a more
rigorous classification of landholding, and a changing perception of
the way in which land was held.[41] It was established more formally
that most lands were held heritably in return for secular, often military,
service, and such lands are said to be held *in fee*. In contrast, ecclesiastical institutions held some land *in alms*, i.e. for religious service. An
example of this toughening of landholding terms is the manner in
which William the Conqueror required his tenants-in-chief (those
holding land directly from the king) to supply specified quotas of
equipped fighting knights for military service as required.[42] The quota
fixed upon the archbishopric of Canterbury in 1070 was sixty knights,
whereupon archbishop Lanfranc immediately subinfeudated more land
from his estate to create a sufficient number of dependent knights to
meet this military obligation. By 1086 nearly 17 per cent of the Canterbury estates (both monastic and episcopal) were held by dependent
knights.[43] This general principle underpins the concept of a 'knight's
fee', whereby a man held land in trust ('enfeoffed') from his superior
lord on the understanding that he should produce one knight for
military service when required.

The legal concept of a knight's fee, which defined the feudal terms on
which manorial land was held, remained highly resilient throughout
the Middle Ages, so that fourteenth- and fifteenth-century documents
regularly contain references to a manor held by 'lord *y*' for 'a knight's
fee' or a 'moiety (fraction) of a knight's fee'. However, the continued
use of the language of fiefs, fees and vassals to describe the terms on
which manors were held was essentially a convenient legal construct,
and the reality on the ground was rather different. For example, a
knight's fee did not equate to a fixed or consistent area of land. By the

40 Little Domesday Book, fol. 369a.

41 Hudson, *Common law*, pp. 89–90.

42 A. Williams, 'How land was held before and after the Conquest', in Williams, ed.,
   Domesday Book studies, pp. 37–8. The description of feudal relationships in this
   section follows orthodox opinion, which has been substantially challenged by S.
   Reynolds, *Fiefs and vassals: the medieval evidence reinterpreted* (Oxford, 1994). This
   debate carries few direct implications for the daily administration of the manor
   after 1200, or its sources, and so is not explored here in any detail.

43 Du Boulay, *Lordship of Canterbury*, pp. 52, 57.

late twelfth century it was envisaged that a manor of five hides was sufficient to constitute a knight's fee, but in practice many were held for much less than this (the 'hide' notionally comprised 120 acres, but represents a fiscal rather than a statute measure). The notion of the knight's fee tells us little about the reality of the late-medieval manor. The military significance of this system diminished in the twelfth century, so that few of the manors held for 'a knight's fee' were actually held by professional warriors: some knights were undoubtedly fighting men, but many manorial lords were not honed fighters but simply local lords of knightly class.[44] This reflects the growing tendency for subinfeudation to occur as a consequence of economic pressures rather than military or feudal necessity. As Richard Britnell has observed, 'the idea of creating new fiefs as a condition of personal service had become anachronistic by 1180. Subinfeudation continued for over a century after this date, but this was a response to the growth of the land market and the reasons for it were financial'.[45]

When manorial documentation becomes abundant in the thirteenth century, it reveals local and regional differences in the extent to which the old estates and territories had become subdivided. Areas of good soil and high population density could support smaller units of lordship than those of poor soil and low population density. Manors on the fertile soils of eastern Norfolk were small and numerous in the early fourteenth century, in direct contrast to the less numerous and significantly larger manors on the infertile sands of south-west and north-west Norfolk.[46] Similarly, aristocratic families and large ecclesiastical institutions tended to resist the forces of fission with reasonable success on lands they continued to hold directly, partly because of their political power and partly because of the internal organisation of their estates.

The discussion so far has focused upon the seigneurial landholding pattern, and its gradual emergence from an earlier system of extensive territories in pre-Conquest England. Unfortunately, historians know little about the ways in which the lord's relationship with his dependent peasants changed during this process of fragmentation, and the

44 S. P. J. Harvey, 'The knight and the knight's fee in England', in R. H. Hilton, ed., *Peasants, knights and heretics: studies in medieval English social history* (Cambridge, 1976), pp. 135–46, 160–73; Du Boulay, *Lordship of Canterbury*, p. 14.

45 R. H. Britnell, *The commercialisation of English society 1000–1500* (Manchester, 1996), p. 129.

46 Campbell, 'Manorial structure', map 1.

extent to which the move to local units of landholding involved the 'manorialisation' of those lordships. In other words, we should not assume that the seigneurial and jurisdictional rights which a lord possessed over his manorial peasantry in the later Middle Ages (sketched briefly in Figure 1, and discussed in more detail in Chapter II) were the same as those which, say, a tenth-century lord possessed over his peasantry. Certainly, peasants throughout the Anglo-Saxon period had owed various dues and obligations to their superior lord, and, for example, the old multiple estates had received ploughing, harvest works and food farms from their peasantry.[47] The Domesday Book records the existence of large numbers of dependent peasants attached to the manor, but we simply cannot be certain what obligations bound them to their lords at this time. Faith suggests that the English peasantry were subjected to greater and more onerous burdens during the twelfth century, and therefore implies that some of the defining jurisdictional characteristics of the late-medieval manor were, in fact, a post-Conquest innovation. In contrast, other historians imply that seigneurial rights over the peasantry did not change significantly in the twelfth century, although the clarification and codification of those rights after *c.* 1160 creates an illusion of change.[48]

It is less contentious to assert that the English manorial system peaked in the thirteenth century. This marked the final phase in a long period of demographic and economic expansion, when new lands were colonised, land values rose, and the population rose to its medieval peak. These conditions – more land and more peasants – were most propitious for the multiplication of manorial units, and encouraged the predominance of the processes of fission over those of fusion. Consequently, it is likely that the total number of manors reached its peak in *c.* 1300. In addition, the emergence of the common law in the late twelfth and early thirteenth centuries clarified the rights of landlords in relation to their lands, and encouraged the codification of the relationship between lord and peasant. Seigneurial estate management became increasingly professional and systematic around the same time, which ensured that manorial resources were more carefully and robustly exploited. As an economic resource, and as a source of income to its lord, the medieval manor was at its peak in the later thirteenth century.

---

47 Faith, *English peasantry*, pp. 11–14.

48 Contrast, for example, Faith, *English peasantry*, pp. 175–7 with Britnell, *Commercialisation of English society*, pp. 70, 74, 134–47.

The process of manorial fragmentation slowed significantly after the thirteenth century until it virtually ceased, as demographic, economic and social conditions changed, and the formal legal definition of manor was tightened.[49] Thereafter, the fusion of manorial units became the dominant process and the manor as an institution underwent a long period of slow decline. The fall in demographic pressure after the arrival of plague in the mid-fourteenth century, the growing confidence and assertiveness of the lower orders of medieval society, and the gradual dissolution of serfdom and its trappings all eased the seigneurial grip upon the manorial regime. Serfdom and villeinage effectively dissolved during the late fourteenth and fifteenth centuries, to be replaced by a more contractual – as opposed to personal – relationship between lord and tenant. By the fifteenth century many manorial records become less detailed and informative, and seigneurial powers of coercion over the manorial tenantry were clearly waning.

The manor's value as an economic resource declined in the later Middle Ages and seigneurial incomes from land diminished significantly. The separate components of individual manors, and especially the mill, the dairy herd, the dovecote, fisheries and parcels of demesne land, were often leased out piecemeal either to other lords or local tenants, and consequently the manor lost some of its coherence as an operational agrarian unit. This decline coincided with the manor's diminishing importance as a medium for controlling serfdom, and the result, to some extent, was a process of 'de-manorialisation'. As a unit of agricultural management and social control, the manor's day had passed by 1500. Of course, land remained the major source of wealth and income in English society, but the prevailing economic conditions encouraged the creation of larger landed holdings. Consequently, the engrossment of manorial units became an increasingly common practice and the functional independence and integrity of individual manors declined. During the sixteenth century, land values, agricultural profits and population levels rose once again, but the manor was not central to estate management in the way it had been in the thirteenth century. In part, this reflected broad changes in estate management, but also the changing landholding structure of English society as more land fell into fewer hands. The process of engrossment is particularly evident between c. 1650 and 1750, when the rate of fusion of manorial units increased.

49 Harvey, *Manorial records* (1st edn, 1995), pp. 2, 55.

Although manorial courts could still be active after c. 1500, their importance in regulating local life was substantially undermined by the rise of parochial government. Successive reforms of local government by the Tudor monarchy bestowed wider powers upon the parish for the issuing of local by-laws, the regulation of agriculture, social control, poor relief, and so on. Consequently, many of the activities that might once have fallen within the jurisdiction of the manor were now assumed by the parish, which itself was accountable to an increasingly centralised system of government.

The pace at, and extent to which, the local influence of the manor declined from the sixteenth century varied considerably from place to place, depending upon local differences in the customary powers and profile of each manor and the attitude of the lord. The manor's function as a unit of agrarian administration diminished most quickly, although its court could remain active in recording transfers of copyhold land, regulating trade and a few other activities until the early nineteenth century. Indeed, the obsession of antiquarian historians of the eighteenth and nineteenth centuries with manorial descents reminds us that the institution still retained some relevance until relatively recent times, and copyhold (a manorial tenure) survived until the 1920s.

Manorial documents

Manorial documents fall into two broad categories. In the first are those which present a 'snapshot' of the various resources of the manor at a given moment, such as a written description of its demesne land or a list of its tenants' obligations. These served as an important source of reference for estate and manorial administrators by providing both detailed and centralised information about manorial assets and a benchmark for assessing the actual and potential yields of the manor. In this category are found surveys, custumals, rentals, extents, terriers and inventories. The second category comprises those documents which record the active management of manorial resources and rights, and their financial returns, over a short period of time, normally a year. These documents were drawn up with the aid of surveys, custumals and so on, and cross-referred to them, but in essence they are concerned with either the day-to-day regulation of manorial jurisdiction or the actual performance and financial yield of resources each year. Not surprisingly, this represents the most voluminous category of extant documents, which principally comprises manorial accounts and court rolls. These are considered in detail in Chapters III and IV. Chapter II considers the first broad category of documents.

From the end of the twelfth century the quantity and quality of documentation emanating from the English manor increased markedly. Some important manorial surveys survive from the twelfth century, accounts appear for the first time in the first decade of the thirteenth century, and by the 1240s manor court rolls were being produced. This explosion of detailed, written, source material relating to local units of landholding and jurisdiction was peculiarly English, and can be explained by a conjunction of powerful forces. Between *c.* 1160 and *c.* 1220 the emergence of an increasingly centralised and cogent system of royal justice, based on the common law, provided a legal context in which titles to land and associated rights were validated, more clearly defined and protected. It also affirmed the importance in law of written precedents and proofs, which in turn encouraged the spread of literacy and the compilation of written records by landlords.[50]

The emergence of the common law coincided with a period of rapid monetary inflation (especially between *c.* 1180 and *c.* 1220) and rising fiscal demands by the Crown upon landlords, which caused growing indebtedness among many of them.[51] Thus a conjunction of economic and legal forces simultaneously encouraged landlords both to increase their incomes by exploiting their landed estates more actively, and to document their activities in greater detail. Consequently, in the first half of the thirteenth century, estate administration in England became more literate, systematic and bureaucratic. This transformation was most dramatic on the estates of the greater landlords, where a decisive shift has been detected from a predominantly rentier, and essentially passive, system of management to one based on enterprising and direct exploitation of individual manors. The early thirteenth century

50 See Pollock and Maitland, *History of English law*; Hudson, *Common law*; S. F. C. Milsom, *Historical foundations of the common law* (1969); P. Brand, *The making of the common law* (1992); P. R. Hyams, *King, lords, and peasants in medieval England: the common law of villeinage in the twelfth and thirteenth centuries* (Oxford, 1980), pp. 162–265; Britnell, *Commercialisation of English society*, pp. 128–51.

51 See P. D. A. Harvey, 'The English inflation of 1180–1220', in Hilton, ed., *Peasants, knights and heretics*, pp. 57–84; P. D. A. Harvey, 'The pipe rolls and the adoption of demesne farming in England', *Economic History Review*, 27 (1974), 345–59; Miller and Hatcher, *Medieval England*, pp. 64–9 and 210–3; K. Biddick, *Pastoral husbandry on a medieval estate* (Los Angeles, 1989), pp. 50–61.

has therefore been described as the beginning of the era of 'high farming', by which historians mean the direct and active management of manors by landlords, a movement which peaked in the late thirteenth century and lasted until the late fourteenth.

The efficiency with which landlords managed their manors, the detail in which they recorded their activities and the extent to which these records have survived varied over both time and place. A social dimension to these variations is also evident, because fewer manorial records have survived from the estates of the lesser landlords, such as the gentry and smaller monastic houses, and most are extant from the estates of the upper nobility and, especially, wealthy monasteries. Surviving documentation is dominated by records derived from the estates of the great Benedictine houses, which were conservative, bureaucratic landlords holding their lands in perpetuity. This security of possession, together with the ample storage space available within their commodious residences, explains why the best and most complete runs of surviving manorial records tend to relate to the grandest monastic houses.

The type of landlord and the location of the estate are clearly important influences upon the contents of manorial sources and their likelihood of survival. Yet, for all the local differences and influences, the most remarkable feature of English manorial records is the consistency of their format and presentation. Every category of manorial document – from surveys to court rolls – conforms broadly to a basic template, regardless of the status of the lord or the location of the manor. The army of jobbing scribes who emerged throughout thirteenth-century England was reared upon standardised formats for laying out manorial documents. The degree of uniformity is so striking that it is tempting to speculate about the existence of medieval management schools for scribes and estate administrators.

II: MANORIAL SURVEYS, EXTENTS AND RENTALS

Introduction

This section considers the form, evolution and usefulness to historians of a group of closely related records: surveys, custumals, extents, terriers and rentals. Indeed, the word 'survey' is sometimes employed by both contemporaries and historians as a generic form to cover all these documents, although technically each source is different. The survey may be defined as a written description of a manor either in summary or minute detail, which before the late sixteenth century was hardly ever accompanied by maps or plans.[1] In its most mature and extended form, it comprises a detailed statement of the customs and services rendered by each manorial tenant [4]. In this guise, the survey can also be known as a 'custumal', although strictly speaking a custumal extends beyond the tenurial obligations of landholders to encompass all the 'customs' of the manor in their broadest sense: including, for example, details of local agricultural practices, such as the pasturing of animals and arrangements for the harvest, and edicts designed to promote good order among residents [8]. An extent is a survey that incorporates a monetary valuation of various elements of the manor [9, 11], and a rental provides a list of tenants and their annual rent charge [14]. Finally, a terrier lists the individual land parcels of a manor according to some topographical order, and describes the precise location of each: it seldom values them [13].

Surveys and extents before *c.* 1300

The survey is the earliest type of document relating to the administration of the manor, which first emerged in the eleventh century and then developed during the next century as a regular aid to estate management. As Paul Harvey wrote in 1976, 'the evolution of the manorial survey has never been investigated: it is work that is badly

---

1 See R. A. Skelton and P. D. A. Harvey, eds, *Local maps and plans from medieval England* (Oxford, 1986).

needed, since much of our understanding of manorial history in the twelfth and thirteenth centuries depends upon these records'.[2] The great Domesday Book of 1086 is essentially a monumental survey of lands and manors across England, containing a brief and outline description of the basic components of each manor and landholding unit [1]. The comprehensiveness of the Domesday survey, at a time when few other records of individual manors survive, greatly enhances its value to historians. Yet its contribution to the development of the manorial survey is also significant, because it utilised the survey on a scale and comprehensiveness previously unknown, and, in so doing, widely demonstrated its potential. Although the Domesday entries for individual manors are severely edited summaries, they were clearly based upon more detailed surveys of individual estates accumulated by the Domesday commissioners. Indeed, some landlords made copies of these background documents for their own use, such as the Exon (Exeter) Domesday and Ely Inquisition.[3] In this respect, the Domesday project helped to encourage and standardise the use of the local survey.

Surveys dating from the twelfth century have survived from around a dozen ecclesiastical estates, which might imply that such landlords put surveys to greatest use or even pioneered them; alternatively, it might simply reflect the accident of survival. Many of these early surveys comprise a very brief statement of the main components of the manor and are therefore relatively uninformative when compared to later ones: references to the demesne are limited and largely confined to its rating for taxation purposes (given in 'hides' or 'carucates'). However, towards the end of the twelfth century many surveys begin to include more information about the composition and obligations of the manorial tenantry [3], a characteristic that becomes even more marked during the first half of the thirteenth century. Consequently, a typical survey of *c.* 1180 is very different to one dating from the mid-thirteenth century [compare, for example, **3** with **4**]. The latter is much more comprehensive in its description of the demesne lands and, especially, the individual landholdings and obligations of the various tenants. A heavy emphasis is placed upon the terms and conditions on which these manorial landholders held their land from

2 This opening passage draws upon P. D. A. Harvey, *Manorial records of Cuxham Oxfordshire, c. 1200–1359*, Oxfordshire Record Society, 50 (1976) pp. 72–8.

3 See, for example, R. Welldon Finn, *Domesday studies: the eastern counties* (1967), pp. 81–104, for a discussion of the Ely Inquisition.

the lord, including descriptions in minute detail of the rents, customs, services and obligations which had to be rendered and performed by individual landholders in return for their land. The unfree landholdings, whose burdens were heaviest, attract particular attention, and considerable space is devoted to the different categories of labour services owed: their form, extent, and duration are recited in great, almost pedantic, detail [4]. The transformation of the survey around the end of the twelfth century reflects both a tighter and more sophisticated management of seigneurial estates, and a rising volume of cases under the common law, which established more precisely the distinctions between different tenures and enhanced the consistency of the written record of land.

Another expanding feature of many thirteenth-century surveys is an extended section on the demesne lands of the manor, especially the arable, often comprising a careful summary of the amount of demesne land which lay in each named field or furlong of the village, and the areas of demesne meadow and pasture. Explicit instructions were issued in 1181 to officials on the estates of St Paul's, London, to compile information about the demesne lands, and after c. 1200 the growing interest among landlords in the direct exploitation of their demesne lands – rather than leasing them out to tenants (see pp. 97–8) – encouraged the production of a detailed and accurate written description of its size and location to facilitate its management. The recording of demesnal details may have originated as a separate operation from the documentation of tenant obligations, but it soon became common practice to record the two sets of details in one survey.

Another significant development in thirteenth-century surveys was the careful measurement of land often, although not universally, in statute acres.[4] Surveys normally expressed the size of landholdings in terms of acres, roods and perches, stating that these measures were based on the statute acre (*acra mensurata*) of sixteen and a half feet to one perch, forty perches to a rood, and four roods to an acre. However, some surveys measured land in customary acres, often referred to as a 'field acre' or an 'acre as it lies' (*acra campestris; acra ut iacet*): these are highly variable local measures which are unlikely to be equivalent to the statute acre. Sometimes tenant land was expressed in units which had some spatial significance but were essentially units of fiscal apportionment rather than measurements of area, such as a hide of

4 A summary of the development of surveying in the Middle Ages is contained in Skelton and Harvey, eds, *Local maps*, pp. 11–19.

land (notionally 120 fiscal acres), a virgate (notionally a quarter of a hide), or as 'defence acres' (*acreware*).

Hence the survey became more technical, formal, detailed and widespread during the course of the thirteenth century. It was compiled under the supervision of senior estate administrators, who drew upon a combination of earlier written documents and the sworn testimony of a jury of local tenants. The time and energy required to produce a full-blown survey was immense, which dictated that the task was not a regular undertaking. When it was undertaken, a survey was often produced for every manor on the seigneurial estate and the final record bound in a single volume. Rougher working copies would have been used on the individual manor, but the original manuscript would have been kept centrally as part of the estate archive. For example, in the thirteenth century the bishop of Ely produced two major surveys of his demesne manors (in 1222 and 1251), both of which were preserved in the bishopric's central archives. The creation of an estate-wide survey was often associated with either the arrival of a new lord or an energetic estate administration, so that in 1429 the election of Thomas Curteys as abbot of Bury St Edmunds triggered the production in the 1430s of highly detailed surveys of the abbatial manors and a much tighter management of the estate.

Finally, the intensified interest in the management of the demesne during the thirteenth century encouraged the production of extents. The extent was an obvious variation of the survey, in that it itemised the principal types of land-use on the demesne (arable, meadow, pasture and so on) and any other resources (rents, mills, woodland, etc.), and also attached a monetary value to each of them. The information is usually presented in a common format: the value of the capital messuage and its constituent parts; the area and value of the demesne arable; the area and value of meadow, pasture and woodland; a list of mills and their annual revenue; secondary sources of income (such as fisheries, warrens); the money rent from the free, and the villein, holdings; the labour dues of the villeins, and a money equivalent; and the revenues of courts and other jurisdictional rights.[5]

The monetary valuations represented the estimated annual rental value of each resource, rather than a capital or asset value, and, although those given in some extents can appear suspiciously rounded,

5 E. A. Kosminsky, *Studies in agrarian history of England in the thirteenth century* (Oxford, 1956), pp. 47–57, provides a detailed discussion of these issues. See also R. V. Lennard, 'What is an extent?', *English Historical Review*, 44 (1929), 256–62.

they were reasonably reliable and accurate. Thus the extent provided estate administrators with an executive summary of the expected financial return each year of the individual assets and jurisdictional rights of the manor.[6] An extent offers the historian a snapshot of the manor's resources and their relative value, and a series of extents from the same manor, spaced across the Middle Ages, can convey a useful picture of dynamic changes if the valuations have been properly updated on each occasion.[7] Many extents have survived as part of the records of inquiry made by the Crown on the death of the king's tenants-in-chief, known as Inquisitions Post Mortem (IPMs).

The detail contained in extents varies considerably. Many (and especially those drawn up as part of an IPM) are perfunctory and generalised, presenting lump sum valuations under broad headings, such as the value of the demesne arable, the mills, the manor court and other perquisites [9]. In contrast, extents drawn up by manorial administrators, as opposed to royal officials, can offer highly detailed and minute information in the fashion of a full-blown survey, providing careful valuations of, for example, each block or individual furlong of demesne arable and each category of labour service [11]. The circumstances behind the production of either 'short' or 'long' forms of the extent were varied. In some cases, the more concise extents were almost certainly updated versions of lengthier, more authoritative, ones. In others, estates which possessed extensive and updated surveys of their manors would probably have little need for equally detailed extents, and would have used shortened extents in close consultation with other estate documents.

Land tenures and personal status on the medieval manor

The main objective of the thirteenth-century survey in its classic form was to provide a written description of the lands held by the manorial tenants, and to record the terms and conditions on which those lands were held. Clearly, an understanding of those basic tenures is essential to understanding the form, and subsequent evolution, of the survey.

6 Harvey, *Manorial records of Cuxham*, p. 75; Harvey, *Manorial records*, British Records Association, 5 (1st edn, 1995) p. 19.

7 B. M. S. Campbell, J. A. Galloway, and M. Murphy, 'Rural land use in the metropolitan hinterland 1270–1339: the evidence of IPMs', *Agricultural History Review*, 40 (1992), 3–6; B. M. S. Campbell, *English seigniorial agriculture 1250–1450* (Cambridge, 2000), pp. 37–41.

The most basic distinction was between free and unfree (also known
as villein, customary and servile) tenure, a distinction which was drawn
with greater precision and formality during the opening decades of
the thirteenth century.[8] This development is reflected in the growing
sophistication and detail of manorial surveys, which began to record
more clearly and precisely the differences between the various categories
of manorial landholders.

The concept of medieval 'free' tenure implies a 'privileged' tenure, i.e.
one which was free from certain obligations. Thus free tenants (*liberi
tenentes*) possessed greater relative freedom from seigneurial control
than free sokemen (*liberi sokemanni*). Less privileged tenures, which
were burdened by a greater weight of obligations, are even more
commonplace, and surveys throughout England record a bewildering
variety of categories of 'unfree' landholders: for example, customars,
customary tenants, tenants in villeinage, villeins, bondmen or cottars
(*custumarii, custumarii tenentes, tenentes in villenagio, villani, bovarii,
bondi, cotarii*).[9] The title to free tenure could be defended in the royal
courts of England, but the title to villein tenure could not.

The distinction between free and unfree tenure was paralleled by a
distinction between personal freedom (*liber homo*) and servility (*nativus,
nativus de sanguine*). Personal status was inherited through the male
line and so one was either born free or unfree, hence the term 'serf by
blood' (*nativus de sanguine*). Reality was inevitably less clear-cut, not
least because 'mixed' marriages were not uncommon. For example, a
serf woman who married a freeman became legally free for the duration
of the marriage. Illegitimate children assumed their mother's status
until the mid-fourteenth century, after which all bastards were deemed
to be free. Furthermore, the interrelationships between tenurial and
personal status could be complicated, but, as a general rule, a freeman
could hold unfree land and be required to fulfill all of its 'servile'
obligations while remaining personally free, but the unfree were
persistently prevented from holding free land.

8 R. M. Smith, 'Women's property rights under customary law: some developments
   in the thirteenth and fourteenth centuries', *Transactions of the Royal Historical
   Society*, 5th series, 36 (1986), 174–5.

9 The discussions in E. Miller and J. Hatcher, *Medieval England: rural society and
   economic change 1086–1348* (1978), pp. 111–28, and S. R. Rigby, *English society in the
   later Middle Ages: class, status and gender* (1995), pp. 34–9 offer good general
   introductions. For the special category of Ancient Demesne, see F. Pollock and F.
   W. Maitland, *The history of English law before the time of Edward I*, 2nd edn
   (Cambridge, 1911), pp. 383–406.

A clear theoretical distinction between free and villein tenures would have been evident to a contemporary student of the common law, and was readily apparent on the ground in the heavily manorialised regions of the Midlands. Elsewhere, however, tenurial reality was complex and varied, and the gradations between free and unfree could be small and obscure in the lightly manorialised areas of East Anglia and south-east England.[10] The authors of surveys were not interested in precise legal distinctions and niceties, for the simple reason that their sole concern was to identify the rents and services due from land-holdings: they concentrated on tenurial obligations, not on whether the nature of those obligations categorised a holding as free or otherwise. However, both contemporaries and historians associate villein tenure with particular dues and services and, for most practical purposes, tenants liable to perform heavy, often weekly, labour services on the demesne, or to render a 'merchet' payment to the lord as a licence to marry their offspring, were deemed to be unfree.[11]

Free tenure assumed a number of forms in the Middle Ages.[12] Many lords held their manors freely in return for either military or religious service, but their free tenants normally held their land as 'socage'. In neither case was the landholder free in the modern sense, because medieval freehold was not *owned* in the same way as modern freehold. This explains why medievalists seldom write that a freeman 'owned' land, and instead use words – such as 'possessed', 'seised' or 'held' – which imply that tenure carried certain obligations to a superior lord which had to be met. Indeed, the superior lord could take steps to reclaim the land if the tenant did not meet those obligations.

Free land could be inherited, purchased by agreement or granted by the holder without seigneurial permission. On acquiring, or 'entering', the land, the new tenant was required to perform homage to the lord, a ceremony which involved the placing of the tenant's hands between those of the lord (or his representative) while kneeling, and the swearing of fealty on oath. This was followed by the payment of a 'relief' (*relevium*) to the lord for entry into the holding, and a formal record of the transfer of tenancy as a written charter. Money rent was

---

10 Miller and Hatcher, *Medieval England*, pp. 111–28; Rigby, *English society*, pp. 27–37; C. C. Dyer, *Lords and peasants in a changing society: the estates of the bishopric of Worcester 680–1500* (Cambridge, 1980), p. 105.

11 E. Miller, *The abbey and bishopric of Ely* (Cambridge, 1951), p. 114.

12 For an introduction to free tenure, see Pollock and Maitland, *History of English law*, pp. 322–56.

the main render on free holdings, although the amount annually payable was relatively fixed and immutable, and the tenant was required
to attend the lord's court. Some free tenures were liable to perform a
few light labour services, normally seasonal works, on the lord's
demesne, and to render a payment as a death duty. After *c.* 1200 the
key features of all freeholdings were the right to defend the title to
the land in the king's courts and the right to alienate (i.e. sell or
grant) the land without seigneurial interference. The entries in surveys
take these rights as given, and concentrate upon the tenant, the size of
the holding, and the rents and services owed to the lord. The presence
of free tenants varied considerably from place to place and estate to
estate, but it is widely assumed that they comprised around 40 per
cent of England's tenant population in *c.* 1300, and that over half of all
tenures were free.

The unfree peasantry was subject to a wider range, and greater weight,
of seigneurial obligations than the free, and surveys are dominated by
meticulous descriptions of these burdens. Landholdings in villeinage
were often more standardised than freeholdings, commonly appearing
as thirty-acre holdings called 'full-lands' or 'virgates'; as fifteen-acre
'half-lands' or 'half-virgates'; or as smallholding 'cotlands'.[13] These
uniform, customary, holdings principally comprised arable land, although
they could also include small quantities of meadow and perhaps
woodland, and invariably came with a messuage. In some parts of the
country the whole 'package' of land and messuage was described as a
'*tenementum*'.

In common law the manorial lord possessed seisin (see p. 27) of villein
land, which theoretically meant that the tenant had no control over
its disposal. Neither villein tenure nor status were protected by the
king's courts, and so a villein could only defend the title to his land in
the lord's own manorial court. At the very least, the tenant was not
allowed to sell, sublet or grant the land either *inter vivos* or *post
mortem* without the lord's permission. Villein land was essentially held
'at the will of the lord', which implied the seigneurial right both to
seize at will a villein holding and its stock, and to determine its
disposal at the death of a tenant. In practice, however, the operation of

13 For an introduction to unfree tenure, see Pollock and Maitland, *History of English
law*, pp. 358–83. Anyone seeking an authoritative and detailed analysis of all
aspects relating to the regulation of customary tenure by manorial authorities,
particularly the legal procedures surrounding disposal and inheritance, must
consult L. R. Poos and L. Bonfield, eds, *Select cases in manorial courts 1250–1550.
Property and family law*, Selden Society, 114 (1997), pp. lxxxv–clxvii.

certain aspects of villeinage was very different to its theory. As with freehold tenure, lords only seized villein land when the tenant had failed to fulfil certain obligations, such as the payment of rents and services. Furthermore, many lands held in villeinage are described as being held by a tenant 'for himself and his heirs' (*sibi et heredibus suis*), which meant that, as long as certain procedures were observed, they could be passed to the tenant's heir without seigneurial interference.

These examples underline the powerful influence exerted by local custom on the operation of villeinage. Custom dictated that villein land could be passed on to an heir without interference and determined whether a single heir or more than one inherited, known respectively as impartible and partible inheritance. Customary law also dictated the temporary arrangements which prevailed when an heir had not yet reached the age of majority (normally 21 years), and the rights of widows and married women to hold land. Married women had no absolute right to hold land under the common law, but manorial custom often protected the wife's access to any dower land if she survived her husband. Indeed, it was increasingly common for some land to be held jointly by husband and wife in order to increase this protection, and for the arrangement to be recorded explicitly in manorial records.[14]

Perhaps the most prominent difference between the theory and practice of villein tenure is the existence of an active market in villein land in many places, including temporary subletting and permanent grants of small parcels of land, and deathbed transfers of entire holdings. The guiding principle was that villein land could be regranted to a named recipient, as long as it was first surrendered formally to the lord. By this formal process, and after its careful and precise recording in the manor court rolls and perhaps a land charter, small parcels and entire holdings of villein land were 'legally' exchanged from one tenant to another, and by the end of the thirteenth century such land transactions were commonplace throughout England and abundant in the eastern and home counties [37, 39].[15]

The rents, customs and obligations attached to villein holdings were varied and complex, but invariably featured some or all of the following: suit of court, annual rents in cash and/or kind, seasonal and weekly labour services, and a range of other feudal obligations such as

14 Smith, 'Women's property rights', 180–90.
15 P. D. A. Harvey, 'Introduction', in Harvey, ed., *The peasant land market in medieval England* (Oxford, 1984), pp. 1–28.

chevage and millsuit (see pp. 31–3). The organisation of unfree land-holdings into standardised units aided the allocation and management of the various and onerous obligations that comprised a substantial part of the rent package owed to the lord. On entering the holding, the tenant swore servile fealty and paid an entry fine (*gersuma*). If the land had been inherited from a deceased relative, then a death duty called a 'heriot' was also payable from the estate of the deceased: this was traditionally the best animal, although sometimes a cash payment was rendered instead.

A small amount of cash rent was often payable annually, normally in equal instalments on two or four designated days (or 'terms') of the year. Other token cash payments are not uncommon, such as 'scotpenny', 'woodfare', 'spenningfee', 'fishsilver' and 'maltsilver', which represented either nominal payments for rights over certain resources or cash commutations of ancient and perhaps arcane customary dues. All cash rents were fixed by custom, so the lord could not adjust them according to the fluctuating market value of land: in this respect, the only adjustable payment was the entry fine rendered on the acquisition of land. Many unfree holdings also paid part of their rent in kind, sometimes as a set measure of grain but often in the form of hens at Christmas and eggs at Easter. The main form of rent from villein tenures was labour services, which were rendered on the lord's demesne. Like some freeholdings, unfree tenures owed seasonal (boon) works at the harvest, for which their workers were often rewarded with the provision of food by the lord. They habitually owed other seasonal works too, such as ploughing and spreading muck in the winter, and mowing hay in the early summer, and could also be liable to carry goods on behalf of the lord at specified times. However, their main burden – and distinguishing feature – was the week work, which required an unfree tenant to perform a number of labour services each week outside the harvest period on the lord's demesne. In some places, extensive labour services formed the main 'rent' component of the holding, and no cash rents were levied.

The exact extent and volume of labour services varied from estate to estate and holding to holding, but they were the most onerous and unpopular of all servile obligations.[16] On some manors, a landholding carried the liability to work on the demesne five times a week during the summer. A tenant might send a representative, such as another

---

16 Miller and Hatcher survey broad differences in unfree burdens from holding to holding and estate to estate in *Medieval England*, pp. 117–33.

family member, rather than perform the work personally, although some works stipulated that each tenant should produce more than one person. Twelfth-century surveys do not articulate the nature of labour services in any detail, which for some historians raises the possibility that they were not a significant demand at this time.[17] Certainly the growth of literacy and estate management in the early thirteenth century, and the shift towards the direct exploitation of demesnes, may have encouraged some reorganisation of the labour services owed by each landholding and dictated the production of a meticulous written description of them. Consequently, many thirteenth-century surveys are dominated by detailed recitals of the labour services owed by tenants, including careful definitions of a single unit of 'work', the type and amount of work required to discharge one 'work', arrangements for illness, and so on [4]. The liability for labour services is therefore recorded in impressive detail in surveys and custumals, while their annual management, utilisation and disposal is recorded in equally impressive detail in manorial accounts [31]. Lords reserved the right to receive a cash payment from their tenants in lieu of labour services, a process known as commutation, and consequently many labour services are often given a cash value in manorial extents for this purpose [9]. The option to take tenants' services in either cash or kind provided the lord with greater operational flexibility.

A range of other obligations and restrictions often applied to villeins. The periodic requirement to perform a manorial office – such as reeve or harvest-reeve – for one year was a widespread burden upon the larger villein landholders. The liability normally rotated annually among the virgaters, which might mean election to office every ten years or so. These offices were unpaid and time-consuming (see pp. 98–9), and a villein might pay a hefty fine rather than undertake them when his turn came. Some landholdings were held by tenants in return for performing specified and specialist services for the lord, such as serving as a master baker, boatman, or maintaining the fabric of a bridge.[18] Landholdings in villeinage could not be 'wasted' by the tenant, either through lopping trees within the messuage or allowing houses or buildings to become dilapidated. On many estates villeins were also required to mill their corn only at the seigneurial mill, where a toll was charged for the privilege. The abundance of private mills and hand mills by the thirteenth century indicates that this

17 Dyer, *Lords and peasants,* pp. 98–9.
18 Miller, *Bishopric of Ely,* p. 126

obligation was not easy to enforce, although intermittent action against non-compliance is often recorded in court rolls. Similarly, some villeins were required to place their sheep within seigneurial folds, an arrangement which permitted lords to supply their demesne arable lands with valuable manure, while others required the lord's permission to sell their beasts of burden.[19]

Villeinage could also imply liability for a range of occasional servile levies or incidents, some of which were personal as well as tenurial.[20] The most important levy, because it constituted a key test of villeinage under the common law, was merchet, payable to the lord on the marriage of a servile woman (although sometimes payable for servile sons too). In practice, this marriage licence was levied mainly on the marriages of those drawn from the upper ranks of villeins rather than on all servile women and was usually charged against the dowry. Consequently, the size of the levy was not fixed, but normally amounted to a few shillings: landless women were often charged only a few pence, while marriage to freemen or outsiders attracted heftier sums.[21] Liability for aid, or tallage, was another onerous servile incident, which theoretically permitted the lord to tax his villeins at will. In practice, the size and regularity of the charge was regulated by custom, varying from an irregular levy on some estates to an annual fixed charge on others. On some estates, it appears to have been first levied in the thirteenth century.[22] It was certainly a lucrative and relatively flexible source of income at Wellingborough (Northamptonshire), yielding £4 in 1258–59 and £14 in 1322–33 [19, 20]. On ecclesiastical estates, the appointment of a new bishop or the election of a new abbot was marked by the levying of a fixed fine, known as a 'recognition', from the servile peasantry.

Capitage or chevage was another head-levy on villeins, sometimes charged annually at a nominal rate against adult males who resided on the manor and did not hold land, but more often charged annually against those who had left the manor. The lord could insist upon this

19 For milling, see R. Holt, *The mills of medieval England* (Oxford, 1988), pp. 36–53; for fold rights, see M. Bailey, *A marginal economy? East Anglian Breckland in the later Middle Ages* (Cambridge, 1989), pp. 65–85.

20 A readable and accessible introduction is H. S. Bennett, *Life on the English manor*, (Cambridge, reissued 1971), pp. 127–50.

21 E. Searle, 'Seigneurial control of women's marriage: the antecedents and function of merchet in England', *Past and Present*, 82 (1979), 3–43; Smith, 'Women's property rights', 168–72; Poos and Bonfield, *Select cases*, pp. clxvii–clxxxi.

22 Pollock and Maitland, *History of English law*, p. 368; Dyer, *Lords and peasants*, p. 103.

form of compensation, because migrating villeins theoretically represented a diminution in the capital assets of the manor. Enforcing chevage payments from flown villeins posed self-evident difficulties, although estate administrators became more persistent in their pursuit of emigrants when tenants became scarce after the Black Death. One suspects that those who did continue to render an annual chevage payment of a few pence or shillings to their lord had a particular interest in doing so, such as a landed inheritance on the manor. Some lords drew up basic ancestral trees of serf families on their manors in order to maintain track of the latter's lineage and whereabouts, and required manorial officials to pursue flown serfs with energy and tenacity.[23] Consequently, manorial court rolls can contain unusually detailed information about the migratory patterns of serfs and their family structures, particularly after the Black Death.

The requirement that serfs seek seigneurial permission to leave the manor was extended further on some manors to those who wished to be ordained or educated. Another common personal levy on serfs was the payment of 'leyrwite' by those women who fornicated outside wedlock, or 'childwyte' for those who gave birth illegitimately, because a bastard child of the villein was deemed to be free.[24] Again, the sum varied but could run to a few shillings. An unfortunate woman at Walsham-le-Willows (Suffolk) who gave birth to bastard twins in 1349, probably as a consequence of the death of her betrothed in the Black Death, was compelled to pay childwite twice.[25] In all these examples, the lord was effectively seeking compensation for the temporary or permanent loss of villein 'stock' from the manor and by extension the loss of valuable dues and obligations from a villein and his progeny. The personal nature of villeinage is also evident when land in villeinage was sold from one lord to another, because the villein who held the land was often sold as part of the transaction. This activity occurred quite frequently in the twelfth century, but was very rare thereafter.

23 E. D. Jones, 'Going round in circles: some new evidence for population in the later Middle Ages', *Journal of Mediaeval History*, 15 (1989), 329–45.

24 Although on some manors the distinction was not clearly drawn, and childwyte was, logically, treated as leyrwite, see Poos and Bonfield, *Select cases*, pp. clxxxi–clxxxiv; P. R. Hyams, *King, lords, and peasants in medieval England: the common law of villeinage in the twelfth and thirteenth centuries* (Oxford, 1980), pp. 3–16 and 25–37; E. D. Jones, 'The medieval leyrwite: a historical note on female fornication', *English Historical Review*, 107 (1992), 945–53.

25 R. Lock, ed., *The court rolls of Walsham-le-Willows*, Suffolk Record Society, 41 (1998), p. 325.

Serfs could legally acquire free status by being knighted, ordained or taking holy orders, but the most common method was to purchase a charter of manumission from their lord, although the charge levied might be hefty (a few pounds). Others who fled the manor and resided in a privileged borough for more than one year were also deemed to be legally free. But the vast majority simply acquired a condition of *de facto* freedom during the course of the late fourteenth and fifteenth centuries, either by leaving the manor and thus residing beyond the lord's jurisdictional clutches or simply by benefiting from the gradual relaxation then dissolution of the burdens and obligations associated with servility.

The gradual demise of villeinage (unfree tenure) and serfdom (personal unfreedom) in the late fourteenth and fifteenth centuries is the most important social development of the era.[26] Faced with a severe shortage of tenants in the century and a half after the Black Death, periods of agricultural depression, and the growing assertiveness of the peasantry, landlords throughout England struggled to find tenants for all of their manorial land. Where no tenant could be found, land was bleakly described as 'lying in the lord's hands'. It lay abandoned and reverted to scrub pasture until a tenant could be found or, rarely, might be consolidated with the demesne. Unfavourable economic conditions for landlords forced them to make their customary tenancies more attractive by removing or not collecting unpopular obligations such as labour services and recognition payments, and therefore resulted in a gradual but widespread relaxation of villeinage. Although seigneurial concessions were not granted readily, the cumulative and permanent impact of piecemeal gestures was immense. Labour services became increasingly difficult to collect and were either allowed to lapse or were formally abolished and commuted for a nominal sum: abolition was often associated with the abandonment of direct exploitation of the demesne by the lord. These difficulties extended to tallage, millsuit, recognition fines and rent payments in kind which eventually suffered the same fate. Heriot for many lands, and merchet and chevage for some serfs, proved more resilient, but leyrwite and liability for manorial office dissolved. Few of the wide range of customary obligations, which had been detailed so meticulously in thirteenth-century surveys, were still

---

26 See R. H. Hilton, *The decline of serfdom in medieval England* (1969); Rigby, *English society*, pp. 80–7, 104–44; R. H. Britnell, *The commercialisation of English society 1000–1500* (Manchester, 1996), pp. 217–23.

levied after the 1450s.[27] Personal servility survived with remarkable resilience on a few estates, where a few serfs by blood were still identified in the sixteenth century. Yet, overall, numbers of serfs were very small by *c.* 1500, because many serf families had either died out or acquired legal or *de facto* freedom: hardly any 'new' serfs were created after 1200.[28]

If the key obligations and services which had once defined villein tenure fell away during the late fourteenth and fifteenth centuries, what then became of it? There can be no definitive answer to this question, because local practices were highly varied and scribes were not always consistent in the formulae they used to describe tenancies. Indeed, unfree tenures during this transitional period are a confusing muddle, and should be readily acknowledged as such. However, the essential point is that the changed economic conditions of the later Middle Ages forced lords to convert a growing proportion of unpopular villein tenures into more attractive, contractual, tenures.

The free and villein tenancies described above can be usefully categorised as non-contractual tenancies, in that they were governed by either common or customary law rather than by specified contractual agreements between the lord and each tenant. Contractual tenures took two principal forms: contractual villein tenures and leaseholds. The differences between the 'non-contractual' and 'contractual' forms of villein tenure can be crudely sketched. The former, as we have seen, were commonplace in the thirteenth century, and were heritable, controlled by local custom, and attracted low, if any, cash rents. Contractual tenures were less common, not heritable, seldom burdened with labour services and often described in late fourteenth- and fifteenth-century documents as 'held at the will of the lord'.[29] This is a particularly unfortunate and confusing term, because *all* villein tenures were theoretically held 'at the will of the lord'. However, non-contractual villein tenures are often described as held 'in villeinage' or 'in bondage' with rights of inheritance 'for him and his heirs', phrases which are invariably absent from contractual villein tenures where 'at the will of the lord', 'according to custom', 'by the rod' or 'by the rolls' are more common. These tenants-at-will rendered little more than an annual cash rent (which was often higher than the cash rents owed by

27 See, for example, Dyer, *Lords and peasants*, pp. 283–91.

28 Pollock and Maitland, *History of English law*, p. 424.

29 Harvey, *Westminster abbey and its estate in the Middle Ages* (Oxford, 1977), p. 245.

heritable villein land) and suit of court, and perhaps an entry fine and a heriot, although the lord could – and occasionally did – seize the land at any time and evict the tenant.[30]

Irrespective of the insecurity of tenants-at-will in legal theory, the general shortage of tenants after c. 1350 meant that, in practice, they enjoyed relative security of occupation. Yet by the end of the fifteenth century many tenants increasingly sought more formal security of tenure and some were granted customary land 'for the life of the tenant'. On the bishopric of Worcester's estates tenancies-at-will were surrendered to the lord and then immediately regranted for a specified life.[31] Another development around this time was for tenants to receive a copy of the court roll entry which recorded the acquisition, terms and conditions of their land. They were then said to hold 'by copy' (*per copiam*). This provided greater security of tenure than a mere tenancy-at-will, which increased further when copyhold tenure began to be recognised in the court of Chancery at the very end of the fifteenth century and ultimately by the courts of common law in the sixteenth century. The developments were neither linear nor consistent, but by these means villein tenure eventually evolved into copyhold tenure.

The second type of contractual tenure to emerge more prominently after c. 1350 was leasehold. Temporary, short-term, leases were occasionally arranged when customary land was unexpectedly seized or abandoned, for example during a plague outbreak, and the lord wished to regrant it as an expedient for a fixed and stipulated cash rent (perhaps for a few months until the harvest) until a more formal and permanent arrangement could be made. This crude form of leasehold is often known as the 'issue' (*exitus*) of land. Alternatively, land which fell untenanted could be exploited temporarily by the lord, in which case a manorial official was directed 'to answer for [its] profits'.

The most common form of leasehold involved holding land on a fixed term (normally of years, but sometimes for a life or lives) for an agreed annual rent. Such tenures are often described as being 'at farm' (*ad firmam*, and the lord was said 'to demise' (*dimissio*) the land), and

30 Harvey, *Westminster abbey*, pp. 246–8.

31 Dyer, *Lords and peasants*, p. 294; Harvey, *Westminster abbey*, p. 280. A useful study of the changes in villein tenure on an Essex manor, which highlights the growing security of contractual tenures after the mid-fifteenth century, is P. R. Schofield, '*Extranei* and the market for customary land on a Westminster abbey manor in the fifteenth century', *Agricultural History Review*, 49 (2001), 1–16.

rendered a stipulated annual rent and, occasionally, an entry fine; they could also include maintenance clauses for buildings and equipment, an important consideration in a period of agrarian depression. The rent level of leaseholds reflected the market value of land more closely than the cash rents attached to free or villein tenures, and so were invariably charged at a higher rate but, as the tenant was subject to no other obligations and enjoyed security for the length of the lease, this form of tenure proved popular. The lessee also possessed the implied right to assign an unexpired portion of a lease to another person. Some villein tenures were converted to leasehold, especially after the Black Death, when tenants proved difficult to find, although this form of tenure was less common than tenancies-at-will.[32] This was a significant concession, because customary land which had been converted to leasehold did not then revert to villeinage. Leasehold was used overwhelmingly whenever lords chose not to exploit all or parts of the demesne directly, because it was a device which offered a market rent, flexibility and little prospect of permanent alienation.

Surveys, rentals and terriers after c. 1300

The classic survey, with its detailed and pedantic recitals of the terms and conditions upon which manorial tenants (and especially villeins) held their land [4], was very much a product of the thirteenth century, when tenurial distinctions were clarified and first codified. Similarly, it was most effective as a management tool where the local land market was relatively static, and standardised peasant landholdings remained largely intact and changed hands infrequently. However, its usefulness was diminished by a highly active land market in free and villein land, where small parcels of land were exchanged frequently and standard holdings were quickly broken down. The growth and intensification of the peasant land market by the end of the thirteenth century in many areas of southern and eastern England meant that many thirteenth-century surveys soon became outdated as a record of manorial landholders, for they depicted a tenurial ideal rather than the complex reality of fragmenting holdings, co-tenancies (often called 'co-parcenars') and temporary sublettings that existed on the ground.

---

32 Harvey, *Westminster abbey*, pp. 249–51. In some cases, villein tenures were first converted to leasehold in the late fourteenth century, and then held as tenancies-at-will, Schofield, 'Extranei', p. 11.

Just as an active land market meant that the landholding structure described in many thirteenth-century surveys soon became outdated, so the decline of villeinage during the fourteenth and fifteenth centuries rendered obsolete their monumental recitals of each landholding's customary terms and conditions of tenure. The growing unpopularity of land held for customs and services, the dissolution of labour services, and the tendency to convert customary land to leasehold or other contractual tenures all reduced the administrative usefulness of earlier surveys. Extents suffered a similar fate. Market conditions in the thirteenth and early fourteenth centuries were essentially inflationary and favourable to landlords, so that the monetary values for land and other manorial resources recorded in extents, although not always precise, at least established a minimum yield that the lord might reasonably expect to receive from the demesne [9, 11]. However, such yields were less predictable or useful after the mid-fourteenth century, when land values could fall dramatically and landlords turned away from exploiting the demesne directly (see pp. 108–10), and consequently detailed extents and fixed valuations became unfashionable: 'the realities of leasing in a fluctuating land market had made the formal valuations of the extent unnecessary and unrealistic'.[33]

As long as manorial rents remained relatively fixed and constant, so the classic surveys and extents of the thirteenth century provided estate officials with an essential reference point for the management of rents. However, such documents became increasingly irrelevant during the course of the fourteenth century, and especially after *c.* 1350, as the level of rental income and the nature of tenures changed rapidly and significantly. The underlying causes of these changes have been described above: the move away from customary rents and services, the breakup of standardised villein holdings, the growing variety of tenures, the piecemeal leasing of the demesne, and sharp shifts in land values, all of which increased the fluidity and variability of the manorial rent roll over relatively short periods of time. Furthermore, cash rents became more important as a source of manorial revenue after *c.* 1350. This is not to argue that landlords were better off in the late Middle Ages (see pp. 108–9), but simply that a growing *proportion* of their manorial income came from cash rents.

33 Harvey, *Manorial records of Cuxham*, p. 78.

The growing importance of, and fluctuations in, rental income necessitated changes in rent management, which were soon reflected in the format and content of manorial records. Negotiating, setting, monitoring, collecting and chasing a fluctuating volume of cash rents became the major task of estate administrators, but the older surveys and extents contained essentially 'static' information that was not very helpful under these new circumstances. They were also expensive documents to produce in an era of labour shortages and rising wages, which forced officials to seek alternatives. Greater use was made of the rental, which was generally a more cursory document [see 14] than the survey, and was primarily focused upon the rental liability of each tenant rather than tenurial details. It possessed the added benefits of being handy, manageable, cheap to produce and readily rewritten to reflect updates to the rent chage. On some estates, subsidiary documents were drawn up to ensure that the sums recorded in rentals were actually collected [16], an important consideration in a slack land market where defaults were commonplace.

Another significant change after *c.* 1350 was the development of the manorial account as an active tool in rent management (the account is explained in detail in Chapter III, but see especially pp. 105–11). The section devoted to 'the farm/lease of land' (*firma terre*) was often perfunctory in early fourteenth-century accounts, but thereafter on many manors expanded greatly in both size and detail. It often contained many, sometimes scores of, detailed entries describing the income due for every small parcel of land held by each tenant on contractual tenancies (often leasehold), and by the early fifteenth century this section could dominate the account and add greatly to its length: in effect, the account incorporated an annual rent roll for contractual tenancies. Individual entries sometimes had glosses added as a superscript in a different hand, noting subsequent changes in the rent charge (such as a negotiated reduction) or the abandonment of the land into the lord's hands (*in manibus domini*). Likewise, the allowances section at the foot of the account (see pp. 110–11), and petitions submitted by rent collectors [27], became more informative and extensive, detailing those rents which remained upaid and, incidentally, revealing how local officials were forced to make *ad hoc* concessions to retain tenants in the post-Black Death era.

The growing irrelevance of earlier surveys to the requirements of late-medieval land management inevitably resulted in changes to the content and format of later fourteenth- and fifteenth-century surveys.

The monumental listings of services and customary obligations attached to the peasant holding largely disappeared in favour of a detailed topographical description of demesne and peasant land. The wider use of various contractual tenures increased the need for a comprehensive and accurate listing of all the manorial lands, and a document that effectively served as a complete 'inventory' of every parcel of land on the manor represented an invaluable store of information irrespective of changes in the tenure of that land. Hence, instead of a statement that tenant *x* held *y* acres, followed by a list of the holding's rents and services, later surveys are more likely to break down and describe each tenant's landholding according to each of its individual, constituent, land parcels pertaining to the manor. Alternatively, the document might be organised on a topographical basis, describing in turn every land parcel on the manor as it lay in the village fields [13].

Late-medieval surveys have more in common with terriers than the grand surveys of the thirteenth century [compare, for example, 4 and 13]. A typical entry might read 'Adam Smith holds two acres of customary land in one piece in Northfield lately (*nuper*) held by Edward Noy and formerly (*quondam*) in the tenure of James Golby. The east abuts on the land held by William Warrener, the north end abuts on the king's highway and the south on the demesne land of the manor'. This format reflected the fact that many of the old, standardised, landholdings had been irretrievably fragmented, and that late-medieval tenants could readily acquire small parcels of land and construct bespoke landholdings on a variety of tenures. However, by carefully and systematically recording some previous tenants of each parcel of land, estate administrators were able to trace its tenurial ancestry back to a standardised holding whose customs and services were documented in an earlier survey.

The changes in land tenancies on the late-medieval manor, and the growing importance of cash rents, presented genuine, and to some extent, novel challenges to landlords and their officials. Another challenge was presented by the strongly adverse economic conditions, especially after *c*. 1375, which forced them to work harder to extract the due revenue from their estates. It would be easy to marshal evidence to support the argument that landlords failed to rise to these challenges: for example, the decline of the extent and the great survey, the proliferation of cheap rentals, the accumulation of rent arrears, and the lengthy petitions for uncollected rents might all be taken to indicate administrative inefficiency and slackness. Yet a more plausible interpretation of this evidence suggests itself. Late fourteenth- and fifteenth-century landlords encouraged their estate officials to manage their rent rolls and tenants more actively, sensitively and closely, and these responses are evident in the changing nature of manorial documents and, indeed, in the changing relationship between those documents. The evolution of the content and layout of surveys, extents, rentals and accounts during this period is strongly indicative of real improvements in, and the growing sophistication of, rentier management by landlords. Historians sometimes recognise and celebrate technological advances more readily than managerial advances, but the social and economic gains that flowed from the latter could be considerable. In this regard, the later Middle Ages was an era of progress and innovation.

Historical uses of surveys and extents

The usefulness of surveys and related documents to historians will be readily apparent from the following extracts, and their primary importance lies in the information they provide about landholding patterns on the medieval manor. Land was the major source of income, wealth and status in medieval society, and therefore the reconstruction of the structure of landholdings on a given manor offers insights into the nature of local society, its distribution of power, and general standards of living among the populace.[34] Likewise, the nature of lordship (its status, whether resident or not, and the number within the vill), the predominant tenurial arrangements (free, unfree, contractual or non-contractual), and the distribution of land among landholders (equitable or polarised) all influenced the nature and disposition of local society to a significant degree (see pp. 8–9), and can be readily reconstructed from surveys and extents. In the absence of censuses of population, surveys provide headcounts of manorial tenants that can be used to construct crude demographic estimates for each manor and to plot local differences in population density.[35]

---

34 Surveys are used extensively in analysing regional differences in landholding patterns before the Black Death in chapter 6 of H. E. Hallam, ed., *The agrarian history of England and Wales: vol. II, 1042–1350* (Cambridge, 1988), pp. 594–715.

35 For example, Hallam, ed., *Agrarian history*, pp. 508–93. Manorial records have been used widely by demographic historians, and the sources for medieval population will be the subject of another volume in the *Manchester Medieval Sources* series, edited by Richard M. Smith.

Surveys also provide the clearest statements about the terms and conditions on which land was held, and therefore define freedom and, in particular, villeinage as a social institution. Villeinage determined the lives of more than half the population of England in *c.* 1300, and its form, spatial variations and temporal changes are essential to understanding medieval society. Court rolls, and to a lesser extent manorial accounts, reveal how villeinage was regulated on the ground, but surveys provide the fixed points for mapping its main features.[36]

The topographical information contained in detailed surveys and terriers of the fourteenth and fifteenth centuries is vital to the reconstruction of field systems, including the location and quality of both demesne and tenant land.[37] Careful analysis of the topographical distribution of landholdings and field names can reveal earlier land-holding patterns, and even the processes of reclamation and colonisation. When combined with research techniques drawn from landscape history and archaeology, surveys can be extremely illuminating about local topography.[38]

Surveys do not reveal much about the household or family structures behind their lists of tenants and landholders, nor do they mention the many landless adults who must have existed in every manor. Nor do they record *all* the land held by an individual, because a tenant may hold land from more than one manor (especially when a village was split between a number of manors). The earlier surveys in particular convey a standardised and perhaps rather simplified picture of land-holding, and fail to acknowledge the existence or effects of subletting, subdivision and co-tenancies. Some surveys may note that a named tenant held a landholding 'with his co-parcenars', but the number of co-tenants and the ways in which the rents and services were divided are seldom recorded. They only provide a snapshot of landholding on the manor, which may well conceal the underlying complexity and reality of the landholding structure.

36 Miller and Hatcher, *Medieval England*, pp. 111–28.

37 A useful discussion, including some detailed examples, of the reconstruction of field systems from surveys, terriers and extents is contained in D. Hall, *The open fields of Northamptonshire* (Northampton, 1995), especially at pp. 42–50. The seminal study of field systems makes extensive use of surveys and terriers: H. L. Gray, *The English field systems* (Cambridge, Mass., 1915).

38 J. Eddison and G. Draper, 'A landscape of medieval reclamation: Walland marsh, Kent', *Landscape History*, 19 (1997), 75–88, is an excellent illustration of the potential for this type of localised research.

The large number of extents produced as part of a royal Inquisition Post Mortem, and their accessibility in published calendars, greatly enhances their importance and value to historians.[39] They emerge in the 1260s and survive in great numbers after the 1290s, and particularly from the first half of the fourteenth century when hundreds were produced each year.[40] They have been used by historians to analyse land values; to compare spatial and temporal variations in land use; to recreate and understand local field systems; and to reconstruct local and regional differences in lordship.[41] The extents from IPMs tend to be less reliable than those produced by manorial administrators, mainly because they were compiled more quickly. Furthermore, there is much variation in the format, scope and detail of IPM extents: 'in some the amounts and values of the different land-uses are given in very rounded figures and summary form, in others they either incorporate information taken directly from manorial accounts and other documentation available at the time or are the product of an exact survey and evaluation'.[42] Inconsistencies and ambiguities complicate the use of this source, and demand caution, but their overall benefits to historians are obvious: 'a comparison of the figures they contain, carried out over a wide area, enables us to capture certain characteristic traits, certain peculiarities which, though vague, are vital. And the results thus obtained assume considerable weight, when confirmed by other sources and conclusions independently arrived at'.[43]

39 *Calendar of Inquisitions Post Mortem and other analogous documents in the Public Record Office (Henry III–Richard II)*, 15 volumes (1901–1970).

40 Campbell, *Seigniorial agriculture*, p. 38.

41 J. A. Raftis, *Assart data and land values* (Toronto, 1974); H. S. A. Fox, 'Some ecological dimensions of medieval field systems', in K. Biddick, ed., *Archaeological approaches to medieval Europe* (Kalamazoo, 1984), pp. 119–58; Campbell, *Seigniorial agriculture*, pp. 55–101; Gray, *English field systems*, pp. 44–7; Kosminsky, *Studies in agrarian history*, pp. 68–151.

42 Campbell, *Seigniorial agriculture*, pp. 38–9.

43 Kosminsky, *Studies in agrarian history*, pp. 57–67 at p. 63. R. F. Hunnisett, 'The reliability of inquisitions as historical evidence', in D. A. Bullough and R. L. Storey, eds, *The study of medieval records* (Oxford, 1971), pp. 206–35.

1   A survey of Shillington, 1086

The earliest surviving survey of most English manors is to be found in the
Domesday Book, although – like all early surveys – the format is short and
highly standardised. This extract is a typical example.

Great Domesday Book, f. 210d. Survey of Shillington (Bedfordshire), 1086.
Latin.

The abbot [of Ramsey] also holds Shillington. It answers for 10 hides.
Land for 14 ploughs. In demesne 2 hides, and there are 2 ploughs
there. And 27 villeins have 12 ploughs. 5 bordars there and 4 serfs.
And a broken mill which renders nothing; meadow for 6 ploughs.
Woodland for 100 pigs. The value is £12, and always as much. This
manor lay in the lordship of St Benedict's church [Ramsey abbey]
before 1066.

2   A survey of Shillington, undated

A later survey of Shillington, originally twelfth century, although still
perfunctory. This contains more information about the descent of the manor
than the Domesday example, but the details of the manorial resources and
tenantry remain frustratingly basic and incomplete.

W. H. Hart and P. A. Lyons, eds, *Cartularium monasterii de Rameseia*, vol. I
(London, 1884), p. 277. Survey of Shillington (Bedfordshire), undated. Latin.

The abbot of Ramsey holds from the king [as a tenant]-in-chief three
carucates of land in Shillington from the grant of Ethelric the bishop
of Dorchester and confirmed by St Edward, William Bastard and
other kings. And just as the said lord holds there ten hides and five
virgates from the king, so the freemen and customary tenants hold
from the same abbot. Their rents are valued annually at [blank].
From meadow [blank], from woodland [blank], from the fishery
[blank], from pasture [blank]. There are two watermills there, which
are valued annually at [blank]. The said abbot has gallows, tumbrell
and view of frankpledge, and all that pertains to the view. And he
owes hideage when required. Patronage of the church is vested in the
abbot. The said manor pertains to the barony of the abbot.

3 Extracts from a survey of the estate of the bishop of Durham, 1183

These extracts contain the complete entries for the featured manors, and are taken from the extensive survey completed in 1183 of the estate of the bishopric of Durham. Once again they are brief, although more emphasis is given here to villein holdings and their dues than in the previous examples [1, 2]. The standardised holdings and renders of villein tenants are striking. Note also that Wilton and Fulforth are being directly exploited by the lord, while the other manors are farmed out to unnamed lessees.

W. Greenwell, ed., *Bolden Buke. A survey of the possessions of the see of Durham in the year 1183*, Surtees Society, 13 (1852), pp. 33, 35. Surveys of Wilton, Fulforth, Crawcrook, Winlaton and Barlow (Co. Durham), 1183. Latin.

In Wilton and Fulforth are 24 oxgangs and a half which the villeins hold, each oxgang of 8 acres and each one renders 2s., one hen and 10 eggs; and they plough and harrow for one day and mow the meadows, and make and move the hay, and with all of these works they receive food. Theobald holds one oxgang, and renders 3s. without work. Hugh holds 2 oxgangs without service, so long as it pleases the bishop. The demesne is in the hands of the bishop. The mill renders 2 marks.

[...] Crawcrook is at farm with the villeins, the demesne and the mill, and with a stock of one plough and one harrow, and it renders 11 marks and a half beyond the assize rents, and the assize rents render 4 marks and half, one cow in milk, 4 chalders of malt and as many of meal and oats, and one castleman, and with Ryton it carts one tun of wine.[44]

[...] Winlaton and Barlow are at farm, with the demesne and the villeins, without stock, and they render £15; and they mow the meadows for 2 days, each villein with one man, and then they have food, and they make and move hay for one day. The marsh, meadow and wood are in the hand of the bishop. The mill renders 5 marks and a half. Sunderland is at farm, and renders 100s. Roger de Audry renders one mark for the mill-dam built on the land of Sunderland.

---

44 Among the dues of the manorial tenants is the requirement to provide one man to perform military duties for the lord at a nearby castle ('castleman'), and to cart a tun of wine for the lord, presumably from a local port such as Newcastle, to one of the bishop's residences. The former is normally associated with free tenants, the latter with villeins.

4 A survey of Hartest, 1251

This is a fine example of a thirteenth-century manorial survey, taken from an estate-wide survey of the bishopric of Ely in 1251 known as the Coucher Book. In many respects, Hartest is a classic manor, characterised by a sizeable demesne, a large proportion of villein holdings, and a bureaucratic ecclesiastical landlord. The demesne lands are described in detail, and the size and customs of archetypal peasant holdings are recorded with careful precision. No valuations are given. The bulk of the survey is given over to a detailed description of the terms on which labour services are owed and discharged, even to the point of covering the arrangements for non-attendance in the event of sickness. The basic unit of labour service was a 'day work', and this survey goes to considerable lengths to define more closely what such a work might reasonably constitute. Whether the pressure for greater clarity and certainty of definition came from tenants or lord is uncertain, although the text reveals that jurors were used to clarify and verify matters. The use of labour services on the demesnes of the bishopric of Ely may well have been at its peak around this time, and this extraordinarily detailed record says much about the landlord's mentality.

Cambridge University Library, EDR G3/27, ff. 162–5. Survey of Hartest (Suffolk), 1251. Latin.

The demesne of this manor is demarcated thus: in a field which is called Appeltoun 80 acres. In a field which is called Northcote 11 acres and 1 rood. In Cubifeld 15 acres. In Edupnesfeld 11 acres 1 rood. In Wodefeld 62½ acres. In a field which is called Elefeld 24 acres. In Horescroft 20½ acres. In Netherhelefeld 55 acres. In a field which is called Thriciakres 30½ acres. In a field which is called Standoun 32½ acres. The total of all arable land 342½ acres measured by the short hundred and the perch of 16½ feet:[45] which can be cultivated by two plough teams whereof both are composed of two stots and six oxen, in accordance with the custom of the vill.

Concerning meadowland that can be mown, that is to say in a meadow called Brademede towards Sumertoun 2 acres. In a meadow which is called Hauebesket 4½ acres. In Standoun Meadow 3 acres. In the other Brademede opposite the gates of the *curia* 4 acres. In Bautoun 3 acres. Sum total of mowable meadows 16½ acres, by the aforesaid perch.

45 The short hundred is comprised of five score (a score is 20), and the long hundred of six score (and therefore 120). Use of the short hundred is more common, but the long hundred sometimes features in manorial accounts when enumerating stock, especially sheep, rabbits and doves. In the original document the scribe will often use the roman numeral C, followed by a superscript 'mi', to signify the short hundred and C^{ma} for the long hundred. For the standard perch, see p. xii.

Concerning several pasture. In Horseclose meadow 1 acre. In land in front of the hall doors and land for sheep 3½ acres. In Brademede at the hall gates 3 roods. In Respesiks 3 roods. In Hasselikall behind the *curia* 1 acre. In Stoudonemede 1½ acres. Total of several pasture, 8½ acres by the aforesaid perch.

Item, be it known that the lord has all the fields and his lands as aforesaid in severalty between the Purification of the Blessed Virgin Mary and the feast of St Michael,[46] except for 2 acres of meadow in Brademede towards Sumercote and 4½ acres in Hauekesthets, in which the neighbours will be able to common after the mowing and carting of the hay.

Concerning woodland. There is a wood there called Homereshay which contains 100 acres also by the aforesaid perch, by the short hundred. There is one grove there which is called Trandeley which contains 12 acres by the aforesaid perch.

Item, be it known that in the whole of this manor, both in lands and in pastures, the lord has his free warren.

Concerning the mill. Item, the lord can, if he should wish, have one windmill there to which all customary tenants owe suit.

Concerning stock. Of stock there can be there 5 cows and one free bull, 20 pigs and one free boar, and 5 score sheep, over and above the aforementioned plough-beasts.[47]

The heirs of Thomas de Burg' hold 20 acres of geldable land from the time of bishop W., that is to say of the demesne, for four shillings by equal portions. John the Shepeneman holds 15 acres of land for 3s. 4d. in equal payments and by the aforesaid customs, except for suit at the hundred court. Osbert son of Godrich holds 4 acres of land for 16d. per annum in equal portions and by the same customs, in accordance with the share of his tenement, except for suit of the hundred.

Reginald son of William the carpenter holds 4 acres of land for 12d. per annum in equal portions and he gives one hen and 4 eggs; and by the same customs as those that the same Osbert does. And he is

---

46 2 February and 29 September. The essential guide to converting dating by saints days and regnal years to the modern calendar is M. Jones, ed., *Handbook of dates for students of English history* (2000).

47 The lord's bull and boar ranged freely among the village cattle, impregnating demesne and peasant stock alike. This benefit to the peasantry was tempered by the lord's right to allow the bull and boar to wander throughout the open fields without restriction or impounding.

charged to find one man in the meadow for one day to lift hay and stack it, without food. The same man holds one sliver of land for 1d. a year at the Michaelmas term [29 September]. Henry the Tailor holds 3 acres of land for 10d. in equal portions and the same customs which Osbert does proportionately. The same holds 2 acres of land for 8d. in equal payments, which piece the present bishop acquired from Robert the Watchman.

Humfrey Huneman holds 4 acres of land for which he makes the ironwork of one plough each year and by the making of ironwork for a second plough yearly he will have half an acre of wheat and half an acre of oats and two oak trees in the wood, that is one in winter and another in summer. And he will shoe the work-horses for a year with the lord's iron and nails. And he owes the same customs as the aforesaid Osbert proportionately. The same holds one acre of land for a rent of 3d. per annum, that is at the feast of St Andrew [30 November], at the Annunciation of the Blessed Mary [25 March], and at the feast of St John the Baptist [24 June]. Michael of Pulham and William of Hoketon hold 5 acres of land, which used to be of Roger of Glemsford, for 14d. per annum in equal portions. Warren son of Edward holds 3 acres of land, which were of the land of the same Roger, for 9d. in equal portions. Walter son of Edward holds one acre of land, which was of the land of the same Roger, for 3d. in equal portions. Eudo Maymund holds one acre of land for 6d. per annum in equal portions.

Concerning customary tenants. John son of Gilbert at Hill holds one virgate of land which contains 30 acres. And he gives in 'hering-selver',[48] 2½d. per annum at the feast of St Andrew, and because of this he will be quit of four works. And he gives one hen at Christmas; and 30 eggs at Easter; and one and a half quarters of fodder-corn at oat-sowing time. And he owes four works every week during the year, except that for every week for the month before the feast of St John [24 June] and also for the month before the feast of Saint Michael [29 September] he owes five works. And the work days are Monday, Tuesday and Wednesday, except for the week before Christmas and the twelve days of Christmas, and two days before Easter, and the weeks of Easter and Whitsun, and all red letter days if they should

---

48 The exact origin and meaning of herringsilver is obscure, but it obviously relates to a payment in lieu of an ancient service involving the provision of herring as rent.

fall on his appointed work-days. So, if such a feast should fall upon a Monday, then he will be quit of two works; and if on a Tuesday or a Wednesday then he will be quit of one work.

And every week from Michaelmas [29 September] until Christmas he will plough as much as he can for one day, without food and work. And he will plough within the same period one and a half acres of 'govelerthe',[49] and will be quit of one work. And in every week between the Purification [2 February] and Easter, namely for 8 weeks, he ought to plough as much as he can for one day, in accordance with the custom of the vill, without food and work.[50]

Item he will plough an acre and a half of 'govelerthe' within the same period, and then will be quit of one work. And be it known that as much as he shall have ploughed by custom and of 'govelerthe', that much he will harrow the oats, without food and work. And as often as there shall be work he will harrow one acre for one work. And as much as he shall have ploughed of 'govelerthe', whether in winter or in Lent, he will sow. And he will go for that purpose supplied by the lord with a seedlip but without food and work. Item he will plough from Trinity until 1st August every week for one day without food and work. And be it known that he is not quit of his works by plough service on account of any feast in the year, except of 'govelerthe' in the manner aforesaid. And be it known that he is to come with five work beasts thrice a year for plough boonworks, the lord providing food. And should he not have any beasts to be yoked, then let him not come.

Item he and all his equals, and all tenants of a virgate of demesne land, and all tenants of 8 acres of land subject to work-service shall mow the lord's meadows for three days with 20 mowers. And to each of the aforesaid mowers there will be allowed three days for one work, And let them spread that which they shall have mown. Item if he should come to lift hay on any of his work days, then it will be allowed to him for one work if it be for an entire day. And if he comes on Thursday, Friday or Saturday, then it shall be counted as nothing

49 Again, the meaning of 'govel' is uncertain, but is clearly a ploughing service to be performed on the lord's demesne land.

50 The number of weeks between 2 February and Easter would vary each year according to the (movable) date of Easter. The point being made is that this ploughing will be performed for eight weeks. The caveat that this labour service is 'without food and work' means that it does not count against the tenant's dues of 'four works every week': in contrast to the 'govelerthe' service, which counts for one work.

towards him. And on account of that mowing they shall have in common one sheep or 12d. And each of them shall have one loaf or, in common, half a quarter of wheat according to their custom; and one cheese and one basketful of salt; and 4d. for drinks; and a bundle of firewood or straw for cooking their food.

Item he and his equals and all tenants of a virgate of demesne land, with the help of the carts of the *curia* if there shall be any, will carry the hay off the meadows to the *curia* without food and work. And all tenants of 8 acres and all cottars shall stack that hay at the *curia* without food or work. And let him find four male labourers for the first harvest boonwork. And he himself shall go also to oversee them that they may do a good job, and they shall have bread and meat to eat and ale to drink. And at the second boonwork two men in like manner with food of the lord. And at the third boonwork, which is called Waterbedrepe, two men similarly with food from the lord and water to drink. And as often as there shall be such work he shall weed for one whole day for one work. And he ought to wash and shear five sheep or ten lambs for one work. And he ought to reap from the govel 4 acres of wheat and 4 acres of oats, binding, stacking and carrying to the *curia* without food and work. And he ought to reap, bind and stack but not carry half an acre of wheat or rye for one work. And if he has manured then it will be allowed to him as a work and a half. And he ought to reap, bind and stack similarly one acre of barley or beans or peas for three works, but not to carry them; and of oats, half an acre for one work only. And as often as the work is on, he will carry the lord's corn in the harvest, as above, with food in moderation from the lord, without work. And he ought to reap stubble for half a day or gather four score sheaves of stubble and bundle and bind and stack, but not carry them, for one work. And he ought to carry dung as often as work shall be ongoing, that is 15 heaps or 7½ cart loads in whatever fields the lord shall wish, and it shall be allowed to him for 4 works. And he shall have for his tumbrel half a bundle of withies for each work-beast.

Item be it known that for every day on which he shall work in the harvest he shall have a small meal, that is to say a loaf and some relish, but nevertheless it shall be accounted to him for a work as above. And he ought to thresh half a quarter of wheat or half a quarter of barley for one work and a half; and half a quarter of barley, beans or peas, or one quarter of oats for one work. And whatever he shall thresh he shall clean and shall carry it to the granary. And the chaff and straw

likewise in whatever place the bailiff shall have assigned to him within
the *curia*, without food and work. And let him come for two quarters
of grain at the lord's granary, and let him make malt from it. And
afterwards let him bring it back, then there shall be allowed to him
one work. And let him do carrying service in accordance with the
roster of his neighbours, with horse and sack, both short and long
journeys; the short journeys as far as Rattlesden, Hitcham, Bury St
Edmunds, Clare, Sudbury and Glemsford and the like, and he will be
credited with one work if he shall have done carrying on his work
day, and if on another day then nothing. The long journeys are as far
as Littleport, [Wood] Ditton, Ely, Brandon, Feltwell, Wetheringsett,
Balsham, Hadstock, Ipswich, Colchester and such places.[51] And each
carrying service will be allowed to him for two works if he shall do
that carriage on a work-day of his and not on any other day. And be it
known that he will carry by each of his services, if there is a task, half a
quarter of wheat or rye or barley or beans or peas; or one quarter of
oats. And it shall be allowed to him as above.

And he shall trench in clear ground one perch five feet in width and to
a depth of five feet; or, in an old trench, one and a half perches of the
same width and depth, as one work. And he ought to split fencing
material or gather withies until the hour of noon in the wood for one
work. Item he ought to split and prepare three bundles of withies in
the wood and carry them as far as the road, for one work. And thereof
he will make two and a half hurdles for one work, and he will carry
them as far as the road; or five hurdles for two works when the task
is needed. And he ought to close up the hedges in the *curia* or the
woodland or elsewhere in the manor from dawn till noon for one
work. And be it that as often as he may split fencing or withies or
hurdles or make hedges, then he shall have one small bundle of lopped
branches or trimmings. And he ought to dig in the *curia* or outside it,
do walling, split firewood, roof houses [with thatch] and clean and do
other small *ad hoc* jobs from 1st August till Whitsun; each day he will
work from dawn till noon for one work; and from Whitsun till 1st
August for one whole day for one work.

His sheep shall not lie in the lord's fold [*sic*]. And he owes suit of mill
if there shall be one on the manor. And he will pay a merchet for his
daughter to be married, and likewise childwyte if she shall have

51 With the exception of Ipswich and Colchester, all of these places are demesne
   manors of the bishopric of Ely. See Miller, *Bishopric of Ely*, for an excellent
   background to the management of the Ely estates at this time.

fornicated and have had a child. And he will give tallage at the lord's will. Nor can he sell his male colt or bull of his own rearing without leave of the lord's bailiff.

Item if the same should become so infirm within the harvest or without it that he shall have been confessed and given communion, then he shall be quit of his works for one month only. But nevertheless he shall do his ploughing outside harvest and his boonworks in harvest. And if he shall be infirm for more than one month then he will not be quit any more. And if he should be so ill for eight days that he shall have been confessed, then he will in the meantime be quit. And if afterwards he recovers from that illness then he will be quit for two days only. And if it should happen a second time he is no more quit.

And if he should die the lord shall have the best beast of the house for a heriot, or 32d. if he shall have no beast, and then his wife shall be free and quit of his works for 30 days only. But nevertheless she shall do her ploughing and her boonworks in harvest as above, and nevertheless his son and heir will make fine with the lord for his relief as best as he shall be able.

Item the same holds 3 acres of land by 6d. per annum in equal portions.

Item be it known that [tenants of] 2 virgates of land ought to plough with their plough for one day in Lent for 'barlibene'[52] and sowing with the lord's barley and harrow without food and work. Item be it known that on the first two days upon which they mow, each of the aforesaid twenty mowers on each of those two days shall have one small bundle of herbage, that is to say as much as he can lift from the ground with his scythe. And if in lifting the herbage he should break the shaft of the scythe or if he should put the other head of the scythe on the ground, then he shall have nothing. But the jurors say that each one ought to have by right in the same manner, on each of those two days, two little bundles. And on the third day on which they mow they shall have no herbage, but their sheep with appurtenances in the manner aforesaid.

John son of Peter holds a virgate of land in the same manner. The same holds a certain part of his curtilage by 6d. in equal portions. John son of Simon holds a virgate of land in the same manner. John of Stapelton holds one virgate of land in the same manner. Henry the reeve holds one virgate of land in the same manner.

52 'Barlibene' appears to be the local name for the spring ploughing service.

Concerning tenants of half-virgates. Richard Pach holds half a virgate of land which contains 15 acres of land. And he gives of herringsilver yearly at the term of St Andrew [30 November] one penny and one farthing; and he will be quit of three works. And he gives one hen at Christmas and 15 eggs at Easter. And of fodder-corn 6 bushels of oats at oat-sowing time. And he owes in every week through the year 3 works, namely on the days of Monday, Tuesday and Wednesday, excepting the week preceding Christmas, the 12 days of Christmas, one day and a half before Easter, and the weeks of Easter and Whitsun, and all red letter days if they should fall upon his work-days. And he is to find one complete plough, whether yoked or not, for 6 days between Michaelmas [29 September] and Christmas and he will plough for those days, as much as he can, without food or work. And in the same period he will plough 3 roods of 'govelerthe' for one work without food. And in the same way he will find one plough, as above, between the Purification of the Blessed Mary [2 February] and Easter for 4 days. And in the same period he will plough 3 roods of 'govelerthe'. And he will go to the lord's granary for seed and will sow and harrow, and it will be allowed to him for one work without food. And be it known that however much he ploughed for oats he shall harrow without food and work, and as often as there shall be work he shall harrow one acre for one work. The same man shall plough between Trinity and 1st August every second week for one day with food and work. And he is to come three times a year with as many beasts as he yokes for the boon-work ploughing, with food from the lord according to the custom of the vill. And if he has nothing to yoke, then let him not come to the said boonworks. And be it known that this man and his three equals are to make one plough and plough with it for one day in Lent for 'barlibene', and will sow and harrow it without food or work.

The same man is to come in common with others to the lord's meadow for mowing for 3 days in the aforesaid manner, and it will be allowed to him for a work as above. And if he should come to lifting the hay as above then it will be allowed to him for a work as above. And he shall have his share of mutton with the others in the meadow as above. And he shall have his herbage likewise as above. And he will carry hay just like John as above. Item he will weed, wash sheep and lambs, and shear just as the said John. And he ought to reap in 'govelrep' for 4 weeks in the harvest, 2 acres of wheat and 2 acres of oats and bind and stack and carry, and there shall be allowed to him

4 works but he will not have food. And he is to find two men for the first harvest boonwork, and one man for the second, and one man for the third. And they will have their food in moderation as aforesaid. And he ought to reap, bind and stack any corn whatsoever for his works just as the aforesaid John, and he will carry corn as often as there shall be that work in the manner aforesaid. And he will mow or gather it just as the said John. And he will carry as much muck, as often as there is that work, as the said John, and it will be allowed to him for three works. And he will have a quarter of a small faggot for making ready his cart. And he ought to thresh any grain whatsoever and clean it and carry it to the granary; and the chaff and straw in like manner as the said John. And he will come to the lord's granary for one quarter of grain, and thereof he will make malt and afterwards return it, and then it will be allowed to him for one work. And he will do his carrying service, in both short and long journeys, in the same manner of the aforesaid John, and it will be allowed to him in the same way. And he ought to ditch, split fencing material or withies, make hurdles and hedges; and he shall have loppings and trimmings, in the same way as the said John. And he ought to dig, wall, split wood, roof houses, clean up, and do other minor and *ad hoc* tasks for his works like John.

His sheep will not lie in the lord's fold. And he owes suit of mill as above. And he will give a fee to have leave for his daughter to marry and will pay childwite for his daughter, and tallage as above, nor may he sell his stallion or bull as above. And if he should become ill as above then he will be quit as above. And if he should die as above then he will give his best beast or 16d. for a heriot, and his wife will be quit for 30 days as above, and his son and heir shall make fine with the lord as best he may for a relief as above.

The same Richard holds half a virgate of land which was of Hugh Musclet in the same manner. William son of Richard half a virgate of land in the same way. The same holds 6 acres of land by 12d. yearly by equal portions. Henry Lamb holds half a virgate of land in the same manner. Warren son of Edward holds half a virgate of land in the same way. The same holds 8 acres of land from the time of Bishop Eustace for 2s. in equal portions. William son of Simon holds half a virgate of land in the same way. The same holds 2 acres of land for 4d. in equal portions. John son of Anketill holds half a virgate of land in the same way. Richard son of Ernald holds half a virgate of land in the same way, and it is appointed that he pay one penny and one farthing more for herringsilver.

Concerning eight-acre tenants. Walter Frede of Clynton holds 8 acres of land and gives one hen at Christmas and 8 eggs at Easter and 3 bushels of foddercorn. And he owes in every week of the year two works, that is to say on Monday and Tuesday, except the week immediately before Christmas, the twelve days of Christmas, one day before Easter, the weeks of Easter and Whitsun, and each red letter day if it shall fall on a Monday only and not otherwise. And he will plough one acre of govel in winter for one work. And in Lent likewise he will plough and will sow some of the lord's corn. And he will harrow one acre of govel for one work. And if he has beasts to yoke let him come to plough boonwork with food provided by the lord as above, but he will do no other ploughing in the year. Item he will mow and do all things in the lord's meadow in common, just like the said John son of Gilbert does above except that he will not carry if he shall stack hay at the *curia* with his equals, without food and work. And he will weed and will wash sheep and lambs and will shear for his works as above. And in 'govelrep' he ought to reap 2 acres of wheat and 2 acres of oats and will bind and stack them in the grange, but will not carry, without food and work. But on the day that he stacks he will have bread and a relish. And he ought to find at each of three boonworks in harvest one man getting food from the lord, as above.

And he ought to reap any corn whatsoever, and bind and stack it for his works like the aforesaid John. And he will have his food on whichever day he shall work in the harvest, and he will reap or gather stubble for his work as above. He will neither carry dung nor make malt but he will thresh for his works as above. And he will do carrying service afoot in turn with his neighbours, short and long journeys, to the same manors and places as the aforesaid John son of Gilbert does above. And he will be credited with his works in the same way. And he will ditch and do fencing and split withies and make hurdles and hedges for his works and shall have loppings and trimmings like the said John. And he ought to dig, wall, split, roof houses, clean up and do other minor and *ad hoc* tasks for his works like the said John, and he ought to dig and wall as has been said. His sheep will not lie in the lord's fold. And he owes mill-suit as above and tallage and merchet and childwite for his daughter as above. Nor may he sell his stallion or bull as above. And if he becomes infirm as above then he will be quit as above. And if he should die as above then he will give 8d. for a heriot, and his wife shall be quit for 30 days as above. And his son and heir will make fine with the lord for his relief to the best of his ability as above.

Agnes Brichaky holds 8 acres of land in the same manner. Ern[?ald] the carpenter holds 8 acres in the same way. Geoffrey of Colne holds 8 acres in the same way. Eudo Underwode holds 8 acres in the same manner. The same holds a certain small meadow with a certain assart for 4d. in equal portions. Thorald the Gardener holds 8 acres of land in the same manner. Richard Pach holds 8 acres of land in the same way. Henry Hevenehey holds 8 acres of land in the same way. The same holds one acre of land for 3d., that is to say at Michaelmas [29 September] and at the feast of St Andrew [30 November] and at the Annunciation of the Blessed Mary [25 March]. William, son of Richard the reeve, holds 8 acres of land in the same way.

Concerning cottars. Roger Thorolde holds one cot-land which contains 4 acres, and he gives one hen at Christmas and 4 eggs at Easter. He gives neither herringsilver nor foddercorn. And he owes in each week through the whole year one work, that is on Monday, and he will not be quit from his work because of any feast except only in the week next before Christmas, and in the twelve days of Christmas, and in the weeks of Easter and Whitsun. And he will plough half an acre of govel in winter for one work and similarly in Lent a half acre for one work and likewise in Lent half an acre and he will sow that and harrow it. And he will go to the lord's granary for the seed as above and it will be allowed to him for one work. And if he has anything to yoke he is to come to a plough boonwork, with food from the lord, just like the said Walter Frede. But he will do no other ploughing during the year. And he will help in the lord's meadows at the lifting and stacking of hay and likewise in the grange, without food and work. And he will weed and will shear sheep and lambs for his works as above. And he will reap one acre of wheat and one acre of oats in 'govelrep', and bind and stook, but not carry or stack. Neither shall he have food nor will it be allowed to him for a work. And he is to find at each of three harvest boonworks one man, with food from the lord as above. Nor will he mow stubble but he will gather it as above. And he shall reap any kind of corn and bind and stack it for his work just like Walter Frede. And on any day when he shall work in harvest he will have his food as above. He will neither carry dung nor make malt nor do carrying service. He ought to do threshing for his work as above. He shall do ditching and fencing and withy-splitting and make hurdles and hedges for his works. And he will have loppings and trimmings as above. And he ought to dig, wall, split wood, roof houses, clean up and do other and *ad hoc* tasks for his works, as above. His sheep will not lie in the lord's fold. And he owes mill-suit as above. And he will give tallage and merchet for his daughter and childwite, as above. Nor can he sell his stallion as above nor his bull as above. And if he should fall ill as above then he will be quit as above. And if he should die as above then he will give 4d. or one ploughshare for a heriot, and his wife will be quit for 30 days from his works as above. And his son and heir shall nevertheless make fine with the lord for his relief as above. The same holds [blank] acres of land by 10d. a year in equal amounts.

Concerning the very small cottars. Richard son of Wyok holds one acre of land and gives one hen at Christmas and one egg at Easter. And he owes in every week of the year one work, that is on Monday except all red letter days and the same weeks as in the case of the aforesaid Roger Torold. He will neither plough nor harrow nor come to plough boonwork nor mow in the meadows nor reap in govelrep nor carry hay or corn or dung, neither will he make malt or do carrying service. Nor will his sheep lie in the lord's fold, nor can he sell his bull or stallion as above. And he ought to weed, reap, ditch, dig, wall, split wood, make hurdles and hedges, and thresh as above, clean and roof houses and do other minor and *ad hoc* tasks for his works like the said Roger Torold. And he owes mill-suit as above. And he will give tallage, merchet and childwite for his daughter, as above. And if he should become ill as above then he will be quit as above. And if he should die as above, then he will give one plough-share for a heriot, and his wife shall be quit of his works for 30 days as above. And his son and heir shall make fine with the lord for his relief as above. Item, be it known that at each of three harvest boon-works he is to find one man as above.

Ralph son of Godine holds one acre of land in the same way. William of Valda holds half an acre of land and gives the lord a hen and an egg. And he owes in every week of the year as many works and the same customs and will work in the same way for his works as the aforesaid Richard Wyoks except also all red letter days and the weeks as above.

And be it known that the lord can make any tenant of 15 acres his reeve if he should so wish. And then that man will be quit of herring-silver, hens, eggs, fodder-corn and all his works and ploughing outside the harvest and boonworks in the harvest. And furthermore he will have half an acre of wheat and half an acre of oats in the harvest, and pasturage on the meers [baulks] in the fields for his horse when he rides around to look after the fields, and leftovers of hay in the meadows, and food between 1st August and Michaelmas [29 September], because he will be messor as well as reeve. And he will have grazing for his horse within the *curia*, and forage and chaff as often as he shall be on the lord's business at market or elsewhere.

Item be it known that the lord can appoint as his forester any tenant of 8 acres, if he shall wish, and then that man will be quit of hens and eggs and fodder-corn and all his customary dues and works only.

Item the lord has right of free warren, and free bull and free boar, and escapes of animals which are called waifs.

The advowson of the church and its gift belong to the bishop of Ely, and it is in the bishopric of Norwich and in the archdeaconry of Sudbury and in the deanery of Thedwastre, excepting for two parts of all the tithes of demesne lands of the pittancer of St Edmunds which the same pittancer holds of the lord bishop in the manor, which tithes the almoner of St Edmunds has yearly.

5   A detailed description of the capital messuage of Willington, 1376

This extract is taken from a 'condition' survey of the capital messuage of the manor, an altogether less common form of survey than the examples given so far. In fact, it emanates from the royal administration of a manor which had escheated into the king's hands on the death of its lord, but whose heir had not yet reached the age of majority. Until that time, the king (in this case, Edward III) could exploit or dispose of the manor (in this case, Willington) as he saw fit. In order to evaluate this temporary asset, royal officials had ordered the king's escheator in Bedfordshire to inspect and report upon it. The resulting, somewhat zealous, survey reveals an unusual amount of detail about the main manorial buildings and their layout, and, in particular, serious neglect and dilapidation.

Calendar of Inquisitions Miscellaneous, 1348–1377, p. 392. Survey of the capital messuage of Willington (Bedfordshire), 8 November 1376. Latin.

Writ to Thomas Sewale, escheator in Bedfordshire and Buckingham-shire, to enquire as to the state of a number of manors, which are in the King's hands after the death of Elizabeth de Mowbray of Axholme, and in the minority of the heir. 10 May 1376 [...]

8 November 1376. In the manor of Willington the principal gate is completely ruined and carried away except the gate staples; the second gate is completely ruined; the third gate, with a watch-tower at the entry to the motte and a drawbridge, is much broken as regards timber, walls and roof. There is a hall of ancient fashion with a pantry, a buttery, a passage and a kitchen annexed, which used to be tiled but are now mostly unroofed, and the timber is old and in bad condition. There is a bakehouse of ancient fashion, old and in bad condition, mostly tiled and the rest unroofed. There is a chamber called Knight's chamber of which the timber is doubtful: it is tiled but needs re-pointing. There is the foundation of another chamber newly laid, that is 'resyns', beams and studs annexed to the said chamber and no more. There is a chamber for the lord with a passage now ruined and nearly razed to the ground for want of both timber and roofing. There is another building called the Nursery, which is tiled but needs pointing and the timber is in very bad condition and almost falling down. There is a building called the Chapel entirely unroofed, but the timber can easily be mended. There is a building called the Garret which used to be a wardrobe for clothes, which is much ruined for want of timber and roofing. There is a watermill of which the building is sufficient but repairs are greatly needed to the wheel and the necessary working parts in the water, and to the floodgates, weir and the foundation of the mill. There is in another place a barn with a haywain house which is completely unroofed and the timber almost fallen to the ground. There is a dovecote kept in reasonable condition. The walls of the manor are of mud and are altogether razed and destroyed. The jurors believe that the whole could be repaired for £100.

6   A description of the capital messuage of Salton, 1479

This short extract from a manorial survey of Salton is much more typical than the previous example [5] of the descriptions of capital messuages which were compiled by estate, rather than royal, administrators, in that it merely describes the existence of buildings rather than their condition. However, such descriptions become more common in later surveys, probably because the lord wished to maintain a detailed record of the buildings within the messuage as an aid to drawing up a leasehold contract.

J. Raine, ed., *The priory of Hexham, vol. 2. The Black Book of 1479*, Surtees Society, 46 (1865), p. 72. Extract from a survey of the manor of Salton (Yorkshire), 1479. Latin.

They hold a certain manor in the vill of Salton where various houses are built, namely one hall with three chambers and a chapel; a kitchen, bakehouse, brewhouse, great stable, an orchard and a garden called the Pengarth. And on the north part of this manor one hall called the Guesthall with a chamber at the end, and the Gatehouse, and one great grange, woodshed, piggery and one maltkiln newly built; an orchard called Kilngarth and a garden called the Bengarth.

7   Inventory of manorial goods and stock at Hemsby, 1352

An obvious extension to a written description of the capital messuage is the compilation of an inventory of the equipment and stock kept within the buildings. Manorial accounts record the annual ebbs and flows of seigneurial grain and animals on the manor, but seldom mention equipment (unless it was bought, sold or repaired). Indeed, inventories of manorial equipment are fairly rare. In 1352, Norwich cathedral priory drew up inventories for each of its demesne manors, and this extract for Hemsby provides exceptional detail about the tools, implements, furnishings and utensils within each of the buildings in the capital messuage.

D. Yaxley, ed., *The prior's manor houses: inventories of eleven of the manor houses of the prior of Norwich made in 1352* (Dereham, 1988), pp. 14–5. Inventory of Hemsby (Norfolk), 1352. Latin.

Hemsby

Item there remain there in the chamber, 2 benches, 1 shield (*'target'*). Item in the steward's chamber, 1 bench. Item in the larder, 2 troughs for salting meat, 1 block for cutting meat. Item in the chapel, 1 wooden altar, 1 superaltar and 1 painted panel above the altar, 1 lectern and 1 bench. Item in the hall, 6 tables, 5 pairs of trestles, 4 benches, 1 worn bowl, 1 laver, 1 broken bar for the fire (*'aundiron'*). Item in the pantry, 1 chest for bread, 1 vat, 2 canvases. Item in the buttery, 2 casks, 4 cades, 2 pairs of trestles, 1 board for cups with trestles. Item in the kitchen, 3 brazen vessels, 1 posnet, 2 worn pans, 1 cauldron, 1 lead vat on the ground, 2 tripods, 1 gridiron, 1 iron roasting spit, 1 mortar with 2 pestles, 1 dresser [for preparing food], 1 flesh hook.

Item in the dairy, 1 bench, 5 eastland tables, 1 table with 2 trestles, 1 table for drying cheese, 5 cheese vats, 2 cheese presses, 1 wooden bucket, 1 churn, 9 dishes, 9 plates, 12 saucers, 2 hanging tables, 1 press, 1 large jug (*'gache'*), 1 broken tong.

Item in the bakehouse, 1 open tub for sieving, 2 hanging lead vats with wooden covers, 1 trough for pastry, 1 moulding board, 6 vats, 4 casks, 2 wide shallow tubs ('*keleres*'), 3 little troughs, 1 bearing-skep [basket], 2 winnowskeps, 3 skeps for carrying malt, 1 sieve for ale, 1 sieve for flour, 1 boulter, 2 shovels for malt, 3 maltstools, 1 bucket bound with iron for the well, 1 spout for the cistern, 1 leaded cistern, 2 hair-cloths for the kiln.

Item in the granary, 2 wooden bushels bound with iron, 2 fans, 2 winnowskeps, 2 shovels for corn, 2 sieves, 4 sacks, 1 cloth for winnowing, 1 peck of straw, 1 '*fleke*' of straw, 6 ploughs of which 4 are old, 6 coulters with 10 shares and 12 collars of leather, 3 pairs of traces, 4 pairs of plough wheels, 4 pairs of traces, 3 harrows.

Item 1 fuel cart with ironed wheels and all the gear; 3 cart bodies for harvest, 1 tumbrel with bare wheels, 1 pair of bare cartwheels, 4 cart saddles, 2 pairs of traces for the cart, 2 pairs of beams, 4 cart-ropes, 5 forks for harvest, 4 forks, 2 spades, 1 shovel, 3 forks for muck, 2 bills, 2 ladders, 14 steps, 1 small ladder, 1 fan, 1 peck for horses, 1 pair of pincers, 1 saw, 1 hook, 1 pack saddle, 12 old axles, 14 sickles. Item 1 new weedhook.

Item in the stable, 10 stotts, 26 cows, 2 heifers, 3 bullocks, 3 bulls, 4 calves of above a year old, 6 calves born this year. Item, 2 boars, 4 sows, 9 pigs, 24 piglets.

Item 16 geese, of which 6 are ganders; 2 cocks, 10 hens; 1 pair of paunces and brassarts [armour], 1 chest plate, 1 helmet, 1 pair of gauntlets and breastplates.

Memorandum of the hut, with hurdles and stakes of the fold.

8   A custumal of the manor of Cockerham, 1326–27

Surveys are sometimes known as custumals, for the obvious reason that they list the rents and customs owed by each manorial tenant. However, in most cases a custumal is a rather different document which lists all the various 'customs' of the manor, including its regulation of agricultural arrangements, retail activities and public order issues. Hence the custumal provided the lord with a handy checklist of local customs, and often drew upon a combination of sworn local testimony and the precedents recorded in other manorial documents (especially court rolls). This example from Cockerham provides a good illustration of the potential of this type of document to historians: the list of customs is rich and varied, offering an excellent insight into many aspects of everyday life. Note, for example, the diverse resource base, providing local residents with peat for fuel, salt pans, extensive pasture for grazing, woodland products, and mussels from the shoreline.

R. Sharpe France, ed., 'Two custumals of the manor of Cockerham, 1326 and 1483', *Transactions of the Lancashire and Cheshire Antiquarian Society*, 64 (1954), pp. 42–7. Custumal of Cockerham (Lancashire), 1326–27. Latin.

The customs of the manor of Cockerham in the county of Lancaster, diocese of York and archdeaconry of Richmond anciently observed in the said manor of Cockerham and ordained from time to time in the court of the same manor of the aforesaid lord, and in a court which was held by Brother William Geryn, cellarer of the monastery of the Blessed Mary of Leicester, in the year of our Lord one thousand three hundred and twenty six and in the first year of the reign of King Edward the third after the conquest of England.

It was ordered that the tenants shall not dig more turves than they can conveniently and sufficiently use for burning, and the fuel from the holdings shall not be provided for strangers under a penalty of half a mark. And the tenants of [Great and Little] Crimbill shall maintain the dikes of the mill pond so that the pond does not burst for the lack of them. And no tenant shall go to other mills. And the tenants of the marsh shall maintain the sea dikes, each of them at his own place under a penalty of half a mark.

Item no tenant shall call any of his neighbours a thief or a robber under a penalty of 40d. And no tenant shall call any of his neighbours a whore, if he does so he shall give the lord 12d.

Item no tenant shall prevent the cattle or animals of his neighbours from being taken into the lord's pound when an offence has been committed under a penalty of 40d. Item no tenant shall dare to put cattle or animals in the lord's pound or in any way drag them out by night, or furtively lead them away, under a penalty of 6s. 8d.

Item no tenant shall implead his neighbour or his fellow for any injury he has suffered in another court outside the aforesaid lordship under a penalty of the seizure of his holding.[53]

Item no tenant shall allow his holding or his houses to fall into ruin under a penalty of making full reparation and seizure of his holding.

---

53 A device designed to ensure that tenants bring cases and business to this manorial court rather than those of other local lords: the severity of the penalty might imply that the manor had suffered in this regard at some time.

No tenant shall bring fuel for his salt cote from outside his holding or take the fuel which has been assigned to one holding to another without the licence of the lord under a penalty of 40d.

No tenant shall sell his turves to anyone without the grant of a licence from the lord under a penalty of 20d.

No tenant shall keep on a marsh, that is to say a common pasture, horses of less value than half a mark which are called in English 'nasaldes' or 'tyttes' under a penalty of 6s. 8d. No tenant shall keep a scabby horse or horses under a penalty of 6s. 8d.

Item no tenant of his own authority shall alter the boundaries of any sands or turf which have been assigned from ancient times under a penalty of half a mark. Item no tenant shall in any way deprive his neighbour of the turf which has been assigned to him under a penalty of half a mark.

Item no tenant shall destroy in any manner the ancient and appointed way on our moss which in English is called Morethweyte or dig turves thereon under a penalty of 40d.

Item none of our tenants whether in our court or outside shall, either as a whole or singly, falsify any inquest under a penalty of paying half a mark to the lord, and similarly to each man who is upon the inquest.

None of our tenants shall in any way remove his neighbour's fences under a penalty of 12d. Item none of our tenants in the place called the Bankhouse shall keep the ditches closed which reach from the moss to the sea, thus causing a flooding of his neighbour's corn, nor shall he prevent those who are concerned from opening them under a penalty of half a mark.

Item no brewer who brews for sale shall refuse to sell ale up to four gallons under a penalty of 6d.

Item anyone holding his tenement for any time after the feast of the Nativity of St John the Baptist [24 June] and not rendering a penny in the manor of the lord shall be held wholly and fully to account for the whole of the following year until the same feast, even though in the meantime he has left his tenement.

Item no tenant shall by himself or his cattle break the dike of the water mill or make a path through the middle of it under a penalty of 40d. for each time.

Item no tenant shall receive servants whether men or women against the will and command of the lord under a penalty of 6s. 8d.

The tenants of Great and Little Crimbill shall maintain and preserve the dike of the aforesaid water mill from harm and breach under a penalty of 40d., each place being responsible for the part of the dike anciently assigned to it under a penalty of the sum aforesaid.

Item each tenant having four acres of arable land shall plough with the lord with one ox twice a year or he shall give the lord 6d., and if he has eight acres he shall give 12d. and so on a mounting scale in proportion to the quantity of his land, 12d. for a plough. And each tenant shall give gifts to the lord in the harvest as they are contained in the rental, or 12d. for each gift and 12d. for each hen. And each tenant shall give ½d. a year for the making of the fold and likewise the elders of the town give 'outlane halfpennies'⁵⁴ for the causeway. And on his death each tenant shall give the lord his best beast.

Item the lord shall be paid one penny for any stray animal belonging to the tenants caught in the corn, the meadow, or the pasture of the lord. And no tenant within the manor of Cockerham shall keep a pig in his house unless it be ringed under a penalty of 40d., but if he shall keep his pigs on the common pasture of Wiyrsdall then he owes [blank] to the warden of the manor for them. And no tenant shall allow the aforesaid pig to enter onto the lord's demesne under a penalty of 40d. for each time, and no tenant shall keep the aforesaid swine within the lord's demesne under a penalty of 40d. for each, always excepting Adam Slaven senior, and Randolph Hoggesson. And the reason for this is that these tenants aforesaid may keep them in the pasture unharmed and free from the interference of their neighbours, the one in the wood of Forton and the other in his own field.

And no tenant of the manor of Cockerham shall live anywhere other than on his holding in the manor of Cockerham with his family, and if he does so his holding will be seized and taken into the lord's hand. And no tenant shall set to farm or in any other way sublet his land, pasture, or moss without licence under pain of the seizure of his holding.

And no one shall keep she-goats within the boundary of the manor of Cockerham, and if they do shall be heavily amerced.

54 The labour services are light compared to those at Hartest [4], and the readily-reckoned values for commuting them imply that the practice was commonplace. The 'outlane halfpennies' are another example of a long-standing commutation of an ancient customary due, perhaps for access or in lieu of a service for maintaining the causeway.

Item whoever has a holding of four acres of land shall bring one ox to plough with the lord's team twice a year or he shall give the lord 12d. for the ox if he does not have it, and should he have eight acres of land he shall bring two oxen or give the lord 2s., and if he has more he shall give more and if less he shall give less according to the number of acres which he holds unless he has a full plough team and then he shall plough with the lord twice a year.

And no one shall fell any trees or cut branches in the lord's woods or receive any who have done so, and if he does he shall be heavily amerced. And when damage of this kind has been done, an inquest of the inhabitants of the wood shall be held in the lord's court to establish who has done the damage, and if they cannot be apprehended by this inquest then the inhabitants will be amerced to the amount of the damage done; a special penalty is imposed however for oak and ash, namely 40d. No tenant of Cockerham shall fell or uproot oak or ash within the bounds and limits of the aforesaid lordship without licence of the lord under a penalty of 40d., and those in the vicinity of this kind of wood-felling shall pay the penalty on those occasions when the offender cannot be had in court. Item no one by himself or another shall fell or uproot the ash trees or willows growing in the copses without the view or licence of the warden of the manor, and if he does so he shall be amerced to double the value of the trees.

No tenant shall hire servants, whether men or women, for the period of hay making until the lord has chosen whom he will at or near 1 August. Tenants summoned to mow with the lord shall come on the day appointed or on the next day immediately following under a penalty of 2s. Item no tenant shall receive any men or women who refuse to reap in the harvest although resident in the lordship and then take themselves off to work elsewhere; and he shall not take any such reapers or binders into his service until the warden of the manor has expressed the wish to have them or not; if he does so he shall be heavily amerced.[55]

Item when all the tenants have been summoned to plough or reap with the lord on a certain day they shall not fail to come on the day on which they were summoned, except when they are reasonably prevented and then they shall come on the morrow of the aforesaid day; if they

---

55 These two customs are designed to protect the harvest workforce on the demesne and the harvest workforce in the village. Labour shortages were most severe in the harvest period.

default then distraint shall be made of all their animals until they submit to the will of the warden.

Item no tenant shall pasture his animals along the dikes of the lord or on his holding, if he does so he shall be heavily amerced.

Item no tenant shall implead or complain against his neighbour in another court or take part with a stranger or relative against his neighbour for any injuries, but he shall abide by the decision of the lord's court; if he disobeys his land shall be taken into the lord's hand until he has made sufficient amends. Item no one shall appear in the court of Gobyr Weyt under pain of a heavy amercement.[56]

No tenant in his digging for turves shall encroach upon the ancient boundaries assigned to the salt marsh as far as a place called the Grene under a penalty of 40d.

No tenant shall trap any of the beasts of free warren with any device or contrivance without the licence of the lord under a penalty of 20d.

No one shall agist in his own, or on the common, pasture with animals called in English 'forinnote', that is to say acquiring profit for him in money, except for the purpose of work of tilling the soil under a penalty of 40d.[57]

No tenant selling meat in the market under the price at which others buy outside shall deny it to his lord. No ale-wife of the aforesaid lord shall sell a gallon of ale at a dearer price than a silver halfpenny so long as the price of a quarter of oats does not exceed 2s. 6d. without the licence of the lord under a penalty of 40d.[58] No tenant of the Bankhouse shall trade his fuel with the strangers who come looking for mussels under a penalty of 40d. It is ordered that no tenant of the Bankhouse shall keep any animals in the pasture for two years excepting only one cow; if he has a horse or a mare there he shall pay 48d. a year to the lord for each of them. And accordingly he shall pay

---

56 Gobyr Weyt is the adjoining manor of Nether Wyreside.

57 'Forrinote' are 'foreign neet', i.e. the cattle of people who do not have commoning rights over the manorial lands. Action to prevent illegal pasturing, and by extension over-grazing and over-stocking of pastures, is widespread in manorial records.

58 Measures to regulate and ensure fair trading practices in local markets were commonplace, and the assize of ale tied its price to prevailing grain prices. Ale in Cockerham was habitually made from oats, an inferior brew to that made from barley: the Brandon and Walsham brewers recorded below [**37, 45**] almost certainly brewed with barley. Oats was probably the dominant spring grain in Cockerham, and barley relatively scarce.

the lord agistment for the other animals which he has and may bring with him but he shall not have geese or pigs or any of that kind.

9 An extent of Framlingham, 1270

A typical example of a short, 'executive', manorial extent, which concentrates upon the various components of the demesne and offers little information about the manorial tenantry. Most 'executive' extents, including this example, were compiled as part of a royal Inquisition Post Mortem. The landed estates of a tenant-in-chief reverted to the king on the tenant's death, and were then granted to the heir after the performance of homage and the payment of a relief, a form of inheritance tax. The amount of money payable as relief was partly determined by the wealth of the estate, and so royal officials drew up a short extent of each manor to ascertain its value. Thousands of manorial extents have survived in IPMs, but because these extents were compiled by royal, not estate, administrators, their accuracy cannot be heavily relied upon: the seigneurial officials had a keen interest in understating the manorial valuations, while the royal officials had to work quickly. For example, a manorial account for Framlingham has survived from 1286–87, where the rental value of the mills and the market tolls was £16, not the £5 recorded in this extent, and where the payment of tallage, overlooked in this document, is recorded. Otherwise, the valuations in this extent compare favourably with income recorded in contemporary accounts.[59]

J. Ridgard, ed., *Medieval Framlingham. Select documents 1270–1524*, Suffolk Records Society, 27 (1985), pp. 19–20. Extent of Framlingham (Suffolk), 1270. Latin.

Extent of the manor of Framlingham, which was formerly held by Roger Bigod deceased, made in the presence of John le Moyne, escheator of the lord King on this side of the Trent and made by 12 sworn jurors: namely John Godsweyn, Richard Hewe, Roger Sewale, Hugo Frebren, Walter le Cok, Robert Bolle, Robert Baldewyne, Robert le Wyte, John Waryn, Robert Tanneys, Ralph Keggel, Patrick le Escot, Robert Fox. Who say on oath that the manor of Framlingham is held from Adam de Bedingfeld rendering for the same 6d.

Item they say that there are 413 acres of [demesne] arable land each year, price per acre 6d.

Item they say that there are from rents of assize of free tenants, £13. Item from custumary tenants, £12 13s. 8½d.

---

59 Kosminsky, *Studies in agrarian history*, pp. 58–63.

Item from tolls and other perquisities of the market, 40s.

Item there are 3 mills, price of each 20s.

Item they say that there are 21 acres of mowable meadow, price of each 2s.

Item there is pasture in the great park and it is valued at 10s. per annum. Item the pasture of Oldefreth valued at 40d. per annum. Item the pasture of Bradhaye valued at 40d. per annum. Item the pasture of Buchhaye worth 40d. per annum.

Item there is a certain wood, from which it is possible to take 3 acres of underwood which are each worth 12d. per annum.

Item that there are 1060 customary harvest works from 1 August to Michaelmas [29 September], price of each 1d. Item there are 3202 [works] from Michaelmas to Pentecost, 1d. each. Item there are 800 summer works, price per work ½d.

Item there are from 160 rents of hens, price per hen 1d. Item there are from 1500 rents of eggs, price per hundred 3d.

Item they say that the fishery is worth 5s. per annum.

Item they say that the pleas and perquisites of the court are worth 50s. per annum.

Item there is a several ditched pasture which is worth 4s. per annum.

Item they say that the advowson of the church belongs to the said manor and is worth 80 marks per annum.

Item they say that Roger Bigod, son of a certain Hugh Bigod, is the nearest heir of the said deceased earl of Norfolk, and is of the age of majority namely 25 years or more.

And the grand total of the extent of this manor is £61 11s. 1½d.

10   An extent of Geddington, 1383

Another short extent, again drawn up by royal officials. In this example, a panel of jurors has been instructed to establish whether the assets of a manor held by the Crown had diminished since an earlier (but undated) assessment. It presented its findings as an extent, which, unusually but informatively, provides a sense of the changing value of the manorial assets over time. Geddington lay in the forest of Rockingham at an important fording point on a major medieval routeway (latterly the A43 trunkroad), which connected the Great North Road at Stamford with the south-west.

Public Record Office, Kew, C145/227/11. Extent of Geddington (Northampton-shire), 12 March 1383. Latin.

Inquisition. Geddington. Thursday before Palm Sunday, 6 Richard II [12 March 1383].

The site of the manor, anciently worth 21s., is now worth no more than 8s., that is for the herbage of the gardens thereof.

There are 200 acres of demesne land belonging to the manor, of which each acre used to be rented at 9d. but is now worth only 4d. per acre. There are 9½ acres of meadow, worth 18d. per acre yearly. There is a wood of great timber whereof the pasture lies in common, of which the profits and commodities, namely pannage, cablish and escapes of animals, used to be worth 100s. but are now worth 10s. only, paid by the men of the fee of St Edmund and Weekley, and of the fee of the church of Geddington in Geddington, for their common in the same wood, because the steward of the king's forest of Rocking-ham has long taken these profits.

Pleas and perquisites of court with view of frankpledge, formerly worth 100s. yearly, are now worth only 45s. net yearly. The market and fair, formerly worth 54s. 8d. yearly, are now of no value because they have ceased to be held for some time past, but the custom called 'thoroughtoll' belonging thereto is worth 6s. 8d. yearly. The common oven and fishery of a several water, formerly worth 46s. 8d. yearly, are now worth only 23s. 4d., the former being leased for 13s. 4d. and the latter for 10s. Three mills, formerly worth 107s., now are worth 71s. net and are so demised at farm.

There is a foreign rent of assize of 33s. 4d. at Cransley and Islip belong-ing to the said manor.[60] There are also rents of assize amounting to £9 17s. 6d. from 39½ virgates of land, and 59s. 3d. for divers harvest and summer works due from the tenants of the said virgates, who have been accustomed to have 'housebote' and 'haybote' from the king's wood there by view of his steward.[61] There are rents of cottars

60 'Foreign' rents, in the sense that they are drawn from outside the manor, are not uncommonly recorded in extents, rentals and accounts. In this case, the lord holds some land in the two named places nearby and, for administrative convenience, its rent is allocated to, and payable at, the demesne manor of Geddington.

61 These common rights are often found in woodland areas, allowing tenants to take sufficient timber to maintain their houses and fencing in good repair: an appropriate and sensible arrangement, but – given the value of timber – liable to abuse.

in Geddington, Glendon and Barford together with small rents of foreign lands, formerly amounting to £7 16s. 4d., but now producing no more than 105s. 2d. for lack of tenants. The manor is therefore worth in all £32 0s. 2d., which is as much farm as the men and tenants of Geddington can fittingly pay, saving their contentment.

11 An extent of Preston Millers, 1321

This long and detailed extent contrasts sharply with the two examples reproduced above [9, 10], and emanates from the lord's own estate administration. The lengthy and careful descriptions of the demesne lands and tenants are very similar in form and content to a classic survey, but the key distinction is the addition of monetary values to each element, particularly the demesne. This particular manor was held by a middling lay landlord. The survival of manorial documents from such estates is poor compared with those of magnates and prelates, but, if this example is typical, it appears that lesser lords also relied upon detailed written records in the administration of their manors. Compare the labour services of the tenants of this manor, and the manner in which they are recorded, with those at Hartest in 1251 [4].

A. E. Wilson, ed., *Custumals of the manors of Laughton, Willingden and Goring,* Sussex Record Society, 60 (1961), pp. 63–8. Extent of the manor of Preston Millers (Sussex), 12 January 1321. Latin.

Extent of the manor of Preston Millers made there on the Sunday next after the Epiphany in the 14th year of the reign of King Edward son of King Edward [12th January 1321], Sir Thomas Tregoz being there, in the presence of William de Wolvercote, knight, Sir Richard de Garboldesham, chaplain, John Peverel, [and] Richard de Sotton, by William de Milliers, William son of Thomas de Preston, freemen, and by Ralph Trys the elder, Ralph le Hunte, Richard Coterel and Adam Swet, custumars, jurors.

They say that the manor is held of the manor of Goring by knight's service as is shown in the extent of the manor of Goring. Also there is there 1 messuage and 3 acres 1 rood of garden, and the pasture of the same garden is worth 5s. and it answers in ordinary years for 1 cask of cider worth 10s.

In Toperesforlang are 7 acres 1 rood of arable land worth 14s. 6d. at 2s. an acre. And an acre can be sown with 3 bushels of wheat, peas or vetches and when sown with beans it can be sown with 6 bushels of beans and when with barley it can be sown with 6 bushels of barley or with 6 bushels of oats.[61] Pytelesfelde contains 12 acres 1½ roods 7 perches worth 24s. 10d. at 2s. an acre and it can be sown in the same way. Le Southale contains 28½ acres 1 rood 3 perches worth 57s. 6½d. at 2s. an acre and can be sown as above. Le Sexacres contains 4 acres 3 roods 7 perches worth 7s. 11½d. at 20d. an acre and is sown as above. Le Nineacres contains 8½ acres ½ rood 13 perches worth 14s. 6¼d. at 20d. Le Swere contains 9 acres 1 rood 11½ perches worth 21s. 8½d. at 2s. 4d. an acre. Le Tretenacres contains 10 acres 8½ perches worth 16s. 9¼d. at. 20d. an acre. Le Stretforlang contains 13½ acres 1 rood 14 perches worth 27s. 8¼d. at 2s. an acre. Le Losfurlang contains 23 acres 5½ perches worth 49s. 11d. at 2s. 2d. an acre. Le Northale contains 11 acres 1½ roods 18 perches worth 22s. 10½d. at 2s. an acre. Le Northlangecroft contains 5 acres 1 rood 1 perches worth 10s. 6d. at 2s. an acre. Le Brembleforlang contains 10 acres ½ rood 11 perches worth 20s. 4½d. at 2s. an acre. The field on the south side of the church contains 4 acres ½ rood 9 perches worth 10s. 5½d. at 2s. 6d. an acre. Le Colverhous contains 3 acres 1 rood 4 perches. worth 8s. 2¼d. at 2s. 6d. an acre. Le Newetrotene contains 2 acres ½ rood 12½ perches worth 5s. 5½d. at 2s. 6d. an acre. The field next to the gate of the manor on the west side contains 6 acres 1½ roods 9 perches worth 16s. ½d. at 2s. 6d. an acre. Baggeroue contains 10½ acres 1 rood 5 perches worth 27s. at 2s. 6d. an acre. Lathemere contains 13½ acres 1½ roods 16 perches worth 32s. 6¼d. at 2s. 4d. an acre. Le Hollatemere contains 5 acres 1 rood 11½ perches worth 5s. 3½d. at 12d. an acre.

They say that there are there 4 acres of meadow in the meadow of Arundel and the hay of that meadow is worth 12s. at 3s. an acre.

They say that the pasture of le Lakedike is worth 8d. yearly. The dyke between Petelesfelde and le Hale is worth 3d. Le Chercheweye with les Sowes is worth 12d. Le Suthaledike is worth 12d. Le Nothaledike is worth 12d. Le Sweredike is worth 5d. The dyke between le Stretefurlang' and le Losseforlang is worth 8d. yearly. The dyke in the middle of le Tenacres is worth 3d. Le Sowes on the west side of Foulescroft is worth 6d. yearly. Baggegrouesdike with the way to the church is worth 5d. Lathemeresdike is worth 5d. Le Pende is worth 2s. There is pasture there for 150 sheep.

61 This statement of the sowing rates of each crop is quite unusual in surveys and extents, though common enough in accounts. The practice here of sowing spring crops such as barley and oats more thickly than wheat (partly as a tactic to smother weeds) is typical, although six bushels per acre is higher than the four bushels often sown on demesnes in south east England.

Ralph le Hunte holds 1 messuage and 6 acres of land in villeinage and owes as rent of assize 4s. 6d. yearly, namely on St Thomas's Day [12 December] 18d. and at Midsummer [24 June] 3s.; and also he owes 2½d. for the hatchyngsulvere at Michaelmas [29 September], and he must reap 10½ acres of whatever kind of corn the bailiff or reeve shall assign to him through the reep-reeve at 5d. an acre; and he must thresh 4 bushels of wheat by level measure after harvest or after Michaelmas [29 September] as it shall please the lord; and he must do a 'water service' (*aquaticare*) on the lord's land for 2 days with 1 man without a meal, and he must do 4 boonworks in the harvest with 1 man with the lord's food, and he must awn (*blestiare*) the lord's barley for 2 days with 1 man without food;[62] and he must provide 1 man to help to make 4 acres of hay in le Castelmede, and he must wash and shear the lord's sheep with the other custumars of the lord.

And he with all the custumars who wash and shear [sheep] shall have 1 fleece, namely the best which he wishes to choose; and he must make malt 3 times a year if the lord wills, and if he makes malt of wheat or barley then he must make 4 bushels and if he makes malt of drage then he must make 6 bushels and if he makes malt of oats then he must make 8 bushels. And he shall give 4 hens on St Thomas's day [12 December] and he must give 6 eggs at Easter, and he must carry the hurdles of the lord's fold from one place to another twice a year, and he shall spread each year 1 row of dung; and he shall give aid and merchet.

Nicholas Haldeby holds 1 messuage and 6 acres of land and he shall do in all renders and services as the aforesaid Ralph. [Likewise] Joan who was the wife of Adam Bartelot. Richard Cotere. Adam atte Tye. Geoffrey atte Southone. Ralph Trys the elder. Ralph le Trys the younger. Henry le Trys. Ralph le Pade. Adam le Waitte.

Henry le Topere holds 1 messuage and 4 acres of land and owes as rent of assize 3s., namely on St Thomas's day [12 December] 12d. and at Midsummer [24 June] 2s. and he owes for Thethcingsulful 1½d. at Michaelmas [29 September];[63] and he must give alternately

---

62 It is not exactly clear what is meant by waterservice, but probably means that the lord does not provide ale for the workers. Awning is the process by which the 'beard' on the ear of barley is removed.

63 An alternative spelling to the 'hatchyngsulver' owed elsewhere by Ralph le Hunte, the 'thetchyingsulfre' owed by William Piscod, and the 'thetchingsulver' owed by Amfird le Putel: a payment in lieu of a customary thatching service of some kind is implied.

in one year 2 hens and in the other year 3 hens on St Thomas's day [12 December], and he must give 4 eggs at Easter; and he must reap and bind 7 acres of corn and he must do 3 boonworks in harvest with 1 man, and he must thresh 3 bushels of wheat by level measure, and he must do a water service on the lord's land for 1½ days; and he must awn the lord's barley for 1½ days and he must provide 1 man to help to make and collect 4 acres of hay with the other custumars, and he must wash and shear the lord's sheep with the other custumars; and he must make malt three times a year if the lord wills and if he makes malt of wheat or barley then he must make 3 bushels and of drage 4 bushels and of oats 6 bushels, and he must hoe the lord's corn for 1½ days, and he must carry the hurdles of the lord's fold from one place to another twice a year, and he must spread one row of dung.

William Piscod holds 1 messuage and 3 acres of land of servile condition and owes as rent of assize yearly 2s. 3d., namely on St Thomas's day [12 December] 9d. and at Midsummer [24 June] 18d., and he owes of thetchingsulfre 1¼d. at Michaelmas [29 September]; and must give 2 hens on St Thomas's day [12 December] and he shall give 3 eggs at Easter; and he must reap and bind 5 acres and 1 rood of corn, and he owes 2 boonworks in harvest, and he must thresh 2 bushels of wheat by level measure after harvest and he must do a water service on the lord's land for 1 day, and he must awn barley for 1 day and hoe the lord's corn for 1 day, and he must wash and shear the lord's sheep, and he must provide 1 man every other year to help to make and collect 4 acres of hay; and he must make malt half as much as Ralph le Hunte, and he shall carry the lord's fold from one place to another once a year, and he must spread half a row of dung.

Cecily who was wife of Henry Wyteby holds as much as the aforesaid William Piscod.

Amfrid le Putel holds 1 messuage and 3 acres of land of servile condition and owes as rent of assize 2s. 3d., namely at St Thomas's day [12 December] 9d. and at Midsummer [24 June] 18d., and he owes 1d. of thetchingsulver at Michaelmas [29 September]; and he must give 2 hens at St Thomas's Day [12 December] and he shall give 3 eggs at Easter; and he must reap and bind 5 acres and 1 rood of corn, and he owes 4 boonworks in harvest, and he must thresh after harvest 2 bushels of corn by level measure and he must do water service on the lord's land for 2 days and he must awn the lord's barley for 2 days, and he must hoe for 2 days, and he must provide 1 man to help make and collect 4 acres of hay, and he must wash and shear the lord's sheep with the other custumars; and he must make malt half as much as Ralph le Hunte, and he must carry the lord's fold from one place to another twice a year, and he must spread ½ row of dung. Roger le Cute holds as much and holds in all renders and services as the aforesaid Amfrid.

Philip Waryn holds 1 messuage and 2 acres of land and owes as rent of assize 2s. 4d., namely on St Thomas's day [12 December] 14d. and at Midsummer 14d. [24 June]; and 2 hens on St Thomas's day [12 December] and 2 eggs at Easter; and he owes 4 boonworks in harvest at the lord's food, and he must assist the thatcher for 2 days so that for 1 day he shall have his meal or 1d. from the lord, and for the other day he shall have nothing, and he must do water service on the lord's land for 2 days; and he must awn the lord's barley for 2 days, and he must hoe for 2 days, and he must provide 1 man to help to make and collect 4 acres of hay, and he must wash and shear the lord's sheep, and he must help to bring in and stack the lord's hay from 4 acres of meadow, and he must carry the lord's fold with other custumars from one place to another twice a year.

Swetejam holds 1 messuage and 1 croft which contains 1 acre of land, and also he holds 1 acre in the field and owes as rent of assize yearly 4s., namely on St Thomas's day [12 December] 2s. and at Midsummer [24 June] 2s.; and he owes 4 boonworks in harvest at the lord's food and suit of court.

John le Nhapekere holds 1 messuage with croft and owes as rent of assize 12d., namely at St Thomas's day [12 December] 6d. and at Midsummer [24 June] 6d.; and he owes 4 boon-works in harvest at the lord's food, and he must do a water service on the lord's land for 2 days; and awn barley for 2 days, and must hoe for 2 days and provide 1 man to help make and collect 4 acres of hay, and he must help to bring in and stack the lord's hay from the aforesaid 4 acres of meadow, and he must wash and shear the lord's sheep with the other custumars, and he must carry the lord's fold from one place to another twice a year, and he must assist the thatcher for 2 days in the same way as Philip Waryn.

Alice daughter of Suetejam holds as much and owes as much of renders and services as the aforesaid John.

John le Forel holds 1 messuage with croft and owes as rent of assize 4s., namely on St Thomas's day [12 December] 2s. and at Midsummer [24 June] 2s.; and every other year 1 hen on St Thomas's day [12

December] and in the same year 1 egg at Easter; and he owes 4 boonworks in harvest at the lord's food, and he must provide 1 man to help make and collect 4 acres of hay, and [he does] suit of court as the custumars.

William Opilhude holds 1 messuage and 2 acres of land and owes as rent of assize 4s. 4d., namely on St Thomas's day [12 December] 2s. 2d. and at Midsummer [24 June] 2s. 2d.; and he owes 1 hen on St Thomas' day [12 December], and he owes 4 boonworks in harvest at the lord's food, and he must furnish 1 man to help make and collect 4 acres of hay.

Robert Oppelhude holds 1 messuage and 4 acres of land and owes as rent of assize 8s. a year, namely at Midsummer [24 June] 4s. and suit of court, and on St Thomas's day [12 December] 4s.

Walter le Tupere holds 1 messuage and 1½ acres of land and owes as rent of assize 2s. 10d. yearly, namely on St Thomas's day [12 December] 17d. and at Midsummer [24 June] 17d.; and he owes 4 boonworks in harvest at the lord's food, and he owes 1 hen on St Thomas's Day [12 December], and he must do water service on the lord's land for 2 days; and he must awn the lord's barley for 2 days, and he must hoe for 2 days, and he must provide 1 man to help to make and collect 4 acres of hay. The same holds 3 acres of le Tuperforlang' and pays 6s. at the same terms.

Walter le Pade holds 1 messuage and 3 acres of land and owes as rent of assize yearly 7s. 7d., namely on St Thomas's day [12 December] 3s. 9d. [sic] and at Midsummer [24 June] 3s. 9½d. and suit of court.

Thomas le Pade holds as much and owes as much as the aforesaid Walter le Pade.

12 Extracts from a terrier of Biddenham, 1347

These two extracts from an early terrier of Biddenham describe individual, but open, parcels of arable (selions) and pasture land belonging to the demesne of the manor according to its location within the village's fields. The land is identified precisely by reference to its abuttals with parcels belonging to other landholders or well-known landmarks in the village. The repeated references to abuttals on the land of Newnham priory indicate the presence of another manorial holding within the village. This document conveys a significant amount of information about the layout and operation of Biddenham's medieval field system, and the distribution of demesne land within it. It evidently contained three open fields operating communally on a three-course rotation. Of particular interest are the descriptions of the small slivers of pasture within the arable fields that served as access routes and turning areas for ploughs, known as baulks and headlands. The use to which these are being put by the lord implies extreme pressure on resources and acute shortages of pasture.

Bedfordshire Record Office, CRT 130/Bid. 5. Terrier of Biddenham (Bedfordshire), 1347. Latin.

Memorandum of land in the south field of Biddenham, which can be sown for two years together.

First season.[64] On the furlong called Mersfurlong, 1 selion lying as 2 roods, next to the land of the prioress of Harrold, 1 selion lying as 2 roods, next to the land of John Malyn, chaplain, 1 selion lying as 2 roods, next to the land of Richard Bedeman on the north, 1 selion lying as 1 rood, next to the land of the convent of Newnham on the north, 1 selion lying as 1 rood, next to the land of John Grendon on the south, 2 selions lying as 1 acre, next to the land of John Sothewyk on the north, 1 selion lying as 1 rood, next to the land of the convent of Newnham.[65]

On short furlong, 1 selion lying as 1 rood, next to the land of John Sothewyk on the south, 1 selion lying as 1 rood, next to the land of John Blanncost on the south, 1 selion lying as 1 rood, next to the land of the convent of Newnham on the north, 1 selion lying as 1 rood, next to the land of John Blanncost on the south, 1 selion lying as 1 rood, next to the land of the convent of Newnham on the north, 1 selion lying as 2 roods, next to the land of Robert Malyn on the south, 1 selion lying as 1 rood, next to the land of John Blanncost on the south, 1 selion lying as 1 rood, next to the land of Robert Wade on the south, 1 selion lying as 1 rood, next to the land of the convent of Newnham on the north.

64 A 'season' or 'shift' is a group of individual land parcels sown alike as a part of a communal cropping pattern. Because the terrier goes on to inform us that three seasons exist, each of two years' duration (followed by an implied year of fallow), and that the three seasons coincide with a south, middle and north field, it follows that the land was being cultivated as a classic three-course rotation on the three open fields. The reference to 'the field called middle furlong', rather than simply 'middle field', might indicate that a third field had been recently created from an earlier two-field system.

65 Note that each selion varies in size, but is unlikely to exceed an acre: the most commonly occurring size in the Middle Ages is two roods.

On the furlong called 'in the far', 2 selions lying as 2 roods, next to the land of the church on the south.

Furlong le Nunnedam, 1 selion lying as 1 rood, next to the land of Robert Wade on the south, 1 selion lying as 2 roods, next to the land of Richard Davy on the south.

Furlong called Barleyland, 1 selion lying as 1 rood, next to the land of William Leche on the north.

Furlong called le Wenland, 1 selion lying as 1 rood, next to the land of the convent of Newnham on the north.

Brodemedefurlong, 1 selion lying as 1 rood, next to the land formerly of William Salmon, 1 selion lying as 1 rood, next to the land of Robert Warde.

TOTAL, 8 acres, of which 6 acres in the lord's hands.

Pesefurlong, 1 selion lying as 1 rood, next to the land of Henry del Ford on the east, 1 selion lying as 1 rood, next to the land of Robert Warde on the south, 1 selion lying as 1 rood, next to the land of William Bylkins on the south, 1 selion lying as 1 rood, next to the land formerly of Thomas Attewall on the south, 1 selion lying as 1 rood, next to the land of William Bylkins on the north, 1 selion lying as 1 rood, next to the land of the convent of Newnham on the north, 1 selion lying as 1 rood, next to the land of Richard de le Crouch on the south, 6 selions lying as 1 acre 3 roods, next to the land of the church on the north.

Darneford, 1 selion lying as 1 rood, next to the land formerly of Roger King on the south.

TOTAL, 3 acres 3 roods.

Deneweyfurlong, 1 selion lying as 1 rood, next to the land of Robert Myle on the south, 1 selion lying as 1 rood, next to the land of John Blanncost on the south, 1 selion lying as 1 rood, next to the land of William Bylkons on the north, 1 selion lying as 1 rood, next to the land of William Bournard on the south, 1 selion lying as 1 rood, next to the land of William Leche on the south, 2 selions lying as 2 roods, next to the land of Thomas Pollard on the south, 2 selions lying as 2 roods, next to the land of John Crouch on the north.

TOTAL, 2 acres 1 rood.

Memorandum of land lying in the field of Biddenham called Middulfurlong lying for the second season which can be sown for two years together

[The document then lists each parcel of demesne land in the same format as above: this section is then followed by another entitled the 'Northfeld of Biddenham lying for the third season, which can be sown for two years together'. The scribe then turns his attention to the demesne pasture]

[...] Pasture lying with the third season sold by William this year: for 1 headland of 2 roods at Kingsmadeheneden, next to the lord's land; for 1 headland of 1 rood at Kingsmadeheneden, next to the lord's land and William Bylkons to the west; for a pasture called le Buttus at Farthul next to church land to the west, 18d.

Pasture for one crop, several in any year, sold by the said William in the aforesaid year:[66] for 3 headlands as 3 roods, next to land of the convent of Newnham at Biddenham mill and Robert le Smith on the south; for 8 headlands, 8 roods, in le Mers next to Sir Richard Bayons on the south, 3s. 6d.; for 10 headlands, 10 roods, in le Mers next to the church on the south, 3s. 6d.; for 1 headland, 2 roods, next to the land of the prioress of Harrold on the south, 12d.; for 1 headland, 2 roods, next to John Maylyn, chaplain, 12d.; for 1 headland, 2 roods, next to Richard Bedeman on the north, 12d.; for 1 headland, 1 rood, next to the land of the prior of Newnham on the north, 7½d.; for 1 headland, 1 rood, 7½d.: for 2 headlands, 2 roods, 8d.; for 2 headlands, 4 roods, 15d.; for 1 headland, 1 rood, ¼d.; for 1 headland, 1 rood; for 1 headland, 6 roods [blank]. TOTAL, 13s. 8¼d.

Pasture, always several, sold by William this year: pasture around Buryinlond, 2s; pasture called le Conyger [blank]. Pasture del Mylnedam at Biddenham bridge.

Meadow for one crop, several in any year, sold by William le Swath in Kynggosmade next the lord's water, 4s. Le Lyttleholm below Fullyngmylnedam, 3d. Le Swath in Sundurmede next the lord's water, 9s. 6d. Ten roods in Sundurmede abutting on le Eyt, 10s. 6d. Oxelene,

66 The repetitive entries relating to these 'sales' of pasture by William, lord of the manor, are specifically for one year only and relate to a crop of pasture rather than of corn. The price per acre is somewhat below the value of the arable. Such 'sales', effectively a one year lease, are very unusual, but, as later examples reveal, care is taken to ensure that the expedient does not disrupt the operation of the communal rotation. 1346 and 1347 were years of harvest failure in many parts of eastern England, which may explain the timing and nature of this activity.

33s. 4d. Syplodeholm, 12s. Le Bryggeholm at the bridge, 6s. 8d. Le Damholm at Fullingmyllne.

Measure of pasture lying with the first season of arable land which can be several for two years together, on the Bromham side: freebord pasture around a wood called Wodecroft, 2 roods 6 perches; pasture balk with a spinney growing round Banlond, 1 rood 31 perches; pasture balk with a spinney growing round Syxakur, 1 rood 16 perches; pasture balk with a spinney growing on the west of Sladedole, 28 perches; pasture balk with a spinney growing on the north of Sladedole, 1 rood 24 perches; pasture balk with a spinney growing on the north side of Grymescroft, 27 perches; del Clovenenbalk and a headland on the north side of Grymescroft, 2 roods 34 perches; Dolemede, 9 perches; 11 headlands against the lord's pasture at Taggebrook, 1 rood 4 perches; freebord pasture of Sarlefrythwood, 37 perches

[the document then goes on to list minute areas of pasture lying within the fields and village of Biddenham in the same format].

13   An extract from a survey of Culford, 1435

Soon after he became abbot of Bury St Edmunds in 1429, William Curteys supervised the production of detailed surveys of all the abbatial manors of this wealthy Benedictine house. Their format and content are not untypical of many fifteenth-century surveys, but have more in common with the terrier of Biddenham [12] than the survey of Hartest [4]. This extract from the survey of Culford is a good example of the increasingly topographical format of late medieval surveys, and comprises a description of the size and location of each parcel of land, rather than a statement of the customary rents and services attached to each landholding. The shift of focus from the standardised land-holding to the individual land parcel reflects the breakup of the old holdings and the growing tendency for tenants to hold land on a variety of more flexible, contractual, tenures. Put simply, estate administrators now required a detailed record of all land parcels, because the terms on which a single parcel of land were held could now change over time. Unusually, this example describes every land parcel lying in the fields of Culford, and not just those pertaining to the abbatial manor, which greatly enhances the document's value to the historian: for example, it is possible to reconstruct Culford's medieval field system. The extract also illustrates the complex structure of the local manorial system, with land parcels of a number of manors – some from different vills – interspersed among each other. Every entry for this furlong is reproduced.

British Library, Add. Ms. 42055, f. 38. Survey of Culford (Suffolk), 1435. Latin.

The quarentena [furlong] at Pokemelledam next to West Stow church.

Easthall [manor] holds 1½ acres abutting on Pokemellepath to the west, one head on the meadow of Easthall called Sotherne to the south, and the other head on the common of Culford at Pokemelle to the north.

The abbot holds 6 acres of demesne between the said land of Easthall to the west, and the lands of Easthall and the rector of West Stow church and of Robert Dobbys to the east, one head on the abbot's meadow to the south, and the other on the common of Culford next to the graveyard of West Stow church to the north.

Robert Dekes of West Stow holds 1 acre between the abbot's land to the west, the land of Lackford manor to the east, and abuts on the land of Easthall to the north.

The manor of Lackford holds 1½ roods and abut as above. Easthall holds 2½ acres and abut on the land of the same manor to the north.

The Hospital of St Edmunds [of St Saviour, Bury St Edmunds] holds 6 acres and abut on the land of Easthall to the north.

Easthall holds 3 roods which is a certain 'buwente' [baulk] between the lands of Robert Dekes and the hospital, and the land of Lackford manor abuts to the south, the land of the rector of West Stow to the north, and abut on Sladewong to the east.

The rector of West Stow holds 2 acres and abut on the abbot's land called Sladewong to the east. Easthall holds 2 acres and abut on the abbot's land called Sladewong to the east.

The rector of West Stow church holds 2 acres between the land of Easthall to the south, the common way next to the graveyard of West Stow church to the north, and on the common way leading from West Stow church to Hordelysmelle to the east.

The abbot holds one piece (*pecia*) of demesne land called Sladewong containing 12 acres between the lands of the hospital to the west, the common heath of Culford called Shortehethe to the east, and abuts on the common way leading from the church to the mill to the north.

The abbot holds one piece of demesne land called 'le Conyngg' containing 4 acres lying in the same field between the land of the rector of West Stow to the north, the common heath of Culford to the south, one head on the Kingsway at West Stow church to the west, and the other on the pasture of the abbot at le Melledam to the east.

14 A rental of Lackford, 1399

A typical rental, albeit from a small, lay, manor. The document summarises the rent charge upon each tenant, whether in cash, kind or services. Each parcel of land, and a previous landholder, is recorded carefully, but little attention is paid to the status of its tenure. The burden of labour services is light, and there are hints that many land parcels are held on contractual tenures: such characteristics are not uncommon in rentals from the late fourteenth century when customary tenure was dissolving. Some land has been recently abandoned 'into the hand(s) of the lord', and no replacement tenant found, which is symptomatic of agricultural recession and depopulation. However, the rental does not allow us to be certain of the real extent to which land and property lay waste and untenanted, because its purpose is to record rental liability and not to survey the status or condition of all the land pertaining to the manor.

Suffolk Record Office, Bury St Edmunds, E3/15.12/3.1. Rental of Lackford (Suffolk), 14 December 1399. Latin.

Lackford. Rental of the manor there made by the tenants of the lord on the day after the feast of St Lucy the virgin in the first year of the reign of Henry IV [14 December 1399], at the terms of Michaelmas and Easter in equal portions.

From Adam Attewell for a tenement called Nokkardes, 4s. per annnum. The same Adam for an orchard called Holdesyerd, 2d. per annum.

From John Page for a tenement in which he lives, 2s. per annum.

From Herbert Buk for a tenement lately 'le Prestyshous', 2s. 6d. per annum. The same Herbert for a grange called Leveredesberne, ¼d. per annum.

From John Chapeleyn for 15 acreware, lately of William Buk, for all services, 10s.[67] The same John for one house called 'Crouch's hous' with one acre of land, 3s. And the same John reaps the lord's corn for one day with one man. And the same John for one orchard called Bolles next to Kingeswell, ¼d. And the same John for one parcel next to the

---

67 John Chapelyn's customary holding is given in 'acreware' rather than statute acres, a common practice in medieval East Anglia. 'Acreware' literally means 'defence acre', refering to an obsolete system of organising military service, and loosely approximated to the statute acre.

gate of the church, 2d. And the same John for one messuage called Bryddes, 1½d. per annum and suit of court.

From Ralph Thommessone for one messuage lately of John Poddyng, ¼d. per annum.

From the abbot of St Edmund for one piece of land containing one perch by width and six by length lying next to the tenement of Ralph Thommessone on one part and the messuage of John Page on the other part, ¼d. per annum.

From John Throston for one built messuage lately of Beatrice Kegge, 3d. per annum.

From Ralph Baldewene for his tenement for all services, 1d. per annum.

From Robert Nokkard for one enclosed orchard lately of Walter Douwe, 1d. per annum.

From Joanna Douwe for one parcel of meadow, ¼d. per annum.

From Herbert Buk for one cottage formerly of Robert Matte, ¼d. per annum.

From Johanna Nokkard for one built messuage with half an acre of land, 12d. per annum.

From Matilda Fuller for one built messuage with half and acre of land, 12d. per annum.

From Nicholas Champayn for one tenement formerly of John Kenche, 2s.

One tenement formerly 'Berwardes' now in the hand of the lord, 2d. per annum.

From the aforesaid Nicholas Champayn for one enclosed orchard formerly of Benedict atte Cherche, 2s. per annum.

From Benedict Schepherde for 16 acreware lately of John Shepherde, 13s. 4d.

From Walter Webbe for two cottages lately of Alex Pepkod, ½d. per annum.[68]

68 Some evidence of Walter Webbe's occupational history is recoverable from other extant sources, where he is recorded as an active weaver with his own, modest, flock of sheep and a sizeable smallholding on the manor. This reiterates the point that rentals only capture an instant of a tenant's landholding career, and give no indication of the economic activity that took place within the messuage or cottage (see p. 114).

From Stephen Chercheman for one cottage with one orchard formerly Nicholas Koman, ¼d. per annum. The same Stephen for one messuage formerly Reynerssonnes, 18d. per annum.

From Joanna Nokkard for one tenement lately of Ralph Orge, 12d. per annum. From the same Joanna for one messuage and one acre of land adjacent lately of William Orge, 6d. per annum and suit of court.

One messuage with one acre of land formerly of Peter Rolf now in the hand of the lord, 8d. And it shall reap four acres of oats at harvest and suit of court, and mow the lord's meadow called 'le Mechemede'. And it shall find one man for one boonwork to reap the lord's corn in the harvest, and give one hen.

William Douwe for one cottage with three acres of land lately of William Poke, 18d. per annum. And owes suit of court, and shall reap one acre of oats, give one hen, and mow the lord's meadow, namely 'le mechemede'. And he shall find one man for one boonwork to reap the lord's corn in the harvest. And the same William for one cottage lately of William Godefrey, ½d. per annum.

From John Flempton for one tenement lately of Henry Aleyn, 3d. per annum and suit of court.

From Matilda Hod for one cottage lately of William Stevenesson, ¼d. per annum.

From John Cheve for one cottage lately of William Jeorge, for all services, ¼d. per annum.

From John Flempton for one cottage lately of William Buk, for all suit and services, ¼d. per annum. And from the same John for one messuage containing one acre of land formerly of John Flempton his father, 20d. per annum. And he owes suit of court twice yearly, and shall reap two acres of 'haverote' in the harvest.[69] Item he shall find one man for one boonwork to reap the lord's corn. Item he shall give one hen each year. The same John for one orchard called 'Salmansattebrege', 8d. per annum for all services.

From Isabel Douwe for one messuage and two acres of land, for all services, 2¼d.

One messuage with half an acre of land lately of Roger Douwe, for all services, 7d. per annum, and suit of court, and mowing the meadow of the lord, now in the hand of the lord.

69 The meaning of 'haverote' is obscure, but probably relates to the oats (*averium*) crop.

From John Hethe for one enclosed orchard containing half a rood of land formerly of Agnes Welkelrons, for all services, ½d. per annum.

From John Hekedon for one piece of land containing two acres lying next to the old way at Cavenham bridge, with suit of court, 6d. per annum.

Total, 51s. 9¼d.

15   An extract from a rental of Cassio, 1332

The manor of Cassio was held by the abbot of St Albans, and at first glance this short extract from one of its rentals appears rather dry and unexceptional. Yet the layout of the entries, finishing with the cornershop by a churchyard, implies strongly that the document is listing contiguous properties along the edge of Watford marketplace. Note that the holdings are held for little more than cash rents, have no agricultural land attached to them, and include some extensions to the properties. Such characteristics are not uncommon in market towns in south-east England, and were obviously attractive to traders. The prevalence of locative, topographical and occupational surnames is also indicative of a market town.

Hertfordshire Record Office: Ms. 6543 ff. 12–13. Rental of Cassio (Hertfordshire), 1332. Latin.

Imaigue Leveston holds one curtilage, which was once William Popelyn's, between the tenement of Henry de Muryden and Henry atte Ashe [no rent given].

John de Muryden holds one curtilage which was William Lovekyn's, and for this he renders 2s. per annum. And it lies between the messuages of John Pak and Nicholas Sperlyng.

Henry atte Ashe holds one messuage, which was once William le Parker's. And for this he renders 6d. per annum.

Isabella, widow of William Personn, holds one built messuage which was once held by Christine Pottere. And for this she renders 18d. per annum.

The same Isabella holds one built messuage annexed to the aforesaid tenement, which was once held by William Cordwainer. And she renders 12d. per annum.

Thomas de Hampton holds one built messuage with a curtilage, and renders 16d. per annum. And he owes suit of court.

Adam le Ironmonger holds one built messuage, and renders 16d. per annum.

Adam le Fox holds one built messuage, which was once held by Reginald Ruddock. And for this he renders 3s. 4d. per annum.

William de la Marche holds one built messuage next to the capital messuage of the same William, and for which he renders 6d. per annum. And the chamberlain of St Alban's owes suit to the court of Cassio for the same tenement.

John le Smyth holds one built messuage, once held by Maurice le Cok, and renders 4s.

William de Nottele holds one messuage which was Richard Waryn's. And for this he renders 1d. per annum.

Walter le Dekne holds one built messuage next to the messuage of John de Wedon. And for this he renders 1d. per annum.

William de Nottele holds one built messuage through Alice his wife, and after the death of Alice it ought to descend to the lord abbot. And renders 18d. per annum.

John le Hostiller holds one built messuage, once held by John Hostiller his father, and renders 15d. per annum. And John, son and heir of Edmund Chilterne owes suit to the court of Cassio twice yearly, and the lord abbot is chief lord. The same John le Hostiller holds one built messuage, once held by Roger Popelet. And for this he renders 16d. per annum.

Robert Spyleman holds one built messuage, once held by John le Bakere, and on this is built his grange and stable. And he renders 3d. per annum. The same Robert holds one shop in the market of Watford, and renders 1d. per annum.

John Schraff holds half a messuage, once held by John le Bakere, and he renders 3d. per annum. Of the fee of the abbot.

William atte Delle holds one built messuage, once held by Simon atte Delle his father and previously by Robert de Staverhulle. And for this he renders 6d. per annum. And he holds from the lord abbot. The same owes 1d. for relaxation of suit of court of Cassio for the same tenement.

Henry Cokedell holds one shop called 'Cornershopp' next to the church-yard, and renders 8d. per annum.

16   Rent payments made by tenants at Willington and Nether Heworth, 1496

Whereas a rental documents the rent liability of each tenant, this centralised estate document from Durham priory details the rent actually received from each tenant. The difference between the rent charge and the rent paid is not always drawn clearly in manorial documents, but could be significant in periods of agricultural depression or peasant rebelliousness. In this example, two tenants, John Unthanke and Robert Robinson, failed to pay the full amount, but an entry marks Robinson as 'quit' of debt: the lord was clearly sensitive to the individual circumstances of each tenant. The tendency for tenants to pay their annual rent in instalments, often on formal occasions such as court sessions, emerges strongly from this document. Interestingly, not all rent was paid in cash, which is more likely to reflect local and temporary shortages of coin rather than the persistence of a barter economy.

R. A. Lomas and A. J. Piper, eds, *Durham cathedral priory rentals, vol. I: Bursar's rentals,* Surtees Society, 198 (1986), pp. 135, 138. Bursar's rent-book entries for Willington and Nether Heworth (Co. Durham), 1495–96. Latin.

Willington

From Robert Ponchon each year, 30s. Of which, 5s. 6d. paid at Jarrow; 3s. 8d. through the hands of Richard Wren; 4s. paid through Richard Wren; 8s. paid at the first tourn; item, 8s. 10d. Quit.[70]

From Robert Robynson each year, 32s. 7½d. Of which, 10s. paid in cash at Jarrow; 5s. through the hands of Richard Wren; 4s. paid at court in the presence of lord Thomas Tipping; 5s. paid through Richard Wren; 5s. paid at the first tourn; item, 12d. Quit [*sic*].

From Richard Wilkinson each year, 30s. Of which, 8s. paid in cash at Jarrow; 2s. 10d. through Richard Wren; item, 2s. 2d. paid; 7s. paid through Richard Wren; 6s. paid at the tourn; item, 4s. Quit.

From John Robinson each year, 30s. Of which, 8s. paid in cash at Jarrow; 4s. paid through Richard Wren; 4s. paid through Richard Wren; 4s. paid at Jarrow; 10s. at the second tourn. Quit.

From George Robinson each year, 30s. Of which, 9s. paid in cash at Jarrow; 4s. through the hands of Richard Wren; 3s. paid in cash; 7s. paid through Richard Wren; item, 3s.; 4s. paid. Quit.

70 The prior of Durham held regular courts at Jarrow, which proved a convenient time and place for tenants from these nearby settlements to pay instalments of rent. Richard Wren was evidently an important and busy official on the prior's estates, since many such instalments were paid through him.

From Thomas Johnson each year, 30s. Of which, 7s. paid in cash at Jarrow; 5s. paid at the court at Jarrow; 6s. through Richard Wren; 6s. paid at Jarrow; item, 6s. Quit.

From William Hunter each year, 30s. Of which, 5s. paid in cash at Jarrow; 4s. through the hands of Richard Wren; 7s. paid in cash; item, 14s. Quit.

Fron John Unthanke each year, 30s. Of which, 4s. paid through Richard Wren; 7s. 10d. paid at the second tourn; 2s. through Richard Wren at Christmas. Thus he owes 10s. 6d.

[...]

Nether Heworth

From William Watson for Pulterclose, 66s. 8d. Of which, 33s. 4d. paid in cash at the third tourn; and he promised to pay 33s. 4d. at the feast of St Cuthbert [20 March]; 33s. 4d. paid in cash. Quit.

From Roland Sotheron each year, 103s. 6d. Of which, 10s. paid in cash at the court at Jarrow; 15s. 6d. in [the form of] 2½ barrels of soap; 6s. 8d. paid at the third tourn; 24s. paid in one barrel of oil; 10s. 4d. paid in cash, and thus he owes 25s. Of which, 13s. 4d. paid through Richard Wren in gold, and 11s. 8d. paid. Quit.

From Thomas Willy each year, 51s. 9d. Of which, 10s. paid at the court at Jarrow in the presence of Richard Wren; 13s. 4d. paid in cash; 2s. 6d. paid afterwards on the same day; 5s. paid in the chapel of Heworth. Thus he owes 10s. 11d., which he pays. Quit.

From Robert Nicholson each year, 51s. 9d. Of which, Cuthbert Fenton paid 8d. in smoked herrings beyond the farm at 'le Schellis'; 6s. 8d. paid through Sir John Gamylsbe at Jarrow; 6s. 8d. paid through Sir John Gamylsbe at Jarrow. Quit.

From William Sotheron for the mill, 20s. Of which, 10s. paid to the terrar,[71] as confirmed by them; 10s. paid through Richard Wren in gold. Quit.

---

71 The terrar was one of the central officers on the Durham priory estates.

17 The lease of Caddington and Kensworth, 1299

Once the decision had been taken to lease a manor to a lessee rather than
exploit it directly, prudence dictated that the terms and conditions of the
lease be stipulated explicitly and in writing. Extant manorial leases from the
twelfth century are rare and perfunctory, but thereafter become more
commonplace and detailed.[72] Many contain basic inventories of the grain and
stock to be returned at the end of the lease, and designate responsibility for
the upkeep of the manorial buildings during the time of the lease. This
example from Caddington is very detailed, and, unusually, involves a lease
from an ecclesiastical institution to one of its own brethren. The dean and
chapter of St Paul's, London, comprised a number of canons, each of whom
had one or more manors from the landed estate assigned to him as his
prebend (i.e. his provision or 'keep'). Many of these prebendary canons held
their manor(s) as freehold, but some, as in this case, were of different status
and held their prebendary manor as leasehold.

C. Gore Chambers, ed., 'Lease of Caddington manor', *Bedfordshire Historical
Record Society*, 1 (1913), pp. 77–89. Lease of Caddington and Kensworth
(Bedfordshire) manors, 1299. Latin.

This is an agreement made between the dean and chapter of the
church of St Paul in London, on the one part and Richard of Gravesend,
archdeacon of London and canon of the said church, namely that the
said dean and chapter lease and make over to the aforesaid Richard
their fellow canon their manors of Caddington and Kensworth at
farm, together with the tithes of the churches of the said vills and all
their rights and appurtenances. To be held of them as long as he lives
and is a canon of the said church and is not a bishop elect [or]
confirmed and serves them well. Rendering them therefore every year
as long as he holds the farm one whole farm in bread and ale, and the
costs of baking and brewing, and alms at every regular and ancient
term, and on the Sunday next after the Exaltation of the Holy Cross
[14 September] he shall render every year at the brewery one week's
bread or two marks. He shall render also every year into the chamber
of St Paul at four terms £13 for Caddington and £20 13s. 4d. for the
manor of Kensworth, namely at the feast of St Michael [29 September]
£8 8s. 4d., and at the festival of the Nativity of our Lord [Christmas]
£8 8s. 4d., and at the festival of the Nativity of St John the Baptist
[24 June] £8 8s. 4d. And for the tithe of the church of Caddington 40
marks and for the tithe of the church of Kensworth 28 marks into the
chamber of St Paul in London yearly at the four terms of the audit of

72 For an example of an early lease, see M. Gibbs, ed., *Early charters of the cathedral
church of St Paul, London*, Camden Society, 3rd series, vol. LVIII (1939), p. 241.

the said chamber, namely at the audit of the Ascension of the Lord 17 marks, at the audit of St Peter Ad vincula [1 August] 17 marks, at the audit of St Martin [11 November] 17 marks and at the audit of the Ashes [Ash Wednesday] 17 marks. And be it known that the said Richard began to make the first payment for the aforesaid churches at the audit of the Ascension of the Lord in the twelve hundred and ninety-ninth year of the same, for the autumn crops next following, for which he will owe nothing when he gives up the said farm. The said Richard shall also have the chancels of the said churches, in so far as concerns the roofing and the glazing of the windows, so sufficiently repaired as often as there be need and so secured that the divine mysteries can be decorously celebrated therein without impediment of rain or wind.[73]

The said Richard shall moreover faithfully preserve the condition of the said manors together with all their ancient rents, customs, dues and services nor shall he remit them for any period to the damage of the church of St Paul, nor shall he free nor sell the serfs of the same. And if any [of the said rents etc.] be dissipated and alienated in his time he shall recover them at his own expense and shall preserve in their integrity all that he finds there, nor shall he make over to farm the aforesaid manors to anyone either covertly or openly; but shall have the same faithfully kept and without fraud by himself and his own servants, so that he does not sell, give or take anything from the woods except only for 'heybote', 'housbote', and 'furbote', and enclosure of the grove between the manor and the church of Caddington, and to make the due deliveries to tenants and this by the view of four good men of the manors and on one side only of the woods.[74] Moreover, all that is upon the land in stock and in buildings, wainage, and foldings and the like, as they are entered below, the said Richard shall, when he gives up occupation of the manors, in person or by his attornies, restore or cause to be restored in as good condition as he received them or better, and whatever improvement shall have been made in his time on the aforesaid manors in buildings, enclosures, ditching, folding, manuring, marling, and other conven-

73 The references within the lease to the tithes of the two parishes reveal that the dean and chapter of St Paul's have appointed themselves as rector of each parish and thus appropriated them (see p. 5). The rector has financial responsibility for the upkeep of the fabric of the chancel, the parishioners for the nave: hence the stipulation in a manorial lease that Richard shall uphold his responsibility as rector.

74 See above, p. 69, for 'housbote' and 'heyboot'; 'furboot', or firebote, is the right to take wood for domestic fuel.

iences in the said matters, shall remain free and quit to the aforesaid church of St Paul, without claim for compensation after he shall have relinquished the aforesaid manors.

The following are the stock and store which the said Richard took over and will restore, namely at Caddington 6 oxen each valued at 8s., eight stots each valued at 6s. 8d., one cow and one bull each valued at 6s. 8d., 150 sheep each valued at 12d., 15 pigs each valued at 12d. Item he received in the said manor 2 great barns, very serviceable and sufficient, one of which is wholly of oak. Item one new barn of beech. Item he received there under one roof a kitchen, a bake-house, and a brew-house roofed with tiles, and provided with a furnace. Item a very serviceable fowl-house. Item a hall, half of it roofed with shingles and the other half with tiles, with a pantry and buttery at the east end, and a small upper room above them, roofed with tiles, and without a garderobe and at the west end of the hall a good large new upper room well roofed with tiles and a garderobe adjoining it. Item a chapel built of stone and roofed with tiles, with a good cellar beneath with a tile-roofed enclosure before the cellar door. Item a tile-roofed passage between the chapel and the hall. Item a granary, very serviceable and well-roofed. Item a new stable, with a good tiled roof, together with a building for cart-horses under the same roof. Item a sufficient upper room over the gateway, and a small stable on one side of it, and a small room on the other side. Item a small tile-roofed building for smith's work. Item a thatched cart-house. Item a thatched dairy. Item a thatched drying-kiln. Item a small thatched room near the herb-garden. Item a sufficiently thatched pigsty. Item a serviceable thatched sheep-cote at Gerdlers with a thatched building for the use of the shepherd. Item a very serviceable sheep-cote near the gate of the manor. Item a well with a wheel, and the roof of the same above it. Item an outer thatched gateway. Item a wind-mill. Item he received in the same manor 60 acres of land well sown with wheat and 80 acres well sown with oats; 105 acres at fallow, 10 of which were manured.

Further, the following are the stock and implements which the said Richard received, and will render up at Kensworth, namely 4 head of cattle each of the value of half a mark, 10 oxen each of the value of 8s., 24 swine and 8 pigs each of the value of 12d., 32 lambs each 6d. Item he received 111 acres of land well sown with wheat and maslin, and 54 acres of oats well sown and 58 acres in fallow.[75] Item he received a

75 Maslin is an equal mixture of wheat and rye seed sown as a winter crop.

small hall with a small chamber at one end and a small very service-able thatched spence at the other end. Item a small very serviceable tile-roofed granary. Item a very serviceable thatched bake-house. Item three serviceable barns. Item one very serviceable cowhouse. Item a very serviceable sheep-cote within the yard and a building for storing straw at one end of it beneath the same roof.

These, moreover, the said Richard received on the feast of St Peter Ad vincula [1 August] in the year 1299, and defrayed at his own expense the cost of the harvest next following, and all these he shall render up on the feast of St Peter Ad vincula whenever he ceases his occupation of the premises and shall be quit of the cost of that harvest saving to himself all the corn and acres sown, to wit, with wheat, barley, oats or peas in excess of the number of acres on which he is bound to leave a crop, as it is above noted. Further, for the faithful observance of this agreement the said Richard pledged his faith to the dean and chapter and found sureties, namely Masters Giles Filol, archdeacon of Colchester, and John de Saint Clair, canons of the said church, and in case of their decease during the term of his farm he will find other fellow-canons as his sureties in their stead. The said Richard also bound himself in all his rents, possessions, and other property, real or personal, wherever found, to make good the aforesaid stock, store and crops, and for the faithful observation of all other aforesaid agreements. Renouncing all privilege of the law courts, all appeal and all remedy at law by which the church of the aforesaid St Paul would be prejudiced in the manner of the premises. In witness, moreover, of the premises, instruments have been drawn up between the aforesaid.

18 The lease of Thorpe Underwood, 1524

A much later lease than the previous example [17], but broadly similar in layout and general content. However, this lease possesses many subtle and sophisticated sub-clauses, indicating that experience made seigneurial admin-istrators cannier at drawing up manorial leases. See, for example, the clause detailing the action to be taken in the event of rent arrears, a recurrent problem during the fifteenth century, and the one permitting travelling representatives of the lord of the manor (the abbot of Fountains) to use the manor as a staging post under terms which are not unfavourable to the lessee.

D. J. H. Michelmore, ed., *The Fountains abbey lease book*, Yorkshire Archaeo-logical Society Record Series, 140 (1979), pp. 107–11. Lease of Thorpe Underwood (Yorkshire), 29 December 1524. English.

Thorpe Underwood. 29 December 16 Henry VIII [1524]. Lease by abbot Marmaduke and the convent of Fountains to Francis Man of Thorpe Underwood and Peter Man his son of their manor or lordship of Thorpe Underwood with all the arable, closes, pastures, meadows and marshes pertaining to it as appears in an annexed bill, except their 'manor place' and grange with other houses within its precincts, also reserving to the abbot and convent the woods and springs belonging to the manor, except that Francis and Peter may have sufficient housbote, axbot, ploughbot, cartbote and fyrebot to hold for forty years, paying £55 5s. 4d. per annum at Martinmas [11 November] and Whitsun.[76] If the rent remains unpaid for forty days, the abbot and convent have the right to distrain for the rent and arrears, and if it is half a year overdue they can re-enter, this lease notwithstanding. If the abbot and convent in the future stay at the manor of Thorpe Underwood for their solace, profit or pleasure, they may take into their hands closes and pasture worth £4 per annum or less for their horses, other brethren and servants, allowing to Francis and Peter as much money as the ground is worth. Francis and Peter are not to sublet without the abbot and convent's assent, licence or agreement, and if the abbot and convent do not agree to Francis and Peter making leases for terms of years, the abbot and convent are to have such parcels of land that Francis and Peter are not able themselves to occupy to let at their pleasure, allowing Francis and Peter the rent, as appears in an annexed bill. Francis and Peter are to repair and maintain all houses belonging to the manor, except for timber which they may take as necessary. The abbot and convent are to have free entry and exit for themselves and their carriages on every part of the manor, except the houses assigned to Francis and Peter, without hindrance from Francis and Peter. Francis and Peter are not to deliver timber to anyone without the abbot and convent's written warrant, and are to deliver such pigeons as are taken at every flight within the manor to the abbot and convent or their deputy, and shall keep to the abbot and convent's use and profit wild boars, deer, herons, pheasants, partridges as well as other fowls and beasts of free warren breeding within the manor, and are not to allow them to be destroyed by any person contrary to the abbot and convent's will and assent, but shall show the abbot and convent any such destruction.[77]

76 See p. 89.

77 Even at this late date the monopoly of free warren (see pp. 4–5) still represented a powerful symbol of seigneurial privilege, and the supply of game from Thorpe Underwood to the abbey's kitchens was obviously well regarded.

By these presents the abbot and convent lease to Francis and Peter such tithes and duties that belong to the chapter of the cathedral church of York by reason of his church of Little Ouseburn, now belonging to the abbot and convent by agreement, and are to take all the said tithes, paying 5 marks per annum to the chapter at Whitsun and Martinmas [11 November] under pain of the fine mentioned in the annexed composition, discharging the abbot and convent of the payment and the penalty, and taking an acquittance from the chapter or his receiver, providing that Francis and Peter are allowed 13s. 4d. per annum on their account for payment of the tithes and for their good service in the future. The abbot and convent grant and confirm Francis and Peter in the office of forestership of the manor for keeping all woods, coppices and springs for the life of the longer liver, on condition that they keep them for the abbot and convent's profit and advantage without waste or destruction by themselves or by anyone with their agreement. They are not to sell any timber without the abbot and convent's assent and licence, except that they may annually coppice and cut the rough 'hagge' of the said woods and springs in faggots after the old measure, proportion and length, some year after the value of 40 marks, £20 less or more as the springs will suffice to bear in their yearly course, and of the said faggots and provents growing and coming of the said coppices and 'hagge', yearly to content and pay the said abbot and their successors 10s. for every thousand, over and above all charges. Francis and Peter are to receive at the customary terms all the abbot and convent's rents in the towns, villages and hamlets specified in the annexed bill, as well as the rents received for the manor of Thorpe, and pay to the dean and chapter of York or their deputy £48 at the feasts of Sts Peter and Paul [29 June] and St Martin [11 November], under the penalty appearing in the annexed composition, discharging the abbot and convent from the payment and the penalty, taking a sufficient acquittance in writing sealed with the seal of the dean and chapter or their receiver. If the abbot and convent or their officers improve any parcels of the towns, villages or hamlets assigned for the payment of rents to the dean and chapter, Francis and Peter are to gather such improvements. Francis and Peter are not to make any lease or promise of any leasehold which is part of the specified towns, villages or hamlets, or take any entry fines, so that such leases are made by the abbot and convent. Francis and Peter are to receive any sums of money given by anyone for the said leaseholds or woods felled which are growing in the said towns, villages and hamlets and all fines, amercements, penalties and other revenues from all courts held there. Francis and Peter are to find bedding and other comforts necessary for the abbot and convent and his other brethren and servants coming to the manor of Thorpe for their solace, if it is not continuously, for which the abbot and convent will give them certain flocks and other rewards as often as necessary. By these presents the abbot and convent grant that Francis and Peter or the longer liver shall be overseers of all necessary repairs in the said towns, villages, hamlets and the manor of Thorpe, felling wood necessary for such repairs, being allowed on their account such sums of money as they pay for the repairs. Francis and Peter, or one of them, are to wait and do service to the abbot and convent and on reasonable warning are to ride with them on their own horses at the abbot and convent's cost.[78] Every year, on reasonable warning, they are to make a true account before such auditors as are assigned to them of all rents, fines, penalties, entry fines, issues and amercements received by them and to pay any arrears charged on their account. For which forestership, overseeing and keeping of woods and the warren of Thorpe Underwood and service to be done the abbot and convent grant to them, for the life of the longer living, a fee of 40s. per annum payable at Whitsun and Martinmas [11 November] with sufficient cloth yearly for a gown of such livery as the abbot and convent may give their other household servants, or else 4s. to be allowed on their account, and furthermore the abbot and convent grant them for the life of the longer living a fee of 10s per annum payable at the said feasts for levying the rents, issues, fines and amercements due to the abbot and convent for the said towns, villages and hamlets for payment to the church of York. The abbot and convent also grant them for the life of the longer living a fee of 6s. 8d. per annum for receiving the rents of the town of Marston, and for keeping the woods there. If Peter dies before Francis, Francis can place the residue of the term in the hands of one of his other sons by virtue of this lease, and if Francis dies before Janet, his wife, and she is not then content to live in the house with her son Peter or his brother, she is to have a sufficient house within the lordship of Thorpe Underwood at Peter or his brother's cost and arable lands, meadow

---

78 An old-fashioned touch in an otherwise very contemporary lease. Leasehold was increasingly popular in the Middle Ages because of its contractual nature, which meant that it did not present any liability on the part of the tenant for personal service to the lord. Yet this leasehold explicitly stipulates that the brothers, as part of their contract, should serve in the abbot's retinue if required, perhaps because they are descended from the villein stock of the manor. Francis and Peter could benefit from their affinity with a figure as powerful as the abbot of Fountains.

and pasture worth £5 per annum, with 'howsebote, fyrebote' and other necessities, without hindrance from Peter or his brother or any other person. Sealed interchangeably. Given in the chapter house at Fountains.

III: MANORIAL ACCOUNTS

Introduction

Manorial accounts build upon the 'static' information contained in surveys, extents and rentals by recording in detail how the individual elements of the manor were managed and what they actually yielded over the agricultural year (normally Michaelmas [29 September] to Michaelmas). As such, a system of manorial accounting represented a logical and obvious development from the use of surveys, and is discernible from the early thirteenth century. The earliest known manorial accounts survive from the bishop of Winchester's estate in the 1200s and 1210s, where they were enrolled with other estate and household records. By the 1230s, enrolled accounts had been superceded by individual and separate account rolls for each manor. In this form, the manorial account (which is known also as a 'minister's account' or *compotus*) soon became widespread on the estates of large ecclesiastical landlords in southern and eastern England. Surviving examples of individual account rolls increase markedly in the 1250s, and become common from the 1270s and 1280s.[1]

The management of the manor

The emergence of manorial accounts corresponded with a substantial change in the management of seigneurial estates in England. In the second half of the twelfth century the greater landlords commonly leased an entire manor to a local lessee for a stipulated annual rent, known as 'a farm': this was sometimes payable in kind, called a 'food

---

1 P. D. A. Harvey, *Manorial records of Cuxham Oxfordshire, c. 1200–1359*, Oxfordshire Record Society, 50 (1976), p. 15; P. D. A. Harvey, 'Mid thirteenth-century accounts from Bury St Edmunds abbey', in A. Gransden, ed., *Bury St Edmunds: medieval art, architecture, archaeology and economy*, British Archaeological Association Conference Transactions, 20 (1998), pp. 130–1. See also F. B. Stitt, 'The medieval minister's account', *Society of Local Archivists' Bulletin*, 11 (1953), 2–8; P. D. A. Harvey, 'Agricultural treatises and manorial accounting in medieval England', *Agricultural History Review*, 20 (1972), 170–82; and B. M. S. Campbell, *English Seigniorial agriculture, 1250–1450* (Cambridge, 2000), pp. 26–36.

farm'. As long as the assets of the manor were not stripped, and as long as the farm was rendered to the lord, the lessee exploited the various components of the manor as he saw fit. No manorial accounts survive from this period when the leasing of manors prevailed. However, from the late twelfth century many landlords moved away from the policy of leasing and instead managed a growing proportion of their manors directly. In effect, landlords ran the demesne as their own agricultural operation, either consuming or selling its produce as appropriate, and collecting the rents due from manorial tenants themselves. This shift to hands-on farming appears to have been a peculiarly English trait, and was virtually unknown on the Continent.[2]

The broad movement towards direct exploitation corresponds closely with the development and spread of the manorial account. Only the humblest landlords administered their manors personally, for most had too many manors and other duties to be directly involved in manorial management themselves. Consequently, the day-to-day running of individual manors on most estates was delegated to local officials, and the manorial account was the means by which their activities were supervised by the landlord.[3] A directly managed manor normally fell under the overall supervision of a single local agent, who effectively served as the farm manager for a year. The post was often occupied by a local landholding peasant, known as the reeve, who was elected annually and compulsarily from the ranks of the unfree tenants. This system of 'elections' was not guaranteed to produce either a willing reeve or a consistent level of service for the lord, and consequently an informal compromise was reached on some manors to allow the same person to serve year after year. On other manors, the local agent was a salaried, and therefore professional, bailiff or serjeant. The reeve/

---

2 For an introduction to this subject, see P. D. A. Harvey, 'The pipe rolls and the adoption of demesne farming in England', *Economic History Review*, 27 (1974); E. Miller and J. Hatcher, *Medieval England: rural society and economic change 1086–1348* (1978), pp. 189–239. The study of medieval estate management has a long pedigree, both for individual manors and whole estates. For example, I. Kershaw, *Bolton priory: the economy of a northern monastery 1286–1325* (Oxford, 1973); J. A. Raftis, *The estates of Ramsey abbey* (Toronto, 1957); C. C. Dyer, *Lords and peasants in a changing society: the estates of the bishopric of Worcester 680–1500* (Cambridge, 1980), pp. 51–83, 113–52; P. D. A. Harvey, *A medieval Oxfordshire village: Cuxham 1240 to 1400* (Oxford, 1965); R. H. Britnell, 'Production for the market on a small fourteenth-century estate', *Economic History Review*, 30 (1977), 53–66; M. Bailey, 'The prior and convent of Ely and their management of the manor of Lakenheath in the fourteenth century', in M. J. Franklin and C. Harper-Bill, eds, *Medieval ecclesiastical studies in honour of Dorothy M. Owen* (Woodbridge, 1995), pp. 1–19.

3 J. S. Drew, 'Manorial accounts of St Swithun's Priory, Winchester', in E. M. Carus-Wilson, ed., *Essays in economic history, vol. II* (1962), p. 15.

bailiff was often supported by a range of other (elected or salaried) officers, frequently drawn from the manorial tenantry, such as a hayward (or *messor*), rent collector, warrener, parker, woodkeeper and granger.

The activities of these manorial officials, under the supervision of the reeve/bailiff, were varied and complex. They bought and sold livestock, decided upon the exact combination of crops to be sown on the demesne, sent grain to the seigneurial household for consumption, leased out mills, negotiated and collected rents, supervised the harvest, and ensured that the labour services of the customary tenants were utilised and performed as required. The responsibility for running the manor was time-consuming, demanding and onerous, and professional bailiffs who performed poorly were quickly replaced.[4] The managerial burdens were especially heavy for the ostensibly 'amateur' reeve. Although it is arguable that the amateur possesses an inalienable right to perform like one, the medieval reeve was judged as a professional and held personally responsible on some thirteenth-century estates for losses incurred through errors of judgement or even a poor harvest caused by the weather, and in some cases his personal assets were seized to pay off debts to the lord.[5]

Despite the possible pitfalls for both lord and peasant, the system of elected reeves proved remarkably resilient until the late fourteenth century. Recent research has shown that reeves and bailiffs regularly made complex and sophisticated decisions about many aspects of demesne management, and it was often these dirty boot officials – rather than the lords or their stewards – who exhibited most commercial and farming acumen on seigneurial estates.[6] Thus, for all the potential liabilities, the office of reeve must have offered rewarding opportunities and experience for the skilled husbandman, and reliable performers were well regarded and rewarded by their lords. A reeve typically received a remission of rent on his landholding, some food and other emoluments during the year of office, and the wily operator must have also exploited other opportunities for profit. Perhaps, like Chaucer's

4 C. Thornton, 'The determinants of land productivity on the bishop of Winchester's demesne of Rimpton, 1208–1403', in B. M. S. Campbell and M. Overton, eds, *Land, labour and livestock: historical studies in European agricultural productivity* (Manchester, 1991), p. 202. See T. F. T. Plucknett, *The medieval bailiff* (1954).

5 Drew, 'St Swithun's', p. 12; N. Denholm-Young, *Seignorial administration in England* (Oxford, 1937), pp. 151–4.

6 D. Stone, 'The management of resources on the demesne farm of Wisbech Barton, 1314–1430' (University of Cambridge, PhD thesis, 1998), pp. 67–9.

reeve in the *Canterbury Tales*, 'he koude bettre than his lord purchase, ful riche he was astored prively'.[7]

The reeve/bailiff of a manor was supervised by estate officials of higher status, although the precise system of management varied from estate to estate.[8] In the thirteenth and fourteenth centuries the lord often delegated this responsibility to one or more stewards, although on the smallest estates he might assume the role himself.[9] A steward often controlled a number of manors, visiting each two or three times during the year. He normally supervised the bigger building projects on the manor, sanctioned extraordinary expenditure, and negotiated with tenants on major or sensitive issues.[10] The expenses incurred by the steward and other visiting estate officials when visiting the manor are frequently recorded in the manorial account, and thus provide a valuable insight into the administrative workings of a particular estate [20]. The steward, and the auditors (pp. 103–4), laid down general policy and directed expenditure or the disposal of produce in specific ways, but within such parameters the reeve/bailiff exercised his own initiative.[11] By the fifteenth century the steward's responsibility for supervising local officials closely had diminished, and control over them was exercised principally through the annual audit of the account instead.

The format of the account

The supervision and record of the actions of the local agents was undertaken through the annual compilation of a manorial account. Its primary purpose was to check and record the flow of money and goods, and to establish the financial position between agent and lord at the end of the accounting year. Consequently, most *compoti* are the reeve's or bailiff's account, although lesser manorial officials sometimes accounted separately.[12] By the second half of the thirteenth century

7 G. Chaucer, *The General Prologue to the Canterbury Tales*, ed. by J. Winney (Cambridge, 1966), p. 70. See also B. M. S. Campbell, 'The livestock of Chaucer's reeve: fact or fiction?', in E. B. De Windt, ed., *The salt of common life: individuality and choice in the medieval town, countryside and church* (Kalamazoo, 1995), pp. 271–4, 302–4.

8 Drew, 'St Swithun's', pp. 25–6; Dyer, *Lords and peasants*, pp. 154–62.

9 Denholm-Young, *Seignorial administration*, pp.136–9.

10 Dyer, *Lords and peasants*, p. 116.

11 Drew, 'St Swithun's', p. 15.

12 R. H. Hilton, ed., *Ministers' accounts of the Warwickshire estates of the Duke of Clarence, 1479–80*, Dugdale Society, 21 (1952), p. xii.

the layout of *compoti* was already highly standardised across the country, which is suggestive of trained staff working from specimen accounts.[13] The front of the account roll (*recto*) detailed financial flows, beginning with a systematic listing of annual and foreign receipts (i.e. those generated 'inside' and 'outside' the manor), and followed by a record of expenditure, foreign expenses and money delivered to the seigneurial household and senior officials. Finally, the outstanding balance between total receipts and expenditure was reckoned.

The other side of the roll (*verso* or dorse) recorded the flows of grain and livestock into, within and out of the manor during the year. The 'receipts' of grain recorded in this section are those from the harvest immediately preceding the start date of the account, less the amount given to the church as tithe (ten per cent, which was taken directly from the field immediately after reaping) and augmented by any purchases during the period covered by the account. Soon after the harvest the demesne grain was stored unthreshed in the demesne grange, and the account records the total amount transferred to the granary (normally threshed) during the accounting year. So, strictly speaking, the grain recorded as received in an account is actually from the harvest held in the previous accounting year: for example, in a *compotus* covering the year Michaelmas 1290 to Michaelmas 1291, the grain recorded as 'issued' or 'received' in the account is that harvested in the late summer of 1290. The disposal of that grain during the accounting year – whether sown as seed corn, fed to animals, sold to market, sent to the lord's household, or destroyed by vermin – is noted with care [20]. The record of grain flows is then normally followed by the record of flows of livestock. Stock is documented by type and age, together with births, cullings, transfers, purchases and deaths. Capital values are not recorded, and any sale prices only appear on the cash side of the account: however, wool weights and dairy yields are sometimes given. The livestock account is often followed by the works account, which details the labour services due from the manorial peasantry and the uses to which they were put [31].

The detail contained in these accounts is highly impressive, and was only attainable by keeping a careful running record of the flows of goods, stock and cash throughout the year. Hence the final account was compiled by drawing upon a range of subsidiary records and working memoranda, such as written notes [24–7] or scored tallies, and supplementary documents, such as rentals, surveys and extents.

13 Harvey, *Manorial records of Cuxham*, p. 40.

It is not uncommon for draft and half-year accounts to survive from some manors.[14]

The concept of accountability, and of allotting responsibility, is central to understanding medieval *compoti.* This represents a significant difference from today's accounting methods, and a modern accountant might be initially nonplussed by manorial accounts. For example, they were not concerned to record actual income and expenditure, to assess fixed assets, to allow for depreciation, or to calculate annual profit and loss in the modern sense. The receipts section essentially detailed what the bailiff or reeve *ought* to have received, and uncollectable items were simply entered as deductions in the expenses section. In addition, capital values of demesne stock and equipment were seldom recorded (although they do appear in manorial inventories), and not everything produced and disposed by the manor within the accounting year, or which was a source of profit, was recorded or given a financial value. For example, when food was sent from a manor to the seigneurial household, the transaction would certainly be recorded in the stock account but not always in the cash account, and the transfer of deer and timber from a manorial park to the household rarely appears anywhere in the *compotus.*

These significant omissions and anomolies underline the point that manorial accounts followed a charge/discharge system of accounting, rather than a system which recorded hard income and expenditure, and was designed to enable the lord to establish accurately the liability of the local agent for money and goods. The 'income' section of the cash account was, in reality, a list of financial charges against the reeve or bailiff, which might include items such as accumulated arrears carried over from the previous account; transfers of grain to the seigneurial household which are given a notional 'sale' value; or rents listed on an earlier rental, some of which had since become defunct and uncollectable. Clearly, none of these relate to actual income or real credits, and where the lord recognised the notional character of such charges, a corresponding sum (say, for 'decayed rents' or 'purchases' of grain for the lord's household) would be entered in the 'expenditure' section of the cash account, representing a counterbalancing discharge from the designated liability.

The final reckoning of the annual balance of charges and discharges was undertaken through a formal audit, the expenses of which are

---

14 Denholm-Young, *Seignorial administration,* p. 134.

regularly recorded in the account itself. A 'view of account' was often conducted in the early summer, in which the figures of the half-year from late September to late March would be scrutinised, and perhaps a provisional full-year account compiled. The formal and full audit of the account of the local agent took place locally rather than centrally, and the adjustments made by the auditors – a charge added here, an allowance conceded there – appear as alterations and marginalia on the final account. The majority of extant *compoti* are audited accounts.

The audit, and the written amendments which appear on the final account, emphasise that the *compotus* constituted 'a dynamic record, a dialogue between local agents and auditors'.[15] Although seldom identified, the auditors were representatives of the seigneurial household whose duty was to ensure that the lord's interests were protected.[16] Before undertaking the audit, they would have scrutinised the accounts of previous years, rentals, surveys and extents to acquire a sense of what they might reasonably expect to find. If the returns or yields fell below their expectations then they might, for example, impose a surcharge on the reeve/bailiff if they felt that he had not secured a satisfactory price when selling stock (or suspected him of not declaring the true price), or they might disallow certain expenses or payments. The policy on some estates was even more stringent, requiring the reeve/bailiff to achieve a specified yield each year in certain areas of agricultural production, and levying a charge if the actual yield fell short of the target. Thus in 1267 the reeve of Stockton (Wiltshire), on the estate of St Swithun's priory, Winchester, was charged 36s. 8d. for 'bad custody' and failing to reach the required wool yield.[17] The system of quotas is less common in the fourteenth and fifteenth centuries, but auditors remained watchful and critical. Those at Bibury (Gloucestershire) questioned most items of expenditure, altering around one third of all entries on the reeve's account of 1387–88.[18]

A good auditor was sceptical by professional inclination, and aware that some reeves – like Chaucer's – reckoned that 'ther was non auditour koude on him winne'.[19] Disputes inevitably occurred between auditors and local officials as they scrutinised individual items on the

15 Harvey, *Manorial records of Cuxham*, pp. 42–3.
16 Denholm-Young, *Seignorial administration*, p. 133.
17 Drew, 'St Swithun's', p. 20.
18 Dyer, *Lords and peasants*, p. 117.
19 Chaucer, *General prologue*, p. 69.

draft account, and much bargaining must have taken place. If the auditors accepted that a charge against the reeve/bailiff was unrealistic, then it might be 'allowed' (i.e. cancelled) or 'respited' (i.e. postponed for collection at a later, unspecified, date). To support their claims at the audit, reeves and bailiffs depended increasingly upon memoranda written by either themselves or local scribes hired at their own expense. Occasionally these memoranda and petitions are sewn to the final account, and provide a valuable source of supplementary information to the historian [**27**]. In addition, by the fourteenth century many manors were using presentment juries in manorial courts (see pp. 173–4) to verify certain information contained in accounts, such as the annual numbers of demesne animals that had 'died of murrain and not of bad custody'. The court could also be employed to fine or coerce tenants who withdrew their rents or labour services, a mechanism which provided manorial officers with some teeth in their dealings with recalcitrant peasants. Similarly, trespasses against the lord's property or stock were pursued through the manorial court.

Once the body of the account had been audited, the auditors balanced the total charge against the total discharge, and recorded the outstanding sum. Occasionally, money was owed by the lord to the reeve/ bailiff (entered as *et sic excedit*), and presumably paid by the auditors immediately. However, it was more common for the charge to exceed the discharge (*et sic debet*). If full settlement of this debt was received at the final audit (*super compotum*), then the reeve/bailiff would be pronounced quit of all debt (*et sic quietus est*). Often, however, the outstanding sum was not paid off entirely, partly because it comprised the debts of previous officials, or items that had proved uncollectable, rather than cash in the local agent's hand [see, for example, **22**]. These arrears would then be carried over to the next year's account, either as a lump sum or itemised according to each individual debtor, until they were either paid or allowed, that is written off, by the auditors (see also pp. 110 and 142 for arrears). The audited *compotus* would then be stored in the lord's household for as long as it was deemed to be useful: accounts were used to monitor estate administration, and to inform future strategies, by officials within the lord's household.[20]

20 Harvey, *Manorial records of Cuxham*, p. 25.

The evolution of the account

The evolution of the manorial account between the early thirteenth and fifteenth centuries, and its detailed workings, have been comprehensively described and explained by Paul Harvey, who usefully identifies three broad phases in their development.[21] Accounts from phase 1 (*c.* 1200–*c.* 1270) were limited to a small number of estates, mainly ecclesiastical, in southern and south eastern England, and were drawn up by central estate administrators: survivals are, typically, enrolled fair copies, and not especially common. Their format was often rudimentary and relatively unstandardised, reflecting different accounting techniques and practices from estate to estate, and the information in them was probably compiled from oral testimony and crude tallies. Indeed, accounts from phase 1 do not always cover an entire year or necessarily commence at Michaelmas, reflecting an early administrative discomfort with the notion of making an annual cut-off point for an operation that was essentially ongoing.[22] The accounts contain condensed entries rather than detailed single items, and the entries are often listed in undifferentiated blocks under the general headings of receipts and expenses [19].

Thousands of accounts have survived from phase 2 (*c.* 1270–*c.* 1380), when they were commonplace on most English estates. Their format is highly consistent, reflecting the widespread adoption of a standardised method of accounting. The degree of standardisation is so impressive and complete that it implies the widespread existence of specimen accounts or, as suggested earlier, some form of management school.[23] Responsibility for drawing up the account had now shifted from the central administrators to the local agent, who employed a local clerk to prepare the account itself. Indeed, the clerk played a central role in marshalling and ordering all the information contained in the account, and consequently a growing body of subsidiary documents was increasingly deployed in this period. The demands made by local agents contributed to the small but growing army of jobbing clerks in

21 Harvey, *Manorial records*, pp. 12–34.

22 Harvey, 'Mid-thirteenth-century accounts', p. 133.

23 Harvey, *Manorial records of Cuxham*, pp. 20–2, 29–30; see above, p. 20. The professionalisation of estate management and accounting during the thirteenth century is evident by the production of treatises for the purpose: D. Oschinsky, ed., *Walter of Henley and other treatises on estate management and accounting* (Oxford, 1971).

late thirteenth-century England.[24] The shift from centralised to localised compilation of accounts is also reflected in tighter financial control
by auditors over *compoti* dating from phase 2 compared with those
from phase 1, and greater dialogue between auditors and local agents.
Consequently, phase 2 accounts include much greater detail about
receipts and expenses, and the information is presented under numerous
subheadings [**20**].

Extant accounts from phase 3 (*c*. 1380–*c*. 1530) are less common, and
considerably less detailed, than those from phase 2. In this phase,
direct demesne husbandry was either severely run down or abandoned,
and labour services were gradually eroded until they disappeared, and
consequently the contents of the account diminished. A manor that
was entirely leased by its lord was covered by a proper leasehold
agreement instead [**17,18**], and the accounts of those manors retained
in direct management were greatly curtailed: the length and detail of
the stock account on the dorse was substantially reduced, and the
running costs associated with the demesne (upkeep of equipment,
harvest expenses, the wages of the *famuli*, repairs, etc.) – which are
richly detailed in the cash section of phase 2 accounts – occupied little
space in phase 3.[25] Indeed, the contracting scale of demesne operations
and the move towards piecemeal leasing is readily apparent in the
reduction in size and detail of sections that relate to the direct
cultivation of the demesne, such as 'sales of corn' and 'harvest
expenses'. In cases where the lord leased the demesne land but retained
other components of the manor in direct cultivation, the lessee (or
farmer) was often required to submit an annual account to the lord,
although, again, the amount of detail was substantially reduced [**22**].
The practice of electing reeves from the unfree tenants eventually
ceased, after which accounts were drawn up either by professional
bailiffs, rent collectors or the demesne lessee. Campbell states that 'by
1450 the era of the manorial account is effectively over', and survivals
are often little more than glorified rent rolls.[26] The method of accounting
for income and expenditure on landed estates was changing, and
accounts in their medieval format are rare after 1500.

24 Z. Razi and R. M. Smith, eds, *Medieval society and the manor court* (Oxford, 1996),
p. 60.
25 For useful discussions on the nature of fifteenth-century accounts, see Hilton,
'Clarence', pp. xv–xxii; Dyer, *Lords and peasants*, pp. 179–90; M. Bailey, *A marginal
economy? East Anglian Breckland in the later Middle Ages* (Cambridge, 1989), pp. 271–6.
26 Campbell, *Seigniorial agriculture*, p. 30.

The three phases in the evolution of the manorial account correspond with broad changes in the management of the estates of England's greater landlords.[27] *Compoti* do not survive from the late twelfth century when the vast majority of manors held by such landlords were leased, and their emergence at the turn of the twelfth and thirteenth centuries corresponded with the shift to direct management of manors on these estates. Accounts therefore arose from the practice of exploiting demesnes directly, even if they were not essential to it. Phase 1 covers the period spanning from the widespread adoption of demesne farming to its peak around 1270. During this period the profitability of agriculture was persistently high.

Phase 2 begins (*c.* 1270) at the peak of direct management and ends (*c.* 1380) as many landlords began a major shift back towards rentier farming. The growing sophistication of accounts in the late thirteenth century is reflected in renewed attempts to incorporate crude calculations of profit and loss for the year. Hence a phrase such as 'profit this year, £13 4s. 10d.' might appear at the foot of the cash account in a different hand. In fact, these rather rudimentary calculations were made after the audit by central administrators (rather than the local agent), and unfortunately the exact premises upon which they were based are obscure. They were evidently constructed by using notional values for the corn and stock produced on the demesne, but these values are seldom known to historians and the calculations certainly did not include any assessment of capital assets.[28]

The notion of profit and loss accounting is documented in the 1230s, but the evidence for it is greatest from the period 1290–1320, which has tempted David Postles to suggest that 'the attempt to measure current profitability may have been no more than an intellectual exercise of a transient nature'.[29] Whatever their purpose and worth, the development of profit/loss calculations indicates that landlords were now regarding their estates and accounting systems from a markedly different perspective. The main reason for compiling the earliest accounts was to minimise fraud by local officials, but by the second half of the thirteenth century landlords were demanding more of their

27 For an introduction to the literature, see Miller and Hatcher, *Medieval England*, pp. 213–39; J. L. Bolton, *The medieval English economy, 1150–1500* (1980), pp. 87–98.

28 Denholm-Young, *Seignorial administration*, p. 129; E. Stone, 'Profit and loss accounting at Norwich Cathedral priory', *T.R.H.S.*, 5th series, 12 (1962), 28–36; D. Postles, 'Perceptions of profit before the leasing of demesnes', *Agricultural History Review*, 34 (1986), 13–15.

29 Harvey, *Manorial records*, p. 28; Postles, 'Perceptions of profit', p. 23.

accounting procedures: instead of asking 'are we being defrauded?', they were beginning to ask 'are we running our estates effectively?', and by these means were seeking to make more informed judgements on the benefits of directly exploiting demesnes.[30]

Economic conditions were distinctly favourable to landlords until the mid-1320s, but gradually deteriorated thereafter and encouraged the greater landlords to turn away by degrees from direct exploitation of their manors and reduce the scale of their operations. Of course, the extent of this movement, and the response of individual landlords and manors, varied considerably over time and place. A common response was to lease those manors which were least conveniently located, or were simply least viable, to a willing lessee for a stipulated annual sum, rather like their predecessors had done in the twelfth century. Even on manors where direct management was retained, it became more common to lease some components of the manor, such as fisheries, woodland, mills and parcels of the demesne arable, to various local tenants in a piecemeal fashion. The scale of leasing (both piecemeal and whole manors) accelerated during deflationary periods, such as the twenty years after *c.* 1325, and the 1380s and 1390s.

In contrast with the widespread adoption of direct demesne farming, which had occurred relatively swiftly between *c.* 1180 and *c.* 1220, the widespread return to leasing in the later Middle Ages was a more piecemeal, varied and gradual process.[31] One explanation for this contrast is that landlords had gained considerable experience in the local management of their estates during the thirteenth century, and had developed more sophisticated systems of accounting, which enabled them to respond more flexibly to the changing economic conditions of the fourteenth century and to make complex and finely balanced decisions about the exploitation of each manor within their estate. Their demands upon the manorial accounting system grew as its potential for informing estate strategy became more apparent, and it is no coincidence that *compoti* dating from phase 2 were more refined, detailed and sophisticated than their predecessors.

Phase 3 in the evolution of manorial accounts (*c.* 1380–*c.* 1530) corresponds broadly with a period of sustained agricultural depression,

30 Stone, 'Profit and loss', pp. 46–7.

31 Such processes are well-documented in many of the estate studies, but see E. Searle, *Lordship and community: Battle abbey and its banlieu, 1066–1538* (Toronto, 1974), pp. 324–37; Raftis, *Ramsey abbey*, pp. 281–301; Harvey, *Westminster abbey and its estates in the Middle Ages* (Oxford, 1977), pp. 148–51.

particularly between the 1440s and 1480s. Local pockets, and short periods, of better conditions existed, and it remained possible for enterprising farmers to make some sort of living out of agriculture, but – in general – rent levels fell to their medieval nadir, tenants were hard to find, customary tenures dissolved, labour services were abandoned, and profit margins in agriculture dwindled. Some landlords responded by encouraging industrial activities on their manors, developing new crops, or shifting to livestock farming (where rising costs could be better contained), but even these enterprises often depended for their success on local conditions and proved to be little more than palliatives.[32] Agricultural incomes fell, and consequently petitions from local agents, especially rent collectors, requesting allowances and respites from charged receipts are commonly attached to phase 3 accounts [27].

The squeezing of agrarian profits and the reduction of landed income in the fifteenth century accelerated and extended the trend towards manorial leasing, because rentier farming was perceived to offer a safer and more predictable source of income than direct farming. This tendency was especially evident on the estates of greater landlords, whose far-flung possessions and fixed administrative overheads presented serious obstacles to reducing the costs involved in direct management. Where landlords did retain demesnes in direct cultivation, stocking levels and the area under crops were substantially reduced.

The return to widespread leasing in the fifteenth century incorporated management strategies which were subtly different to those employed in the twelfth century, because landlords had now acquired both the expertise and the information to manage their estates more effectively. Extant twelfth-century manorial leases are rare, and tend to be cursory and rather imprecise about the terms and conditions of the tenancy, reflecting a rudimentary system of estate administration and less use of the written record. In contrast, manorial leases dating from the fifteenth and early sixteenth centuries are commonplace, relatively long, and often contain features such as stock inventories and maintenance clauses [17, 18].

The ubiquity of detailed manorial leases in the fifteenth century, and the continued use of accounts long after the demesne had ceased to be exploited directly, indicates strongly that landlords had become more stringent and effective administrators of their rental income. This characteristic is also evident on those occasions when landlords chose not to lease a manor in its entirety for a stipulated rent to a named lessee, but preferred a more flexible and sophisticated approach in which individual manorial components were leased on different terms to different tenants. Thus part of the demesne arable might be leased in parcels of differing sizes to a number of tenants, whose tenancies terminated at different dates; the demesne meadows might be similarly leased, while certain larger pastures were retained directly to support a demesne sheep flock; the manorial court might be run by the lord's officials, and the wood leased to one tenant, and the warren to another.

This policy of retaining some elements in hand but leasing many components of the manor separately, and of continuing to collect rent from landholding tenants directly, means that phase 3 accounts are concerned mainly with rent management. This policy obviously required more administrative effort than merely leasing the entire manor to one person or a consortium, because rent collectors and bailiffs had to be supervised, tenants sought, and leases negotiated (see above, pp. 39–41). However, it did enable landlords to retain greater control over their manorial assets, and to squeeze more income from them in a testing economic climate. The Paston letters reveal clearly how fifteenth-century landlords had to be flexible and responsive just to keep tenants, let alone secure new ones.[33]

The unfavourable economic conditions, and the inherent weakness of the landlord's position, contributed significantly to escalating arrears, which are a distinctive feature of phase 3 accounts. The size and persistence of arrears in this period underline the difficulties of collecting rents, leases, fines and amercements on many manors.[34] Arrears should be regarded as part of the ongoing dialogue between the local official and the auditors, and could include a mixture of notional charges, realistic debts and long-standing items for which auditors reckoned the official should still be held liable. The latter might include, for example, rent that had not been paid for years and was unlikely to be collected, but which the auditors refused to write off. Arrears, therefore, reveal as much about accounting policy on a manor as they do about economic reality, and must be interpreted with caution. Many phase 1 and 2 accounts simply record arrears as an unspecified lump sum, but from the late fourteenth century they are

---

33 R. H. Britnell, 'The Pastons and their Norfolk', *Agricultural History Review*, 36 (1988), 132–44.

34 Dyer, *Lords and peasants*, pp. 179–87.

increasingly broken down at the foot of the account into smaller items in order to keep track of the personal liability of named officials, merchants and tenants [20, 22].

The individual manorial *compotus* disappears rather abruptly in the early sixteenth century, which reflects a genuine change in managerial practice more than survival rates. The dissolution of the great monastic houses in the late 1530s may have been a contributory factor in the decline, because they had first devised the *compotus* and then put it to greatest use. Yet the shift away from direct seigneurial husbandry, the diminution of feudal dues, and the decline in the manor's role as a unit of agricultural management all reduced the need to draw up separate accounts for individual manors. The gradual disappearance of 'amateur' local officials drawn from the manorial tenantry, and their replacement by salaried rent collectors and bailiffs who probably worked for the same lord on more than one manor, moved the managerial emphasis back toward the centre of estates. Thereafter, information about individual manors was still recorded, but was increasingly integrated into centralised and composite estate records. The sixteenth-century shift towards the centralised control and exploitation of landed estates, run by a professional administration, is evident in the emergence of specialist books which detailed the management of specific commodities across the estate, such as sheep and cattle.[35]

Historical uses of the account

It is clear from this brief introduction to the form and development of the manorial account that the exact exploitation of individual manors depended greatly upon the type, size and location of the estate, and the status of the lord. A similar point applies to the survival rate of *compoti*, which is highest on certain types of estate and in certain areas of the country. For example, few accounts have survived from the smallest lay estates, despite the fact that many such manors were often managed directly between the eleventh and fifteenth centuries. Minor lords certainly used accounts to supervise their manorial affairs, but they were less likely to keep those accounts for long periods for reasons of space and necessity. Consequently, the documentary record is poorest for the most numerous, and perhaps most enterprising, category of manor.

35 P. Edwards, *Farming. Sources for local historians* (1991), pp. 32–5.

The majority of extant *compoti* derive from the manors of larger ecclesiastical or lay estates, where structures of estate administration were most developed (and bureaucratic). In Norfolk seventy per cent of extant accounts are from ecclesiastical manors, yet lay outnumbered ecclesiastical manors in the county by four to one. The survival pattern of accounts is most complete from the estates of large, 'perpetual', institutions with the facilities to store a large archive, rather than from lesser lay estates prone to disruption and dispersal. Yet it might also reflect the fact that Benedictine monasteries and bishoprics in south and east England both pioneered the manorial account and also put it to greater use than any other medieval landlord: we cannot be certain, given the unevenness in the survival of records. We can be more certain that a manor's location influenced the survival rate of its accounts. For example, very few *compoti* are extant from upland areas and north-west England, probably because the problem of geo-graphical isolation discouraged landlords from managing such manors directly, and, of course, accounts were a product of direct management. Most survivals are from central, southern and eastern England, where the coverage is good: over 2,000 manorial accounts for Norfolk are extant from the period 1238–1450, covering perhaps fifteen per cent of the county's medieval manors.[36]

Although the uneven survival pattern of manorial accounts is disappointing, the extant *compoti* present historians with invaluable, incomparable and abundant information about a wide range of eco-nomic and agricultural activities in medieval England. Much of this information comprises raw economic data, the basic building-blocks with which historians construct, and attempt to understand, changes in the medieval economy: wage rates for different categories of labour, prices of agricultural and other produce, rent levels, and land occupancy. The two medieval volumes of the *Agrarian History of England and Wales*, which survey variations in agrarian characteristics and fortunes by region, are largely based on the raw information contained within scores of *compoti*.[37]

The details about demesne husbandry in manorial accounts are extremely revealing, and provide insights into medieval farm manage-ment which are better than those provided by agrarian sources from

36 Campbell, *Seigniorial farming*, pp. 32–3.

37 H. E. Hallam, ed., *The agrarian history of England and Wales: vol II, 1042–1350* (Cambridge, 1988); E. Miller, ed., *The agrarian history of England and Wales, III: 1348–1500* (Cambridge, 1991).

the early modern period. The type, quantity and proportion of sown crops, the method and intensity of ground preparation, and the balance between arable and pasture farming are readily ascertained from many *compoti*: some even provide details of the proportion of demesne arable under cultivation [29]. Where consecutive accounts survive for the same manor, annual grain yields are calculable and patterns of product disposal can be identified, which allows historians to assess whether manors were geared principally to the market or to the production of crops for seigneurial consumption (and whether market forces made them more productive). Similar assessments of livestock farming – local specialisms, productivity and commercial orientation – are also possible.

Thus manorial accounts permit historians to reconstruct many of the essential features of medieval, albeit demesne, agriculture: spatial and temporal patterns in farming practice, field systems, land productivity, and the nature of agricultural production and disposal.[38] The internal workings of a medieval farm are graphically exposed, and we also see something of the local farming practices within which it operated. However, the accounts seldom provide any explanation for the agrarian policies adopted by the manorial demesne, and so little is known directly about the external forces that were conditioning the local responses. Occasionally, a low yield or an unusual decision may be justified by a terse reference to, for example, extreme weather conditions,[39] but, in general, historians have to explain for themselves the observed agricultural activities of particular manor. Economic and commercial factors were obviously influential, but the specific requirements of the lord's household for food or cash were also important. For example, a large static household, such as a monastery, was more likely to seek bulky provisions from its closest demesne manors and cash from its furthest.[40]

38 For a discussion of this use for accounts, see B. M. S. Campbell, J. A. Galloway, D. Keene and M. Murphy, *A medieval capital and its grain supply: agrarian production and distribution in the London region c. 1300*, Historical Geography Research Series, 30 (1993), pp. 18–22; Campbell and J. P. Power, 'Mapping the agricultural geography of medieval England', *Journal of Historical Geography*, 15 (189), 24–39; Campbell, 'Measuring the commercialisation of seigneurial agriculture c. 1300', in R. H. Britnell and Campbell, eds, *A commercialising economy: England 1086 to 1300* (Manchester, 1995), pp. 132–93.

39 J. Z. Titow, 'Evidence of weather in the account rolls of the bishopric of Winchester, 1209–1350', *Economic History Review*, 12 (1960), 360–407.

40 Miller and Hatcher, *Medieval England*, pp. 198–204.

Furthermore, accounts represent neither fully nor accurately the farming strategies deployed on local peasant farms, nor depict the full range of local economic activities. It is often assumed that enterprise and conditions on the demesne are more or less representative of those on neighbouring farms, but hardly any evidence of peasant farms exists with which to test this assumption. Similarly, accounts may provide a hint of local industrial activity, by mentioning income from seigneurial mineral rights or a fulling mill, but they certainly understate its local extent and importance. The majority of medieval handicrafts took place primarily in domestic locations, yet *compoti* only record the rent due from landholdings and not the activities that took place within them.

For all that *compoti* do not reveal, the scope that they create for research into a wide range of economic issues is considerable. A single *compotus*, or a handful dating from across the late Middle Ages, can provide a robust profile of the manor's agrarian characteristics, while a good run of accounts enable dynamic trends and movements to be charted in detail. The nature of accounts, and the large number of surviving examples, permits a wide range of topics to be studied over long chronological spans and broad geographical areas. For example, recent research by Bruce Campbell has provided a national framework within which local agricultural information can be placed and understood. By sampling 1,900 accounts from 870 manors dating between 1250 and 1449, Campbell has compiled a comprehensive national database of crops and livestock on demesnes, which has enabled him to sketch the broad spatial and temporal differences in seigneurial farming systems and techniques across medieval England. This method of aggregative 'snapshot profiling' reveals the existence of a number of distinct categories of regional farming systems, where the product and intensity of agriculture – the degree of specialisation and technical involution – were markedly different. Although extensive forms of agriculture predominated across the country as a whole, the intensity of agrarian production and its commercial orientation is impressive in some places, and the most precocious regions were those with cheap access to large urban centres, high population densities, and limited institutional constraints. Campbell's monumental work in charting the contours of medieval farming systems provides an essential backdrop to any local research into manorial accounts. 'With the national picture established in outline, the challenge must now be to extend and refine the classifications ... the exercise needs to be repeated at a more detailed scale in order to bring into sharper focus the local as well as regional variations by which medieval farming systems were so plainly characterised'.[41]

Other historians have employed manorial accounts to understand the nature of, and changes in, the management of individual seigneurial estates during the later Middle Ages. Wide-ranging studies such as these were especially popular in the 1960s and 1970s, although the recent preference has been for more detailed research into smaller groups of well-documented manors. Christopher Dyer's formidable study of the estates of the bishops of Worcester provides an excellent example of the former, and offers much useful, general, commentary on the management and exploitation of manorial resources.[42] In particular, he employs numerous *compoti* from over a dozen demesne manors to chart the changing balance between arable and pastoral farming, and between rentier and direct management, during the later Middle Ages, and relates these changes to the activities and managerial attitudes of successive bishops, and to overall levels of estate income. They are also employed to reveal changing rent levels and patterns of land tenure, and to explore the implications for lord-peasant relations across the estate as serfdom withered away in the fourteenth and fifteenth centuries.

A good series of *compoti* from a single manor presents considerable potential for detailed research, and David Stone's work on the bishop of Ely's well-documented manor of Wisbech Barton (Cambridgeshire) provides a fine example. He charts and then explains subtle changes in demesne farming strategies over the short and medium terms, and in so doing reveals the remarkably sophisticated and careful management of the demesne in response to a range of changing external economic stimuli. For example, the balance and intensity of crop production was highly sensitive to shifts in grain prices, indicating considerable commercial awareness and shrewdness by the reeve. Between 1300 and 1348 wheat was sown mainly as a cash crop at Wisbech, and its production was strongly influenced by prevailing wheat prices. Yet Stone reveals how fluctuations in local wheat prices also impacted upon the demesnal area devoted to crops other than wheat. When wheat prices rose, the area under legumes was increased in order to enrich the soil in preparation for next year's wheat crop: when they slumped, the returns from the production of mixtill (a wheat-rye

41 Campbell and Power, 'Mapping the agricultural geography', pp. 242, 227–32.
42 Dyer, *Lords and peasants*.

mixture) rose, and the balance of crops sown was adjusted accordingly. It is also evident that the reeve shrewdly held back some of the manor's wheat surpluses until the summer months when prices were highest.[43]

Only detailed and painstaking research such as this can reveal the varied and complex combination of commercial, domestic and economic forces that influenced demesne farm management over the short to medium terms, and – in the process – provide fundamental insights into the nature of the medieval economy. The very existence of manorial accounts provides a detailed knowledge of the agrarian economy of medieval England which vastly exceeds that of any other place in the medieval world, especially between *c*. 1250 and *c*. 1420 when they are most informative.

19   An account of Wellingborough, 1258–59

A good example of an early (phase 1) account from Wellingborough (Northamptonshire), a sizeable and important manor belonging to the wealthy Benedictine abbey of Crowland (Lincolnshire). Its layout is largely undifferentiated, for both receipts and expenses are presented in unbroken blocks without subheadings. The entries on the cash side of the account are very perfunctory, and the receipts in particular are uninformative when compared with later accounts where petty items are painstakingly recorded [20]. In contrast, the grain and stock accounts are relatively full. No works account is included, although it is evident from the harvest expenses that labour services were widely used in this year. However, a modest inventory of agricultural implements is included, which is not common in manorial accounts.

F. M. Page, ed., *Wellingborough manorial accounts, 1258–1323. From the account rolls of Crowland abbey,* Northamptonshire Record Society, 8 (1935), pp. 1–3. *Compotus* of Wellingborough, (Northamptonshire), 9 October 1258 to 10 November 1259. Latin.

Wellingborough. Note that Roger the reeve of Wellingborough on the Friday before the feast of St Martin in the 4th year of the lord Ralph the Abbot [10 November 1259], renders his account of all receipts and expenses from the Sunday before the feast of St Dionisius in his 3rd year [9 October 1258] until the said day.[44]

---

43 Stone, 'Wisbech Barton', chapters 2, 3, and 4.

44 Both the dates and the period covered by this account are unconventional, indicating that the standardised Michaelmas to Michaelmas account did not become overwhelmingly adopted until the later years of phase 1 accounts.

Receipts

From farms and rents of all kinds through the whole year, maltsilver
and tithe of hay and 'gressilver', £39 7s. 5½d. From aid [tallage] last
year £4. Item from aid this year £12. Item from perquisites and
fines, £9 15s. 0d. From garden produce sold, 30s. Item from cheese
sold, 60s. Item from stubble and straw in the *curia* sold, 32s. Item
from the hides of one ox and three cows sold, 5s. 7d. Item from 11
quarters and 3 bushels of barley sold, 56s. 10½d.

Total £74 6s. 11d.

Expenses thence

Issued to the lord Hugo, £48 13s. 5¼d. by 7 tallies.[45] Item for the
expenses of the ploughs and the wages of the smith per annum, 35s.
5½d. Item in buying 3 horses for the ploughs, 20s. 2d. Item for the
upkeep of the fold, 2s 2d. Item for the expenses of the dairy, 15d. Item
in buying 2 horses for the cart, 17s. Item for the expenses of the
carters, 5s. 5¼d. Item for scythe ale, 2s. Item for the expenses of the
stewards per annum, 3s. 5d. Item to the maltster, 26d. Item for
shoeing the horses of the stewards and Laurence of Manneb' and
others, 3s. 7½d. Item for the expenses of the servants and reeve, and
of the boonworkers and for all the supervisors in the harvest, 38s.
10½d. Item for small articles of the manor 8s. 13¼d. Item for
threshing 19 quarters of wheat and all [other] grain, and winnowing
[it], 77s. 8d. Item for charcoal bought, 5s. Item for buying coffers and
lids for the chapel, 17s. 7d. Item for dressing the skins of lambs, and
for fowls bought, 12s 3½d. Item for grain bought, that is to say 1
quarter of wheat, 6 quarters of rye and 14 quarters of oats, £4 6s. 1d.
Item for thatching the chancery and other houses in the *curia*, 20s.
11d. Item for the expenses of the lord Gilbert of Preston, 8s. 3½d.
Item for the expenses of Gilbert de Cheyle on two occasions, 6s. 2d.
Item for the expenses of the lord prior of Freston and other
supervisors, that is to say the lord G. de Lamar' and the constable of
Northampton and others, 15s. 6d. Item for work about the pond and
the ditch round the granary, 13s. Item to a certain goldsmith of
Northampton, by the lord's command, 15s. by tally. Item to the lord
R. de Wicl'cal' towards [his visit to] Oxford, by the lord's command,
8s. 5d. Item to John Lorimer of Northampton, 9s. 6d. Item to P. de

---

45 I.e. paid in cash to the seigneurial household as confirmed by seven separate tallies,
   effectively a crude form of receipt.

Silebi for the tithe of Uphall, 8s. Item for the wages of 13 *famuli* from Michaelmas [29 September] to Ascension day [22 May], 8s. 8d. Item for the wages of the *famuli* in the harvest, 52s. 8d. Item [paid] at Finedon for rent, 8d. Item allowed for the land of Robert Launcelyn, half a mark. Item for the reeve's allowance, 4s. Item for the allowance for the house of Walter Clerk, 18d.

Total £74. 15s 9¼d.

All things therefore being added, subtracted and allowed, the lord owes to the reeve 8s. 10¼d. And the same reeve must settle everything contained in this account roll, and the wages of the servants as entered in this roll, that is to say up to this reckoning day.

Issues of the Granary

Of wheat. Issue of wheat, 129 quarters with all the increment.[46] Item received from Addington, 5 quarters by tally.[47] Item bought one quarter. Total 120 and 15 quarters.

Of which, expended in seed, 20½ quarters. Item in bread for the visits of the lord on three occasions, 4½ quarters and one bushel. Item sent to Crowland, 92 quarters by tally. Item to Morborne, ½ quarter without tally. Item given to the wife of John Spigernel, one quarter. Item to Geoffrey Cithared as a gift of the lord, ½ quarter. Item to the smith as a gift of the lord, ½ quarter. Item for the expenses of the servants and supervisors, and of the boonworkers, until the Michaelmas before the account [is rendered], 15 quarters and one bushel. Equal.[48]

Of rye. Issue of rye, with increment, 83 quarters. Item bought, 6 quarters. Total 89 quarters.

Of which, expended in seed, 21 quarters and one bushel. Item sent to Crowland, 40 quarters by tally. Item issued to the *famuli*, up to the

---

46 The 'issue' of grain is that transferred from the barn into the granary after threshing, and in this case relates to the harvest from the summer of 1258. Increment of grain refers to the use of heaped rather than flat measures (see n. 60, p. 133). In contrast, an increment of *malt* would refer to the expansion in the volume of barley or oats when fired to make malt. See Harvey, *Cuxham*, pp. 52–5.

47 Addington, like Morbone below, was a demesne manor of the abbey. Modest transfers of grain between demesne manors in direct cultivation were not uncommon, sometimes as a device to improve the quality of seed corn.

48 The amount issued 'equals' the amount expended.

Michaelmas before the account [is rendered], 15½ quarters.[49] Item for bread for the three visits of the lord, 3½ quarters and one bushel. Item for the expenses of the *curia* up to the Michaelmas before the account [is rendered], 7½ quarters. Item to Henry Carpenter as a gift of the lord, ½ quarter. Item to Roger the ditcher as a gift of the lord, ½ quarter. Equal.

Of barley. Issue of barley, with all the increment, 199½ quarters and ½ bushel. Item received from Addington 15 quarters by tally. Total 214½ quarters and ½ bushel.

Of which, expended in seed, 37 quarters. Item to the smith, one quarter. Item sold 11 quarters and 1½ bushels. Item sent to Crowland, 26 quarters by tally. Item sent to Crowland as malt, 95 quarters. Item issued for the *famuli* up to the Michaelmas before the account [is rendered], 40½ quarters and ½ bushel. Item in feeding the pigs, 2½ quarters. Item brewed for the visit of the lord on three occasions, 9 quarters. Total 222 quarters and one bushel. And so he [the reeve] correctly answers.

Of drage. Issue of drage with increment, 146½ quarters. Item received from Addington, 17½ quarters by tally. Total, 164 quarters.

Of which, sent to Crowland, 155½ quarters by 2 tallies. Item issued to the *famuli*, 3 quarters. Item for bread for the *curia*, ½ quarter. Item brewed for the visit of the lord on 3 occasions, 9 quarters. Item issued to Nicholas son of Michael, by the lord's command, 4 quarters. Total 172 quarters, and so he [the reeve] correctly answers.

Of oats. Issue of oats, with increment, 126 quarters. Item, received from Addington, 5½ quarters by tally. Item bought, 14 quarters, as above. Total, 145½ quarters.

Of which, expended in seed, 72½ quarters and 1 bushel. Item for flour, 1½ quarters. Item for fodder for the horses of the *curia* for the whole year, 42½ quarters. Item for fodder for the 3 horses of the lord on three visits, 11½ quarters. Item for fodder for the steward and supervisors for the whole year, 10 quarters. Item to Geoffrey le Harpur as a gift from the lord, one quarter. Item for vetches issued to the *famuli*, 7 quarters. Total, 140 and 51 quarters and 1 bushel and so correct. And be it known that the issue to the *famuli* is made up to the

---

49 The *famuli* received grain as part of their wages. For an interesting study of similar payments see C. Dyer, 'Changes in diet in the late Middle Ages: the case of harvest workers', *Agricultural History Review*, 36 (1988), 21–37.

Michaelmas [29 September] before the account [is rendered], that is to say, 66 quarters and ½ bushel.

Of beans. Issue of beans and peas, 6 quarters. And of increment, ½ quarter.

Of which, expended in seed, 6 quarters. Item for potage, ½ quarter. Equal.

Stock. There remain in the *curia* 3 carthorses and 8 horses for the ploughs, of which 3 are mares. Item, 16 oxen. Item one bull. Item 16 cows. Item there remain 12 three year-old calves, of which 6 are male and 6 female of whom three are accounted above among the cows. Item there remain 12 two year-old calves, of which 6 are male and 6 female. Item there remain 12 of this year's calves. Item there remain in the *curia* one boar, 3 sows and 2 pigs. Item 15 pigs over a year old. Item 8 suckling pigs. Total pigs, 29.

Item he accounts for 35 ewes brought forward from the last account, of which 26 had murrain. Whence remain 9 ewes. Item he accounts for 22 castrated wethers. Of which 19 had murrain, whence remain 3 wethers. Item he accounts for 19 of last year's lambs. Of which 15 had murrain, whence remain 4 ewes. Hence there remain in all 13 ewes. Item there remain of this year's issue 9 lambs. Of which one is male and 8 female.

Item there remain in the *curia* 3 geese and 3 ganders. Item 12 hens and 3 cocks. Item, 4 ducks.

Implements. There remain in the *curia* 4 iron bars with 4 ropes. Item 4 iron forks with 4 pairs of traces. Item 4 iron threshing-sledges and 3 manure-forks. Item 2 jars and 2 barrels. Item 8 vats and 2 tins. Item, 2 brass bowls and 2 jugs. Item one wash-tub and one measure for grain, and 2 plates and one tripod. Item 2 halters with one cloth. Item 12 ploughs of which 4 have all the harness. Item 6 crates. Item 2 baskets for carrying and 2 for sowing. Item 8 sacks and 2 winnowing fans, and 2 ladders and 2 tubs and 2 vats in the bakehouse and 1 lock.

20   An account of Wellingborough, 1321–22

A later account from the same manor of Wellingborough, this time dating from phase 2. It is significantly longer than the first example [19], due mainly to the detailed itemisation of individual receipts and expenses under separate subheadings. The different style and content reflects an administrative shift in responsibility for the construction of accounts from central to local officials, and the benefits to historians of this shift are evident from the most cursory glance: even the pot of mustard bought to complement the ploughmen's lunches is recorded. There is still no works account [31], but the stock account is very full and provides useful insights into the operation of a small demesne dairy. Much can be gleaned about the administration of the abbot of Crowland's estate from the incidental references in the account, from the transfers of money to Crowland and the movement of cash around other manors on the estate, to the exceptionally detailed section on 'stewards' expenses'. Wellingborough was evidently deployed as the main administrative centre for an outlying part of Crowland abbey's lands.

F. M. Page, ed., *Wellingborough manorial accounts, 1258–1323. From the account rolls of Crowland abbey,* Northamptonshire Record Society, 8 (1935), pp. 122–35. *Compotus* of Wellingborough (Northamptonshire), 29 September 1321 to 29 September 1322 [F. M. Page has 1322–23 in her printed edition, but all the individual dates recorded within the account fit the accounting year 1321–22]. Latin.

Wellingborough. The account of John Fiden reeve of the abbot of Crowland for his manor of Wellingborough from the feast of St Michael in the 19th year of Simon the abbot until the feast of St Michael next following [29 September 1321 to 29 September 1322].

Arrears. Whence he renders account for £13 7s. 93d. arrears of his account of last year. Total £13 7s. 93d.

Rent of assize. Item he answers for 56s. 8½d. from rent of assize of free tenants per annum. And for 7s. 4d. from 12 virgates of sokeland per annum. And for £12 12s. from the assized rent of customary works per annum. And for £14 11s. 4d. from the assized rent of the molmen per annum. And for 37s. rent from the five-acre men per annum. And for £6 10s. 3¼d. from the assized rent of the cottars (*cotsetles*) per annum, whence 3s. is from one free tenant. Total £38 14s. 7¾d.

Farms.[50] Item he answers for 13s. 4d. from a certain custom called 'gressilver'. And for 17s. 2d. from divers plots of meadow and tofts leased at farm. And for 100s. from the tithe of hay this year. And for 4s. 3d. from 'longaverage' throughout the year. And for 2s. 9d. from 'frangeware' throughout the year. And for 10d. from 'woodaverage' throughout the year. And for 54s. from the carrying services of the

---

50 In medieval usage the word 'farm' signifies a contractual tenure, and especially land held on leasehold, in contrast to its modern meaning (pp. 35–7).

customary tenants, at farm this year.[51] And for 35s. from 140 carrying
services belonging to the toft-sokemen leased at farm this year, at the
price of 3d. per carrying service. And for £11 13s. 4d. from two water
mills with 2 plots of meadow adjacent leased at farm for 10 years, this
being the second. And for 16s. from the fulling mill leased at farm this
year. And for 20s. from the market tolls, perquisites of the market
court, and stalls this year. And for 26s. 8d. from 4 common ovens this
year. Total £26 3s. 3¼d.

Fines and perquisites. Item he renders [account for] £7 0s. 2d. received
from one court held on the Saturday after the feast of All Saints [5
November 1321]. And for 21s. 7d. received from one court held on
the Thursday of the morrow of St Hilary [14 January 1322]. And for
49s. 9d. received from one court held on the Thursday of the feast of
the Annunciation of the Blessed Mary [25 March 1322]. And for 70s.
9d. received from one court held on the Saturday of the feast of the
Apostles Philip and James [1 May 1322]. And for 63s. 2d. received
from one court held on the Monday of the morrow of St James [26
July 1322]. Total £17 5s. 5d.

Aid [tallage] of the homage. Item he renders account for £14 received
from the aid of the homage this year. Total £14.

Sale of grain. Item he renders account for 21½d. received from 2
bushels of wheat sold. And for 3s. 4d. received from ½ quarter of
'rednot' sold.[52] And for 27s. 4d. received from 5 quarters 1 bushel of
barley, sold at the price of 5s. 4d. per quarter. And for 5s. 6d. received
from 1 quarter of barley sold. And for 67s. 6d. received from 9
quarters of barley, sold at the price of 5s. 6d. per quarter. And for 10s.
received from 1½ quarters of peas, sold at the price of ½ mark per
quarter. And for 2s. 7d. received from the quarter of vetches sold to
Robert Bate on the authority of Richard de Keten'. And for 8s. 8d.
received from 2 quarters of vetches sold. And for 9s. received from 1

51 Most of these obscure customary dues seem to relate to either ancient pasturing
   rights ('gressilver') or forms of carrying service ('woodaverage'), but these entries
   indicate that the latter are no longer performed personally. The 54s. received for
   carrying services means that the reeve has commuted them to a cash payment this
   year.

52 A winter sown crop. An extended 'sales of grain' section signifies to the reader
   immediately that the demesne is under direct exploitation. Some accounts provide
   details of the destination of sold grain, the purchaser and the month in which the
   sale took place. See D. L. Farmer, 'Two Wiltshire manors and their markets',
   Agricultural History Review, 37 (1989), 1–11.

quarter 1 bushel of vetches sold. And for 8s. received from 2 quarters
of oats sold at the price of 4s. per quarter. Total £7 3s. 8½d.

Issues of the manor. Item he renders account for 2s. received from grass
in Calvesholm sold. And for 18d. received from 2 parcels of herbage.
And for 4d. received from *folesavers.* And for 9s. received from one
virgate of meadow sold. And for 11s. 6d. from hay sold. And for 9s.
from stubble sold. And for 4s. 3d. received from 4 lambskins sold. And
for 12½d. from 1 lambskin sold. And for 15s. received from sale of the
produce of the garden. And for 7s. 9½d. received from 6 stone 1
quarter of cheese sold, at the price of 15d. per stone. And for 8s. 6d.
received from 'harrowing silver'. And for 15d. received from one stone
of butter sold. And for 3s. 10d. received from four pasture-rights sold
in the Haye. Item he renders [account] for 2s. 6d. received from 4
horse hides sold. Total 79s. 6d.

Foreign receipts. And for 46s. received from William de Thorp, collector,
for the wages of the *famuli.* Total 46s.

Sales beyond the account [super compotum]. Item he answers for 29s. 6d.
from divers things sold beyond the account. Total 29s. 6d.

Grand total, £124 9s. 10½d.

Allowances and defaults. Item he claims allowance of 4½d. for *frangware*
from the lord Alan son of Warin of Wilby, because the tenement is in
the hands of the lord John of Wilby. Item he claims allowance of 20s.
for the rent of John Seymour of Hardwick for the two terms of
Michaelmas and Easter. And of 2s. for the amercement of Roger
Burghard, excused by the lord abbot.[53] And for 6d. for the amercement of Richard Elyot because he lives on the fief of the lord John of
Wilby. And of 10s. for his own rent since he is reeve. And of 3d. from
Henry of Irenland since he is a stranger and without guarantors. And
of 2d. from Geoffrey Dagge of Irencr' since he is a stranger and calls
no guarantors. And of 13s. 4d. for the amercement of John Deistere,
since it was excused by Brother Robert of Luffenham. And of 6d. for
the amercement of William Der since he is a stranger and went away
without guarantors. Item 17½d. in default of the rent for one soke
above the brook, since the land is in the lord's hands. In default of
rent for one virgate of land called Yioiesyard 3d. through the heir of
Ada of Suypeston. And 3d. for the amercement of John Taylor for the

53 For amercements, see pp. 176-7.

[mill] grinding-fee since he lives on the fief of John Elys of Ashby. Total 29s. 1d.

Upkeep of the ploughs. For the smith's wages for the irons of the ploughs and the shoeing of the horses and carthorses throughout the year, through a standing agreement 42s. For newly covering 7 ploughs on occasions, 12½d. For the wages of two carpenters felling 2 trees and working on the timber for ploughs for three days by task 15d., to each 2½d. per day. For two 'sway-stones', 1d. For one pair of sheets, 1½d. For five headstalls and 2 reins, 4d. For the wages of 2 carpenters working on the ploughs and harrows, and timber for the ploughs and harrows, for six and a half days by task 2s. 3d. In buying rods, *thistres*, and buckles for the *taubote*, 2s. 4d.[54] Item for 2 headstalls and 2 reins, 3d. For hiring one boy for the plough while one of the *famuli* sowed beans and peas for three days, 12d. For two carpenters making two new ploughs for one day by task, 5d. For hiring one boy for the plough while one of the *famuli* sowed barley for three days 2¼d., at ¾d. per day. For hiring one boy for the harrow for three days, 2¼d. For 3 headstalls and 3 *fadine* bought for reins, and girths of thick cord, 2½d. For making three new ploughs, 7½d. Total 51s. 5d.

Item he accounts for the expenses of one plough-ale for 47 ploughs on the Monday before the feast of the apostles Simon and Jude [26 October 1322]. For bread he accounts above. For ale, 6s. 6d. For one quarter of beef, 18d. For mutton, 6d. For mustard, 1d. Item in the expenses of one plough-ale for the boonwork on the Monday after the Annunciation [29 March 1322] for 24 ploughs, with other men of the vill assisting there that day. For bread, 12d. For ale, 5s. 10d. For 240½ herrings bought wholesale, 2s. 9½d. For two whitings, 11d. For mustard, 2d. Item for the expenses of 2 ploughing boonworks on the Thursday after the Annunciation [1 April 1322]. For bread, 7d. For ale, 6d. For herrings and fish, 3½d. For mustard, ¼d. Item there was given to 6 ploughmen from the sokes at the barley-sowing three gallons of ale [costing] 6d., on the command of Richard de Keten'. Item he accounts for 12d. for the shoeing of oxen this year. Total 22s. 2¼d.

Upkeep of carts. For putting axles to 3 carts, 6d. For buying 4 measures of cloutnails, 2s. 4d. Item for buying 312 cloutnails, 4d. Item for buying iron mounts and rods for the staves and rungs of the ladders, 2½d. For buying 2 ells of hemp-cloth and canvas for making

54 These terms refer to various components of the harness.

the cart-harness, 8d. Item for mending four horse-collars and 2 cart-horse saddles, 3d. Item for buying four headstalls, 4d. For buying three nails for the carts, 3d. For buying 6 *widings*, 4d. Item for buying a rope and rear-cord for a cart, 4d. For buying one saddle for a cart, 2s. 6d. For buying grease for the carts, 7½d. For mending four old saddles and for eight pounds of flock bought for them, and for mending 6 collars and buying three pairs of tubed pipes [for the harness], 22d. For one pair of thripples and for putting them on, 2d. For one *cartkypo*, 2d. For 2 pairs of *cartescriles*, 2d. For the wages of 1 carpenter mending carts for 1 day by task, 2¼d. Total 11s. 2½d.

Upkeep of houses. For buying nine bundles of planks for the stable and in [buying] nine short beams, 6s. For making an enclosure for the hen house by task, 9d. For the wages of one thatcher thatching the house for 1 day by task, 2½d. For buying three trees from Richard de Keten' for making the stable, 21d. For cementing and carpentering the stable, 11s. 6d. by contract. For [buying] 10 quarters of lime, 5s. 10d. at the price of 7d. per quarter. For the wages of one tiler for pointing the room of the abbot through a standing agreement, 6s. For his wages for pointing the long house and the great gates, 7s. For the wages of one thatcher for thatching the ruined larder and the chapel, and the house called the cheesehouse, through a standing agreement, 4s. 6d. For buying rods for fastening the thatch of the larder, 1d. Item he accounts for a payment to the mason working at the oven, on the authority of Richard de Keten', 5s. 4d. Item for a payment to John Martin the mason, on the authority of Richard de Keten', for fetching stone to the site of the aforesaid oven, 16d. Item given to the masons and their team on the command of Richard of Glatton, 2d. For buying hasps, hinges and nails for the wood-work of the said oven, 6½d. For buying three cartloads of brushwood for making the bedding of the ewes at the sheep-fold and for thatching the said sheep-fold securely on account of the wind, and for the expenses of the manor on account of the visit of the steward and for bread baked for the *curia* and the plough ale, 18d. For making 360 spike-nails for the gate and doors of the manor and for the sheep-cote, 7½d. Item for the wages of one carpenter cutting up timber at the sheep-cote and for fixing new timber and securing the old timber, and for mending the walls through a standing agreement, in gross, 15d. For mending the locks of the door of the room at the top of the hall, and of the bakehouse door and of the barnyard gate, 3d. For one lock bought for the door of the hall, 4d. For the wages of 2 carpenters fixing buttresses in the garret for 1 day by task, 5d. For two thatchers thatching the cow-shed and stable for 11 days by task 4s. 1½d., for each day 2¼d. For their three servants for the same time 2s. 6d., of whom 2 took 2d. per day and the third servant ¾d. Item for the wages of one tiler mending the tiles of the knight's room, the abbot's room, and the kitchen, 2s. 6d. In cementing and thatching the house called the garret through a standing agreement, 20d. For buying rods for fastening the thatch of the stable, 2d. For one mason working for two days on the walls of the herb garden in front of the hall by task, 5d. For his one servant for 2 days, 2d. For one man making the bedding of the ewes for three days by task, 5d. For mending the door of the kitchen with a hinge and grease, 2d. Total 67s. 10½d.

[No heading] Item for buying three manure-forks, 3½d. For buying three irons for 2 spades and a threshing-sledge, 4d. For buying one iron fork and iron for a manure-fork, 2½d. Item he accounts for the expenses in spreading 500 cartloads of manure 2s. 1d., on the authority of Richard de Keten', giving for each hundred cartloads 5d. For buying straw from Richard de Keten' for sustaining the animals of the manor, 16s. For buying two horse-hide thongs, 2d. For buying 3 fastenings for the great gates and cross-bars and nails, 4d. For buying 21 rods of hemp cloth for making sacks, 4s., at the price of 2¼d. per rod. For buying thread to sew up the said sacks, 1d. For buying 2 thressels and 2 trowels, 4d. For one pound of oatmeal, 5½d. For tallow and garlic, 2d. For hiring one boy for 4 days to mind the cottars' sheep while the shepherd drove 160 hoggets to Langtoft, 4d. For the expenses of two men driving the said hoggets there, 5d. For buying one bushel of hemp seed, 5d. For ladders, ½d. For two carpenters and one locksmith working and making a roof over the great pigeon-cote for one day by task, 9d. For one mason and 1 thatcher working on the same pigeon-cote for 2 days by task, 12d. For mending the chains of the manor and for the wages of the smith for making the iron-work, 5d. For hiring one boy to mind the sheep in winter from Ash Wednesday in the manor until the Tuesday called Hockday 5d., because the shepherd of the manor went away at Ash Wednesday. Total 28s. 6d.

[No heading] For buying eight swivels, 2½d. For dressing the hides of 1 mare and 1 foal, 12d. For driving nine young cattle and 1 foal to the marsh, 4½d. For making one piece of wall from the gable of the kiln towards the house of John of Morborne, 2½d. For making ten halters from rope in stock, 5d. For mending one brass plate and one brass pot, stopping up 2 holes, 3d. For making one lead gutter between the

granary and the porch, 1d. For castrating 17 young pigs, 5d. For making five quarters of [illegible], 10d. For buying 1 sieve, 1½d. For two thatchers thatching stacks of peas for six days by task, 2s. 6d., to each 22d. per day. For buying 6 bushels of salt for the use of the manor and for the visits of the steward and other supervisors and for the use of the dairy 5s., at the price of 10d. per bushel. For buying 9½ quarters of bran to feed the pigs 6s. 4d., at the price of 8d. per quarter. Total 16s. 10d.

Upkeep of the fold. For buying 28 hurdles for the fold, 2s. 11d. at the price of 12d. each. Item he reckons for buying grease and tar, 6s. 1½d. Total 9s. 0½d.

Purchase of stock. For buying one horse for the cart, 6s. For buying 1 sow 2s. 7d., on the authority of brother R. de Luffenham and of R. de Keten. Total 8s. 7d.

Upkeep of the dairy. For three tin plates, 3d. For 2 tin bowls, 2d. Item for buying four pans for cheese, 8d. Item for buying one gallon press, 8d. Total 21d.

Hoeing. Item he accounts [for expenses of] hoeing, 11s. 1½d. Total 11s. 1½d.

Reaping. Item he accounts for 2s. given to 34 men of the sokes who reaped. Total 2s.

Wages of the famuli. For the wages of 1 carter, eight ploughmen, 1 cowherd and 1 shepherd per annum, 36s. 8d., to each 3s. 4d. For the wages of the dairymaid 2s. For the wages of 1 gardener for the winter and Lent terms, 8d. Item for the wages of a second shepherd for the winter term, 4d. For the wages of William Christian the beadle from Hockday [12 April] to Michaelmas [29 September], 2s. For the wages of the swineherd per annum, 20d. Total 41s. 4d.

Expenses of the stewards. Item he accounts for the expenses of the stewards with clerks and others with them at one court after Michaelmas, and for their expenses going towards Oakington, 8s. 11¾d.[55] Item for the expenses of the steward with clerks and others with him

---

55 Oakington (Cambridgeshire), another demesne manor of the abbey. Brother Robert of Luffenham is mentioned repeatedly in this expenses section, and was clearly one of the senior monks at Crowland with considerable responsibility for the management of the abbey's estates. Richard de Ketton also recurs, and was probably a lay steward in the service of the abbey.

on the Thursday of the morrow of St Hilary [14 January 1322] 5s. 5d. For the expenses of the steward at one court on the Thursday of the morrow of the Annunciation of the Blessed Mary [26 March 1322], and for their expenses going towards Oakington, 4s. 8d. For the expenses of the stewards at one court on the Saturday of the feast of the apostles St Philip and St James [1 May 1322], and for their expenses going towards Oakington 7s. 10¾d. For the expenses of the stewards at one court about the feast of St James [25 July 1322] and for their expenses going towards Oakington 15s. 1d. For the visit of brothers Robert of Luffenham and Robert de Sculthorpe with three boys on the Thursday after the feast of St Nicholas [10 December 1321]. For bread, 2d. For ale, 8d. For herrings and fish, 6d. For wine, 7d. For candles, 1d. For ointment, 1d. For shoeing the horses, 1d. For the visit of brother Robert de Luffenham and Simon de la Fen on the Saturday before the Purification [30 January 1322] coming to supper with three boys and for their lodging till the morning. For bread, 9d. For ale, 8d. For [damaged], 5d. For meat, bacon from stock. Item for herrings consumed at supper on the Saturday, 12d. For the visit of brother Robert of Luffenham and Robert the clerk on the Wednesday after the Annunciation of the Blessed Mary [31 March 1322] coming for the arrears of Thomas Boun, Roger Burghard, and John the reeve. For bread for the boy, 2d. For the dogs, 3d. For ale for the boys, 3d. For buying two rods of coarse cloth at the same time to send to Crowland, 5d. For the visit of brother Robert of Luffenham and of John [damaged] with boys on the Wednesday after the feast of St Philip and St James [28 July 1322] and for their lodging till the morning. For ale, 4d. For *memisia*, 3½d. For candles, ½d. For the visit of brother Robert de Luffenham staying at Northampton on St Lawrence's day [10 August 1322] on the abbot's business. For one gallon of wine, 6d. For the visit of brother Robert of Luffenham, Geoffrey Pampilon and Robert the clerk with four boys and 4 horses on the Wednesday after the feast of the Exaltation of the Holy Cross [15 September 1322] to the Thursday, and going to Northampton in the morning. Item for their lodging on the Friday. For bread, 8d. For ale, 6d. For dried fish and herrings, 6d. For candles, 1d. For [illegible], 1d. For shoeing the horses, 8d. For making the saddles and [illegible] of Robert the clerk, 8d. Total 52s.

[odd sections of the following paragraphs are illegible, and are marked thus …]

Item he accounts for expenditure in the visits of brother Luke de Stanford and Richard de Glatton with four boys … after Michaelmas coming to supper and for their lodging till the morning ... 3d. For ale, 9d. For heifer's meat, 8d. For pork and veal, 6d. For larks, 2d. For one and a half gallons and 1 pint of wine, 3d. For the visit of master John the rector ... and Richard de Glatton to audit the account on the Monday ... Evangelist [19 October 1321] and for their lodging on the following Tuesday and Wednesday. For bread 2s. 2d. For ale, 15½d. For heifer's meat, 8d. For pork, 7d. For veal, 3d. For herrings and fish, 3d. For larks, 2¼d. For eggs, 1½d. For mustard, pepper, saffron and ... 1½d. Item for the expenses of Robert the clerk on the Saturday of the eve of St Luke the Evangelist [17 October 1321] until the Monday of Richard de Glatton's arrival, for two days and for his lodging after the departure of Richard de Glatton on the Thursday following until the Tuesday, for five days for compiling the account ... . For bread, 4d. For ale, 7d. For meat, 6d. For herrings and fish, 4d. For eggs, 1d. For 2 lbs. of candles, 4d. Item ... person(s) released and hanged.

For the visit of Richard de Glatton, Richard de Haredon, with others of the neighbourhood on the Thursday after the feast of St Hugh [19 November 1321]. For bread, 9d. ... 1s. 8d. For meat, 15d. For ... and pepper, 2½d. Item he accounts for the visit of master John Rector of Twywell and Richard de Glatton on the Saturday before Ash Wednesday [20 February 1322] with three boys carrying the abbot's letter concerning dragging and fishing in the pond. For bread, 6d. For ale, 6d. For herrings and fish, 4d. For eggs, ½d. For milk, ½d. For mustard and candles, ½d. For the visit of the rector and R. de Glatton on the Saturday before the feast of St Paul [23 January 1322]. For bread for the boys and dogs, 2d. For ale, 4½d. Item he accounts for the visit of the lord archdeacon of Northampton in his visitation on the Thursday in Easter week with a servant and boys. For bread, 6d. For ale, 8d. For eggs, 2d. For bacon, 2d. For the visit of Henry de Castro on the Wednesday before Christmas [23 December 1321], 6d. For the visit of John son of Robert Joseph and Richard de Pinchello on Ash Wednesday [24 February 1322] looking for Henry as far as Langtoft, 4d. For the visit of [?] and one boy carrying two letters, of which one was to go to the sheriff of Northampton on behalf of the abbot's tenants of Peakirk, 3d. For 2lbs. of candles bought for the supervisors, 4½d. For shoeing the horse of Richard de Glatton from time to time, 6d. Total 23s. 6¼d.

Item 1s. given to John de Thom' the bailiff of the hundred at [?the hanging] of persons, on the authority of Richard de Glatton and

Richard de Keten'. Item 4d given to Thomas servant of Richard de
Keten' for taking larks to the abbot of Crowland, on the authority of
Richart de Keten'. Item 4d. given to Roger de Deye going to Whaplode
to ask for the Crowland carts to carry grain to Crowland. For the
expenses of three men driving pigs ... to Crowland and for boats
taken across the river to Crowland, and for rope bought to tie the pigs
to the boat, 19d. For the expenses of the reeve taking the Michaelmas
rent and perquisites of the court to Crowland with one boy and one
horse, 18d. Item for taking ... of 2 foals in the marsh and for their
expenses at Wellingborough, 6d. For the expenses of 4 men going to
Crowland with 4 horses and taking 86 hens and 16 capons, 16d. Item
given to Crowland to ... For carting 24 quarters of wheat to Addington,
4s., by authority of Richard de Keten', for each quarter 2d. In buying
one dozen platters, three goblets, 12 plates, and 12 saucers for the
supervisors, 8d. For the expenses of the Crowland carters taking
grain to Crowland [and] to Morborne with other carters of Hoyland
on 14 occasions.[56] For bread he has accounted before. For ale, 16d.
Item for meat, 17d. Item ... for the carters of Crowland, 1½d. In buying
grease and issuing it to them for the carts, 3d. Item given to the bailiff
of the lord king in Wansford ... of one horse taking the hens of ... 3d.
Item for toll paid for the carts at the bridges of Thrapston, 3d. For
the expenses of the reeve going with a cart and one horse to carry the
Wellingborough peas to Morborne and to Yaxley, and for boats to
take the peas to Crowland 1s.[57] Item 15d. given to John Pope the clerk
for writing the office of Corpus Christi on the command of the lord
archdeacon of Northampton in his visitation.[58] Item for the expenses
of the reeve and 1 horse with a boy taking the Easter rent with the
perquisites of the court to Crowland, 1s. Item 1s. given to Robert son
of John and Richard son of Ralph Carter and their fellow labourers
going to Crowland at the Purification [of the Blessed Virgin Mary],

---

56 Hoyland is a demesne farm close to Crowland.

57 Wansford, on the Great North Road, was a demesne manor of the abbey. Medieval
   Yaxley (Cambridgeshire) was an inland port on the river Nene providing a navig-
   able link with Crowland via the fenland water system. Thrapston (Northamptonshire)
   was an important bridging point of the Nene between Wellingborough and Peter-
   borough.

58 This refers to the regular archdeacon's inspection of the parish church to ensure
   the proper provision for, and delivery of, christian worship. The devotion to
   Corpus Christi was introduced to England in 1318, and this entry probably marks
   its arrival in the archdeaconry, R. Hutton, *The rise and fall of merry England: the
   ritual year 1400–1700* (Oxford, 1994), p. 54. Other references in the account to the
   collection of tithes reveals that the parochial church of Wellingborough had been
   appropriated by the abbey, see p. 5.

by authority of Richard de Keten' on command of the lord. Item given
to Richard de Keten' as expenses for taking to Crowland the 100s. [of
the tithe of hay]. Item 3d. to one boy going to Crowland on the
Sunday before Michaelmas [27 September], on command of brother
Robert de Luffenham. For hiring one cart in the harvest to carry 3
quarters of rye to Yaxley, 2s. 6d. on authority of Richard de Keten'.
Item 4d. given to the manorial carters carrying grain in autumn as far
as Yaxley to buy bread for their horses on the way as they had no
fodder. Item 5d. given to one boy minding the sheep of the cottars
while the shepherd looked for three of Robert Joseph's goats in the
marsh, since they were lost for 5 days owing to rainstorms. Item 6d.
given to Richard Taylor, cowherd of the manor, for driving one foal
and four bullocks from Crowland to Wellingborough and for boats
and the expenses of the animals and his expenses. Item 3¾d. given to
one boy minding the animals of the manor at that time. Item for the
expenses of the reeve taking £5 to Crowland on the Tuesday in the
week of Pentecost, 8d. Item for two loaves and 2 gallons of ale, 6d.,
given to Thomas Boun, John Benot, John Wichened and their fellows
since they gave half a mark in order that they might not collect the
100s. of the tithe of hay, on command of Robert de Luffenham. Item
for minding the tithe of grain at Hardwick, 4d. Total 24s. 11¼d.

Money transferred. Item he accounts for £84 4s. 3d. paid to the
receiver of Crowland by 22 tallies. Item he accounts for 13s. 4d. paid
to master Gilbert of Middleton, archdeacon of Northampton, on his
visitation. Item he accounts for 9s. paid to the rector of Hardwick as
his stipend, by receipt. Item to John de Sceutinor for his salary, 20s.
Item he accounts for 2s. 6d. paid to the dean of Rothwell for taxation
of the church of Wellingborough, by receipt. Item he accounts for 33s.
paid to Richard de Keten', by command of a writ. Item paid to the
rector of Finedon in quittance of the rent of the main millpond of
Finedon, 8d. Total £88 2s. 9d.

Grand total of all expenses, including monies transferred, £108 4s. 3¾d.

And thus he owes £16 5s. 6¾d., of which 13s. 6d. is in the hands of
the executors of W. de Thorp as arrears of the said William. 19s. 4d.
is in the hands of Thomas Boun for 4 quarters and 2½ bushels of wheat
sold upon the account as appears at the foot of the preceding account.
And £10 is in the hands of the same Thomas as the arrears of the
years 16 and 17 of the lord abbot ... And 24s. 9d. is in the hands of
Roger Berughard.

And so John owes the lord 68s. 1¾d., of which 33s. 8d. is allowed to him for divers things sold upon him and subtracted from him. And so he owes as clear balance, 34s. 5¾d, of which 4s. 5¾d. is excused. And he owes as clear balance, 30s.

[Marginal note]: It is commanded that the executors of William de Thorp, Thomas Boun and Roger Berughard come to ... show the tallies of money paid out from arrears etc., not allowed to them out of the said arrears.

Wellingborough. It is not put in the grange as Richard de Keten', to whom the grain was sent in gross, has accounted for his time.

Issues of wheat. Of which John Fiden reeve of Wellingborough rendered account for 58 quarters 3 bushels of wheat received from Richard de Keten'.

Of which, for the expenses of the steward at one court after Michaelmas, 5 bushels of wheat. Item issued to John de Thame the bailiff of the hundred on the authority of Richard de Glatton and Richard de Keten', 2 bushels. Item sent to Crowland, 56 quarters 6 bushels. Item sold, 2 bushels. Sold beyond the account, 4 bushels for 3s. 6d.[59] Equal.

Issues of 'rednot'. Item he renders account for 52 quarters 7 bushels of rednot received from Richard de Keten'.

Of which, baked for one plough-ale on the Monday before the feast of the apostles St Simon and St Jude [26 October 1321] for 47 ploughs, 1 quarter. Item baked for the carters of Crowland and the carters of Holland taking grain to Morborne, 2 bushels. Item baked for one plough-ale on the Monday after the Annunciation of the Blessed Mary [29 March 1322], 1 quarter. Item issued to Robert the Smith according to contract for repairing the ironwork of the carts this year, 2 bushels and no more because he had 2 bushels of peas. Item 1 quarter given to the bailiff travelling on the authority of Richard de Keten'. Sent to Crowland, 49 quarters. Sold 1 quarter. Sold beyond the account, 2 bushels for 22d. Equal.

Issues of barley. Item he renders account for 45 quarters of barley received from Richard de Keten'.

Of which, 5 quarters made into malt. Item baked for one plough-ale on the Monday after the Annunciation of the Blessed Mary [29 March

---

59 Sales beyond the account were part of the final reckoning with the auditors (p. 104).

1322], 1 bushel. For feeding the geese and goslings, 2 bushels. For feeding 8 of this year's new calves, 3 bushels. Item issued to the reeve of Morborne for seed, 20 quarters by tally. Item issued to the reeve of Addington, 2 quarters by tally. Item 1 quarter given to Simon at the gate of Northampton, by authority of Richard de Keten', as a tip [*avantagium*] for the 20 quarters by the razed measure bought by him from the said Richard.[60] Item 6 bushels of barley given as a tip on 15 quarters sold. Sold, 15 quarters 1 bushel. Sold upon the account 3 bushels for 2s. Equal.

Issues of peas. Item he renders account for 60 quarters of peas received from Richard de Keten'.

Of which, for fattening 21 pigs from the Sunday after the feast of St Luke the Evangelist until the feast of St Martin [25 October to 11 November 1321], by command of a writ, and from the feast of St Martin until the feast of St Andrew [11 to 30 November 1321], for a total of six weeks, by order of Richard de Glatton, 10½ quarters, for each pig ½ quarter, and the large quantities are due to the great hospitality [*sic*]. Item for the potage of the *famuli*, 4 bushels. Item given to the poor in potage, 2 quarters. Item for potage for one plough-ale on the Monday after the Annunciation of the Blessed Mary [29 March 1322], 1 bushel of peas. Item to Robert Smith for repairing the ironwork of the ploughs as above, 2 bushels. Item given to two *famuli* minding the horses of the manor while grazing at night in summer, by authority of Richard de Keten', 2 bushels. Item sent to Crowland 42 quarters 1 bushel, by 2 tallies, of which 10 quarters were issued to John the Granarer. Item issued to the reeve of Addington 2½ quarters. Sold beyond the account, 2 bushels for 20d. Item sold 1½ quarters. Equal.

Issues of vetches. Item he renders account for 6 quarters of vetches received from Richard de Keten'. And for 5 quarters received as throw-outs from the oats as appears elsewhere in the oats.

Of which, for feeding the pigs and piglets of the manor during the winter season and in the summertime, because they were sick with measles, 4 quarters 2 bushels. So much expended this year because the farmer had all the grain of the manor whence the reeve had nothing.

60 Razed, i.e. flat, as opposed to heaped measure. Wholesales of corn normally attracted an advantage, a tip, to the merchant calculated at one quarter for every 20 sold, see R. H. Britnell, '*Advantagium mercatoris*: a custom in medieval English trade', *Nottingham Medieval Studies*, 24 (1980), 37–50.

Item issued to the reeve of Addington, 2 quarters. Item issued to William Christian for his supervision of the threshers for one month, and the reapers also, and for guarding the meadows for 5 weeks, on authority of Richard de Keten', ½ quarter. Item given as a tip on the sale of 4 quarters 1 bushel, and for threshing them in the granary because he received [them] by the razed measure, 1 bushel of vetches. Item sold, 4 quarters 1 bushel. And equal.

Issues of oats. Item he renders account for 155 quarters 1 bushel 1 peck of oats, whence 5 quarters are of vetches thrown out, which were received from Richard de Keten' from the issues of the granary. And for 7 quarters 1 bushel received in twenty eight and a half sheave of oats, of which each counts as 2 bushels. Total, 162 quarters 2 bushels 1 peck.

Of which, he accounts for rejects, as above, 5 quarters of *bolemong.* Item for flour made for the potage of the *famuli,* 4 quarters. Item for the fodder of 7 cart horses from Michaelmas until the Sunday before the feast of St Dunstan [29 September 1321 to 16 May 1322] for 32 weeks and 4 days, 33 quarters 2 bushels, for each horse per night 1 measure, of which six make a bushel. Item he accounts for the fodder of 12 horses from the feast of All Saints until Palm Sunday [1 November 1321 to 4 April 1322] for 22 weeks, 38½ quarters of oats, giving 12 horses 2 bushels per night. Item he accounts for the said 12 horses from Palm Sunday until the Friday on the eve of the feast of the apostles Philip and James [4 to 30 April 1322] when they went to grass, for three weeks and five days, 4 quarters 7 bushels, giving the 12 horses 1½ bushels per night. Item he accounts for the fodder of three cart horses harrowing for 8 to 9 weeks, 1 quarter, to each of the nine 1 measure. Item he accounts for the fodder of 5 horses of brother Robert de Luffenham, Robert de Gruntr', Richard de Glatton and Robert Clerk at one view after Michaelmas [29 September] for two days, 1 quarter 2 measures. Item he accounts for the fodder of three horses of brother Robert de Luffenham and Robert Clerk at one court on the Thursday of the morrow of St Hilary [14 January 1322], staying for 2 nights, 1 quarter. Item he accounts for the fodder of three horses of brother Robert de Luffenham and Robert Clerk, at one court on the Monday after the Annunciation of the Blessed Mary [29 March 1322], 1 quarter. Item for the fodder of their horses staying from the Tuesday to the Wednesday following, 2 bushels of oats. Item for the fodder of 2 horses of brother Robert de Luffenham, one horse of John Messenger, one horse of Robert Clerk, and 1 horse of William son of Robert Grauncr' at one view after Easter, ½ quarter. Item he accounts for the fodder of 2 horses of brother Robert de Luffenham and Robert de Sculthorpe on the Saturday and Sunday before the feast of St Nicholas [29/30 November 1321], 2 bushels. Item he accounts for the fodder of two horses of the steward, brother Robert and Simon de le Fen from the Saturday until the Sunday before the Purification [30/31 January 1322], 3 bushels. Item he accounts for the fodder of three horses of the steward, brother Robert and John Messenger on the Wednesday after the feast of St Philip and St James [5 May 1322] coming to supper and to breakfast on the Thursday, 3 bushels. Item he accounts for the fodder of three horses of brother Luke de Stanford and Richard de Glatton on the Wednesday after Michaelmas [30 September 1321] and in the morning, 3 bushels. Item he accounts for the fodder of two horses of the rector of Twywell and Richard de Glatton staying on the Monday of the morrow of St Luke the Evangelist [19 October 1321], and in the morning to audit the account of the manor, 2 bushels of oats. For the fodder of the horse of Robert Clerk staying at Wellingborough to compile the account of the manor, for 10 days, 3 bushels. For the fodder of three horses of Lord Hugh de Gorham about the feast of St Nicholas [6 December 1321] coming for 2 nights, 3 bushels. For the fodder of ten horses of the lord Alexander de Montfort, 5 bushels. For the fodder of the horses of master John de Twywell and Richard de Glatton at the surrender of 2 persons, 1 bushel. Item for the fodder of the carthorses of Crowland and the carthorses of Hoyland carrying the grain of Wellingborough to Crowland, 5 quarters, 3 bushels, 1 quarter by tally against Hugh the Carter. Item he accounts for fodder of the horses of the rector of Twywell and Richard de Glatton on the Friday and Saturday before the feast of St Paul the apostle [23 January 1322], 2 bushels. Item he accounts for the fodder of 16 horses of the lord archdeacon in his visitation, 3 bushels. Item for feeding the hens and capons, 2 bushels. For feeding the doves, 3 bushels. For the fodder of the horses of Richard de Cheyle, ½ quarter. Item for the fodder of four horses taking 86 hens and 16 capons to Crowland, ½ quarter. For the fodder of the cart horses of the manor taking peas to Morborne and other grain of the manor to Crowland and oats for seed to Asewick from time to time, 2½ quarters. Item issued to the sheriff of Northampton, 2 quarters by authority of Richard de Keten'. Item to Simon Lanncelyn, under-sheriff of Northampton, 1 quarter by authority of Richard de Keten'. Item issued to the reeve of Morborne, 20 quarters by tally. Item issued to the reeve of Asewick, 20 quarters on command of brother Robert de Luffenham. Item sent to Crowland, 5 quarters 3 bushels by tally against Colard the granarer. For the fodder of oxen and calves, 7 quarters 1 bushel received as above in 28 sheaves, and half a sheaf from Richard de Keten'. Sold beyond the account, 2 quarters for 8s. 8d. at the price of 4s. 4d. per quarter. Equal.

Issues of malt. Item he renders account for 5 quarters of malt received, made as above. Of increment nothing because *beby* and nothing germinated.

Of which, for the expenses of one court after Michaelmas, 1 quarter by authority of Richard de Keten'. Sent to Crowland, 4 quarters by tally against Colard the granarer.

Account of stock

Carthorses. Item he renders account for 6 cart horses received from remainders.[61] Total 6.

Of which, 2 died of murrain, by accidental murrain as is testified by the rolls of court. Total 2. And there remain 4.

Horses. Item he renders account for 12 horses received from remainders. And for 2 horses received from foals, and for 1 horse received from purchases, and for one horse received from waifs. Total 16.

Of which, in murrain 4, from the above cause. Total 4. And there remain 12 by the indenture.

Foals. Item he renders account for 2 over the age of one year from remainders. Total 2.

In murrain, 1 from the above cause. Total 1. And there remains 1 aged two years and male.

Oxen. Item he renders account for 4 oxen received from remainders. Total 4. And there remain 4 by the indenture.

Cows. Item he renders account for nine cows and 1 bull received from remainders. Total 10. And there remain 9 cows, of which 1 is sterile, and 1 bull.

---

61 In this context 'remainder' means brought forward from the previous account: the phrase is commonplace in stock accounts. Another common phrase in stock accounts, as evidenced by the entry for calves below, is 'received from issue', meaning animals that were born to manorial stock during the period covered by the account.

Cattle. Item he accounts for 10 cattle aged over one year received from remainders, of which 5 are male. Total 10.

Of which, 10 were sent to the marsh at Crowland by authority of Richard de Keten', of which 5 had murrain there by testimony as above. Total 5. And there remain 5 cattle according to the indenture, of which 3 are male.

Calves. Item he renders account for 8 calves received from issue. Total 8. And there remain 8 aged over one year, of which 5 are male.

Hoggets. Item he renders account for 145 female hoggets received from remainders. Total 145.

Of which in murrain 5, and the skins were sold. Item sent to Langtoft 145 [*sic*] by tally. Total 145. And none remain.

Boars and sows. Item he renders account for 2 boars and 4 sows received from remainders, and for 1 sow bought and for 1 boar recruited from the pigs as elsewhere. Total 8.

Of which, in murrain 1 sow. Neutered, 2 sows [*sic*] and they are joined with the pigs as below because they ate their young. Total 3. And there remain 3 boars and 2 sows by the indenture.

Pigs. Item he renders account for 21 pigs received from remainders, and 16 from recruits from the young pigs as elsewhere, and from sows as above, 2. Total 39.

Of which upgraded as above with the boars, 1. Killed for the plough-ale on the Monday before the apostles Simon and Jude [26 October 1321], 1. Item killed at the feast of St Martin [11 November 1321] for the larder for the stewards and supervisors, 2. Sent to Crowland, 19 by tally. In murrain, 2. Total 25. And there remain 14.

Young pigs. Item he renders account for 13 young pigs received from the issue of the month of November, and for 5 young pigs from the issue of the month of March, and for 6 young pigs bought together with one sow. And for 12 from the issue beyond the account, each sow answering for 3 issue. Total 36.

Of which, for the expenses [i.e. consumption] of Brother Luke de Stanford and Richard de Glatton on the Thursday after Michaelmas [1 October 1321], 1. For the expenses of the people of the neighbour-hood, on the Thursday after the feast of St Hugh [19 November 1321], at the surrender of 2 persons who were hanged, 2. And for one court on the morrow of St Hilary [14 January 1322], 2. In murrain, 8 in the month of December, the cause as above. Sold beyond the account 12 for 4s. at the price of 4d. per pig. Total 25.[62] And there remain 5 young pigs of the month of March and 5 young pigs of the month of August from purchases.

Geese. Item he renders account for 17 geese received from remainders, of which 16 are female and 1 a gander. And for 15 geese received from the issue of the manorial goose-house. And for 2 geese received from rent. Total 34.

Of which, for the expenses of the steward at one court after Michaelmas, 1. Item for the expenses of the steward at one court on the Thursday of the morrow of St Hilary [14 January 1322], 1. For the expenses of Brother Luke de Stanford and Richard de Glatton, 1. For the expenses of the Rector of Twywell and Richard de Glatton for compiling the account of the manor ... of the account of the nineteenth year ... 2. For the expenses of the people of the neighbourhood at the surrender of persons who ... Item ... at the surrender of 5 persons, 1 goose. For the expenses of one ... For the expenses of one court after Michaelmas and for their lodging ... In murrain, 6. Total 19. And there remain 4 of which 3 are female and 1 a gander.

Capons. Item he renders account for 24 capons from rent and chevage.[63] Total 24, of which in default of chevage, 6. For the expenses for the surrender of the persons, 1. Sent to Crowland, 16 by tally and none remain.

Hens. Item he renders account for 30 hens received from remainders, of which two are cocks, and for 94 hens arising from rent. Total 124 hens, of which for the expenses of the steward for holding the court, 6 hens. For the expenses of brother Luke de Stanford, Richard de Glatton, master John rector of Twywell, and for one plough-ale, 6 hens. Sent to Crowland, 86 hens. In murrain, 2 hens. Total 120 hens. And there remain 4, of which 1 is a cock.

Issues of the dovecotes. Item he answers for 152 doves as the issue of 2 dovecotes throughout the year. And for 328 as issue beyond the account, of which each pigeon house answers for 6s. 8d. Total 480.

62 The sale of so many young pigs beyond the account is unusual, and raises the possibility this entry represents a charge against the reeve for failing to achieve a specified target rather than genuine sales. See p. 103.

63 One capon was customarily the annual levy for chevage (see pp. 32–3).

Of which, for the expenses at the *curia*, 40. For the expenses of the steward and supervisors, 50. For the expenses of the plough-ale, 30. Sent to Crowland, 60. Item allowed to him on account of the bad season, 100. Sold beyond the account, 200 for 5s. 6d. at the price of 1d. for 3 pigeons.[64]

Issue of the dairy.[65] Item he renders account for 28 stone of cheese received from the yield of 8 cows of the manor, of which rowen cheese 7 stone. Total 28 stone.

Of which, for the expenses of the steward for holding four courts, 2 stone. Item for the expenses of the stewards at one court held on the Saturday after Michaelmas in the twentieth year of Simon the abbot [2 October 1322] and for their lodging for the Assize at Northampton, 1 stone. Item for the expenses of brother Robert de Luffenham, Peter Pampilon, John Messenger and Simon de le Fen with their boys on their many visits, 2 stone. For the visit of the Rector of Twywell, brother Luke de Stanford and Richard de Glatton on their many visits with their boys, and Robert Clerk for his lodging in order to compile the account of the manor, 1 stone. For the expenses of 1 plough-ale on the Monday before the feast of the apostles St Simon and St Jude [26 October 1321], ½ stone. For the expenses of the carters taking grain to Crowland on 14 occasions, 2 stone. For the expenses of the reeve, Henry de Keten', the bailiffs of the lord king, and other supervisors, 3 stone. Issued to Richard de Keten' for feeding the harvest-workers, 10 stone. Sold, 6 stone 1 quarter. Sold beyond the account, 6 stone for 2s. 6d. Total 28 stone. And nothing remains.

Butter. Item he renders account for 6 stone of butter received from the yield of the cows of the manor. Total 6 stone.

Of which, for the expenses of the steward with a clerk and boys on their many visits, 1 stone. Item for the expenses of Brother Luke de Stanford, Richard de Glatton, the bailiffs of the lord king, and the reeve and other supervisors, 1 stone. Item issued to Richard de Keten' for feeding the harvest-workers, 3 stone. Item sold 1 stone. Total 6 stone. And nothing remains.

64 A more obvious example of the imposition of a quota system upon the reeve than n. 62 above.

65 Many manors preferred to lease out their demesne cow herds even at the peak of direct exploitation, but this stock account – admittedly for a small dairy – shows that the Wellingborough herd was worked directly.

Hides. Item he renders account for 6 horse-hides and the hide of 1 foal received from animals dead of murrain as above. Total 7. Of which 2 hides were dressed and a half was ... (?). Item sold 4. Total 7. And there remains ½.

21   An account of Morton, 1479–80

A good example of a phase 3 account from a lay estate, at a time when it was temporarily held by the Crown. In contrast to those from phases 1 and 2 [**19** and **20**], this account has no lengthy sections on sales of corn, costs of upkeeping equipment, harvest wages, etc., which immediately signals that the arable demesne lands are leased. Indeed, the lease of the demesne merits a separate section under receipts. The collection of rents and running of the manorial court are undertaken directly, but all other economic resources are rented out. No arrears are recorded, which is unusual for accounts of this period, but internal references to a new rental imply that the rent charge has been recently re-evaluated and, implicitly, that earlier debts had been cancelled or restructured.

R. H. Hilton, ed., *Ministers' accounts of the Warwickshire estates of the Duke of Clarence, 1479–80*, Dugdale Society, 21 (1952), pp. 66–9. *Compotus* of Morton (Warwickshire), Michaelmas [29 September] 1479 to Michaelmas 1480. Latin.

Morton. Account of Thomas Savage, reeve there for the same time.

Arrears. None, because he was quit of his account in the preceding year, as appears at its foot.

Rent of assize. But he answers for £24 14s. 6d. for rent of assize there this year, as appears in a new rental made last year, with increment of rent, payable there at four annual terms, of which 1d. from a pair of spurs payable at Easter. And for 9d. for the price of 3 capons issuing from rent there annually payable at Pentecost, namely for this feast when it falls within the aforesaid period. And for 2s. 8d. for the rent of the dovecote there, namely from increment of rent of the same, as appears in the aforesaid rental, beyond the ancient 4d. rent for the same as recorded in last year's account. Total, £24 17s. 11d.

Sale of corn and stock. He does not answer for any profits issuing from the sale of corn and stock there during this period, because no sales of this kind occurred there within this time, by the oath of the said accountant. Total, nothing.

Issues of the manor. Nor does he answer for any issues of the meadows
called Haddon, Pruttesmede, Rosham, Astmede, Sullesmede, Newemede;
or one *frisce* pasture at Churchehull; divers headlands at le Hallebroke;
or of pastures, whether at le Buryhum, or at the windmill, or a certain
pasture of two acres of demesne land lying on le Lowe and under the
grove there, namely for the period of this account, because they are
leased to the farmer of the demesne lands within his lease detailed below.
Total, nothing.

Lease of demesne land. But he answers for 106s. 8d. for the lease of the
site of the manor there, thus leased to Henry Hopkyn with all
demesne lands, meadows, grazing and pastures pertaining to this manor,
together with all customs, and he ought to render £8 6s. 8d. per
annum. Total, 106s. 8d.

Perquisites of the courts.[66] And for 2s. 8d. for the perquisites of one view
of frankpledge there, held on the Thursday after the feast of All Saints
in the 19th year of the present king [4 November 1479], as appears
by the same rolls produced and examined beyond the account. And for
3s. for the perquisites of one view of frankpledge with a court held
there on the Tuesday next before the feast of the Annunciation of the
Blessed Virgin Mary in the 20th year of the said king [21 March
1480], as appears by the same rolls similarly produced and examined
beyond the account. Total, 5s. 8d.

Grand total of charges, £30 10s. 3d.

Of which,

Allowances with decayed rents. The same accounts for allowances of
rents for lands and tenements lying in the hands of the lord king for
lack of tenants, and for rents of tenants there discharged by the
former lord, the deceased earl [of Warwick, d.1471], as it is alleged
by Nicholas Roddy, the steward there, just as is testified by a certain
rental renewed last year, with the issues of lands and tenements lying
decayed in the hands of the lord king, beyond £14 16s. 10d. levied
[from rents] as appears in a certain bill produced beyond last year's
account, £10 1s. 1d.

---

66 The manor court is still run directly by the seigneurial administrators, even
though most of the manor is leased: an arrangement that was not uncommon in the
fifteenth century.

Purchases of corn, with stipend of the reeve and the steward's expenses. And in 1 quarter of wheat bought for a gift to the Master of St John's, Warwick, from his alms granted by the ancestors of the late lord there, price 5s. And in 1 quarter of barley similarly bought for a gift to the said Master from the said alms, price as above 5s. And in the stipend of his reeve for his office this year, 13s. 4d. And in expenses of the steward holding courts there this year, together with 4d. paid for parchment for the court rolls, as is fully recorded in the same rolls produced beyond the account, 3s. 8d. Total, 27s.

Repairs. And in divers agreements, costs and expenses incurred through making and undertaking all necessary repairs and rectifying various defects within the said manor, as appears itemised in one paper bill given and examined beyond this account, 34s. 8½d. Total, 34s. 8½d.

Transfers of monies. And in transfers of money by the said accountant to John Luthyngton, receiver of the lord king there, as appears in one bill given and examined beyond this account, £6 6s. 8d. And in money by the same accountant similarly given to the same receiver beyond this account in the presence of the auditors, £9 0s. ½d. Total, £17 7s. 5½d.

Which total corresponds with his total charges noted above, and he is quit.

22   An account of Haselor, 1484–85

This example contains a number of characteristics common to fifteenth-century accounts: an extensive section of 'allowances', revealing falling rents and abandoned holdings, and mounting arrears, which are broken down in detail at the foot of the account. The breakdown of arrears normally details the amounts owed by each individual debtor, although large single items (for example the lease of the demesne arable or the purchase 'on credit' of the wool clip) are sometimes identified. Some of the arrears date back decades, and the auditors' expectation of collecting them is clearly unrealistic. This section provides a more accurate sense of the cash actually collected, and is therefore central to understanding the annual yield of the manor. Note the expenditure on the repairs of various manorial buildings, which remained a seigneurial obligation during the lease of the demesne, and the use of bills at the audit – including by the demesne lessee – to verify earlier transfers of money.

D. Styles, ed., *Ministers' accounts of the Collegiate church of St Mary, Warwick, 1432–1485*, Dugdale Society, 26, (1969), pp. 172–7. *Compotus* of Haselor (Warwickshire), 14 April 1484 to 14 April 1485. Latin.

Manor of Haselor. Account of John Perkyns, bailiff there, for the whole year as above.

Arrears. Item, the accountant answers for £47 3s. 1d. from arrears of the last account of the preceeding year, just as appears at the foot of that account. Total, £47 3s. 1d.

Rents of assize. And for £15 1s. 2½d. received from the rents of the tenants there per annum, payable at two annual terms namely at Michaelmas [29 September] and the Annunciation of the Blessed Virgin Mary [25 March], as appears in the rental. Total, £15 1s. 2½d.

Minute [petty] rents. For 1lb pepper issuing from the rent of John Trussell for the meadow called Milleham. Paid at Christmas, nothing for record here because in the fee of the auditors. For 1lb of cumin seed issuing from the rent of William Whitynton for a messuage and a virgate of land in Haselor each year, payable at Christmas, nothing here because this year it was delivered to lord Oliver Alwode. But he answers for 1d. for the value of 6 wooden plates from the rent of the abbot of Evesham payable each year at Christmas. And for 6d. received for the rent of 2 capons issuing from the rent of the said abbot, rendered on Christmas eve, as well as 12d. from rent of the same abbot owed above in rents of assize. For one pair of spurs for rent there as appears in the rental, nothing for record here because repaid to the lord of Upton for a certain rent as appears in the rental. Total, 7d.

Lease of the demesne lands. And for £6 13s. 4d. received from the lease of the site of the manor there, with all lands, meadows, pastures and rights of pasture belonging to the demesne, and all its other appurtenances whatsoever, thus leased to Nicholas Thommes for the term of 7 years, rendering this total annually to the dean and chapter and all their successors, namely at Christmas, the Annunication of the Blessed Virgin Mary [25 March], the Nativity of John the Baptist [24 June], and Michaelmas [29 September] in equal portions. Total, £6 13s. 4d.

Increments of rent. And for 3s. received from increment of two crofts there, of which one is called Cornecrofte and the other Grescrofte, lately in the tenure of Geoffrey Perkyns, which is in addition to 5s. of ancient rent received from rents found beyond the account by examination of the rentals, and one hen and two chickens.

Sale of wood. And for £13 received from sale of the wood there this year, as sold to Thomas Rows of Ragley. Total, £13.

Perquisites of court. And for 4d. received from the perquisites of the court held there this year. Total, 4d.

Grand total of receipts and arrears, £82 4s. 10½d.

Allowances of rent. Of which, he accounts in allowances of rent of one messuage and one virgate of land in Walcote, lately in the tenure of Richard Bemond, which ought to render 18s. per annum and is now leased to John Perkyns for 14s., and thus 4s. in allowance. And in allowance of rent of one messuage and one virgate of land in Walcote, lately in the tenure of Henry Perkyns which ought to render 18s. and is now leased for 14s. 8d., and thus in allowance 3s. 4d. And in allowance of rent of one messuage and one virgate of land in Walcote called Brownesplace with one parcel of land under Wythycombe, lately in the tenure of Nicholas Jones which ought to render 19s. and is now leased to John Lane for the use of his son for 15s. 8d., and thus in decay 3s. 4d. And in allowance of rent of one messuage and one virgate of land in Walcote, lately in the tenure of William Sever which ought to render 15s. per annum and is now leased for 14s. 8d., and thus in decay 4d. And in allowance of rent of one messuage and one virgate of land in Haselore, lately in the tenure of Nicholas Adams and previously Adam Wilkins, and is now leased to John Perkyns for 14s. 8d., and thus in decay 3s. 4d. And in rents released by the dean and chapter to the tenants of 5 messuages and virgates of customary land there which ought to render 18s. per annum, and now leased for 14s. 8d., in addition to the said messuages and virgates of land allowed above. Namely, in allowance of the rent of one messuage and virgate of land lately of Adam Wilkyns, now in the tenure of Robert Lane; another messuage and virgate of customary land in Walcote, lately of Peter Shepherd and now in the tenure of Geoffrey Perkyns; another messuage and virgate lately in the tenure of Robert Corbett in Walcote, and now in the tenure of John Tommez; and another messuage with one virgate of customary land lately in the tenure of Nicholas Mathew, now in the tenure of John Adebury, and thus in allowance of the said 5 messuages and virgates of customary land, out of consideration of the said dean and chapter due to a revaluation by the lord, namely for each messuage and virgate per annum, 3s. 4d., as appears in a certain rental renewed there in the month of April in the 17th year of king Henry VI [1439], and kept in the treasury of the church of the Blessed

Mary, 16s. 8d. And by advice release of the rent of one messuage and a half virgate of land in Walcote lately in the tenure of Robert Wylkyns for 9s. per annum and now leased to the same for 7s. 4d. per annum, and one messuage and a half virgate of land formerly of John Jones in Walcote for 9s. per annum, and now leased to Henry Perkyns for 7s. 4d. per annum: and thus in allowance of rent, 6s. 8d. And in allowance of rent of one toft and one dovecote, and two separate parcels of meadow, one called Cambuttes and the other Lytull Pylham, lately in the tenure of William Pynson and afterwards in the tenure of the vicar there, which are charged above at 18s. and are leased to William Hare for 13s. 4d., and thus the shortfall of rent this year is 4s. 8d. And allowance of the rent of one meadow called Camme charged above at 13s. 4d. lately in the tenure of William Huggez and now leased to Thomas Tommez for 10s., and thus 3s. 4d. in decay of rent this year. And allowance of the rent of a certain parcel of *frysce* land lying under the wide wood, lately in the tenure of Thomas Lane and now in the hands of the lord, and nothing is levied from it, 12d. Total, 46s. 8d.

Wages of the bailiff, with expenses of the steward. And in his wages, accounting for himself through his office, for collecting rents and leases there just as allowed in the preceeding account, 10s. And for a reward given to the same John for custody of the wood, for his diligence and reliability in his general work, as in the preceeding [account], 3s. 4d. And in expenses of the steward when holding the court there this year, 5s. 7d.

Repairs to manorial buildings, with the fencing of the wood. And paid for repairs made on the chancel of the church there, with 3s. paid to the vicar for proctorial expenses this year as appears in an item shown beyond this account, 4s. 5d.[67] And paid to Richard Gibbes for making 56 perches of hedging, at 1d. per perch, 4s. 8d. And paid to Thomas Trap for 40 perches of hedging made, at 1d. per perch, 3s. 4d. And paid to Thomas Sever and John Wilkes for making 84 perches of hedging, paid as above, 7s. And paid to Richard Hymmyng for making 49 perches of hedging, 4s. 1d. Total, 23s. 6d.

Transfers of money. And he accounts for monies transferred to lord John Gilbert, canon and treasurer of the collegiate church of the Blessed Mary, for money owed by Nicholas Tommez farmer of the

---

67 The upkeep of the chancel of the parish church was the responsibility of the rector. This, and other references to payments made to the vicar, indicate that the dean and chapter had impropriated Haselor church.

demesne land there, as confirmed by a bill made on the feast of the apostles Sts Simon and Jude [26 October], 66s. 8d. And to the same treasurer for money owed by the said Nicholas Tommes, as in the final bill for the above, 13s. 4d. And to the same treasurer for money owed by the same Nicholas beyond this account, witnessed by the subtreasurer, 35s. 6d.

And to the same treasurer for money owed by John Perkyns, collector of rent there this year, as confirmed by a bill shown beyond this account which was made on the feast of St Andrew the apostle [30 November] this year as recognised by the said treasurer, £7 13d. And to the same treasurer for money owed by John Perkyns for payment made to the vicar there for his pension this year for three terms, namely Christmas 16s. 8d., the Purification of the Blessed Virgin Mary [2 February], 16s. 8d., and the Annunciation [25 March], 16s. 8d. And to the same treasurer for money owed by the same John for part sales of the wood called Withicombe this year, £8. Total, £23 6s. 7d.

Grand total of payments and transfers, £27 15s. 8d. And they [the dean and chapter] are owed £54 9s. 2½d.

Of which, allowed to Nicholas Tommes, farmer, for repairs to the manorial buildings this year as confirmed by an item shown at this account, considered and ordered in front of the canons, 11s. 2d.

And they are owed £53 18s.½d. Of which, he accounts for payment to the lord of Upton for release of suit of his court this year, 4d. And thus they are owed £53 17s. 8½d.

Of this, on Robert Adams, formerly farmer there for his old arrears, £17 9s. 4d. On Richard Farmour for arrears of wood lately sold to him, 72s. 8d. On Thomas Mase, lately farmer there, for his arrears, £6 15s. 11d. On Henry Gibbs for sales of wood 37 years ago, 15s. 11d. On Cecil Whityngton for an unpaid heriot, 9s. On Nicholas Sever for an amercement imposed on him by the rolls of the court, 6s. 8d. On William Bedell for unpaid rent over the preceding 15 years at 12d. per annum, 15s. On the executors of the will of [blank] Whityngton for his heriot, 12s. On John Gibbes, lately collector of rent, for his arrears, £4 2s. 11d. On Nicholas Tommes, the present farmer, £7 0s. 3d. On John Perkyns, the present bailiff and collector of rents, £11 18s. ½d., of which £5 is for the sale of wood this year, and £6 18s. ½d. for rents.

23   A rectorial account of Pawlett, 1496–97

This is a conventional manorial account, but does not technically relate to a manor. In fact, the holding is a well-endowed parochial rectory, which had been long since impropriated by St Augustine's monastery in Bristol. However, as the glebe land was large enough to run as a small demesne, and as some land pertaining to the church of Pawlett had been granted to tenants for rents and services, the monastery was administering this rectory as a small manor. Note that the court was not held this year, presumably due to lack of business (see p. 187).

A. Sabin, ed., *Some manorial accounts of St Augustine's abbey, Bristol,* Bristol Record Society, 32 (1960), pp. 35–8. *Compotus* of Pawlett (Somerset), Michaelmas 1496 to Michaelmas 1497. Latin.

Pawlett. The account of Thomas Baldewyn, farmer [lessee] there, from Michaelmas in the 12th year of the reign of Henry VII until the same feast in the 13th year.

Arrears. None, because in accordance with the completion of last year's account the aforesaid accountant was quit, as appears at its foot. Total, nothing.

Issues of the manor. He does not answer for 6s. 8d. received from annual rents there, because they are conceded to the aforesaid farmer within his lease. Total, nothing.

Sale of grain. Nor for any issues from the sale of grain there, because all of this grain belongs to the aforesaid farmer as part of the lease recorded below. Total, nothing.

Lease. But he answers for £20 10s. received from the lease of the parsonage [rectory] there with all spiritualities and temporalities except capons and hens. Thus leased to the aforesaid farmer per annum. Total, £20 10s.

Sale of stock. And for 6s. received from the sale of 24 capons sold to the steward for the lord abbot's entertainment, as appears elsewhere, price per capon, 3d. And for 4s. received for 24 hens sold to the same steward, as appears there, price per hen, 2d. Total, 10s.

Perquisites of the court. He does not answer for any profits issuing from the perquisites of court there this year, because none were held there during the year. Total, nothing.

Grand total of receipts, £21.

Necessary expenses. He does not claim allowance for any monies paid this year as certain necessary expenses, because he is required to do this as part of the contract of his aforementioned lease. Total, nothing.

Foreign payments. But he accounts for monies paid to the hundred of Northpederton to discharge the abbot from suit [of court] there for the year, 2s. Total, 2s.

Repairs. And in monies paid for a quarter part of the repairs undertaken on a certain bridge there called le Quenebrigye this year, 2s. 8d. And in monies paid to repair two lattices on a certain wall in the oxhouse for two days, taking 6d. per day, with 11d. paid to a certain labourer making 35 perches of seawall there at the end this year, 55s. Total, 60s. 7d.

Foreign transfers. And in monies paid to the steward for the lord abbot's entertainment, for the cost of 24 capons and 24 hens as mentioned above, this year, 10s. Total, 10s.

Transfers of monies. And in monies transfered to brother John Nuland, treasurer of the monastery of St Augustine by Bristol, for his lease before the closure of this account at various times, £11 13s. 4d. And on another occasion beyond this account, 114s. 1d. Thus, in total, £17 7s. 5d.

Grand total of allowances and payments, £21. Which corresponds with his total charge above, and thus he is quit.

Stock

Grain. The parsonage does not answer for 20 quarters of wheat, 30 quarters of beans and 24 quarters of oats, which was rendered in a previous year, as recorded elsewhere in a certain lease, because the same parsonage is leased this year at farm for money, as above. Total, nothing.

Oats flour with mustard grain. Nor does he answer for 4 quarters of oats flour and 4 quarters of mustard grain for the same reason. Total, nothing.

Payments to the famuli. Nor does he answer for the provision of grain to the *famuli*, because the keep of the *famuli* is the responsibility of the farmer. Total, nothing.

Affers. But he answers for two female affers, of which one is valued at 10s. and the other at 2s., received from the remainders [i.e. carried over] of the 4th year preceeding in custody as recorded elsewhere. Total, two female affers. Which remain in the custody of the said farmer, and to be valued at the end of his lease as to their price, etc.

Colts. Nothing, because the issues of the above affers belong to the farmer as appears in his contract. Total, nothing.

Oxen. But he answers for 7 oxen received from the remainders of the 4th year preceeding in the custody of the farmer, price per head 16s. Total, 7 oxen. Which remain as recorded above.

Bull. And for 1 bull received from remainders of the 4th year preceeding in the custody of the said farmer, price 7s. Total, 1 bull. Which remains as recorded above.

Cows. And for 7 cows received from remainders of the 4th year preceeding in the custody of the said farmer, price per head 10s. Total, 7 cows. Which remain as recorded above.

Sow. And for 1 sow received from remainders of the 4th year preceeding in the custody of the said farmer. Total, 1 sow. Which remains as recorded above.

Geese. And for 5 unmated geese received from remainders of the 4th year preceeding in the custody of the said farmer. Total, 5 geese. Which remain as recorded above.

Capons. And for 24 capons received from the lease of the aforesaid farmer each year paid at Easter. Total, 24 capons. Which were sold as above, and equals.

Hens and chickens. And for 24 hens and chickens received from the lease of the aforesaid farmer each year paid at Christmas. Total, 24 hens. Which were sold as above, and equals.

Hens eggs. He does not answer for 300 hens' eggs which ought to be rendered from a certain farm each year, because they are included within his farm. Total, nothing.

Cheese. He does not answer for 200 stones of cheese which ought to be rendered from a certain farm each year, for the same reason as immediately above. Total, nothing.

Hay. He does not answer for hay or herbage there, because included within his aforesaid farm to sustain the lord's animals. Total, nothing.

Deadstock. But he answers for one grain-cart with one pair of wheels with iron rims, valued on first receipt at 26s. 8d. And for one dung-cart with one pair of iron-rimmed wheels, received from remainders of the 27th year preceeding in the custody of the said farmer. Total as appears, and remain as recorded above.

Examined and approved.

Subsidiary documents to the account

The wide scope of manorial accounts, and the level of detail they provide, dictated that local agents perforce kept track of the day-to-day flows of money and goods through a variety of subsidiary documents of varying status. This is particularly true of phase 2 and 3 accounts, where the onus of account production rested more on the local agents than central administration. Some of these documents were little more than crude personal memoranda, but others assumed a central role in justifying and verifying decisions to the auditors, and maintaining an exact record of certain categories of income and expenditure. Few of these subsidiaries have survived, for the simple reason that their usefulness ceased after the audit, but their widespread use is evidenced by regular references to them in audited accounts [21, 22]. Fortunately, some have survived as schedules sewn as attachments to the final account, and these examples provide a valuable insight into the process of compiling later manorial accounts.

24   An agistment roll for Esholt park, 1395

A short list of cattle grazed by local people in the deer park of Esholt, where no communal pasturing rights existed. The manor was therefore justified in charging for the right, which, judging from the total revenue of 30s. 5d., provided a useful supplementary income. Very little is known about stocks of deer in deer parks, because accounts rarely mention them, but an implication from this document is that the lady of the manor permitted some locals to raise the odd deer calf with her own herd, an unusual privilege. Of course, this document would not include any reference to the demesne deer, because they grazed in the park by right.

British Library, Add. Roll 41656, agistment roll for Esholt park (Yorkshire), 1395.

Agistments of cattle in the park of Esholt in the summer of the eighteenth year of the reign of King Richard II after the conquest [1395].

And from Roger de Hawksworth for 2 oxen, [illegible]. And from John Batty of Calverley for 1 ox, [illegible]. And from Adam Carletun of Esholt for 2 cows, 2s. 4d. And from John Connes of Baildon for 1 cow, 14d. And from Thomas Bysshop of Hawksworth for 5 heifers, 2s. 11d., and from the same for 3 stirks there, 2s. And from John de Guiseley for 2 foals there, 2s. And from Walter Nanson of Yeadon for 1 foal, 12d. And from Hugh de Folyfoot of Rawdon for 3 oxen, 3s. And from Thomas Jackson of Horsforth for 2 cows, 2s., and from the same Thomas for two deer calves, 12d. And from John de More for 2 oxen from the Sunday of Holy Trinity [6 June] until the feast of St Peter Advincula [1 August], 20d. And from Caril de Wradlay for 3 deer calves, 18d. And from Richard Saunderson for 1 deer calf, 6d. And from John del Wode of Guiseley for 1 deer calf, 6d. From Thomas de Thenore for 2 mares, 4s. From William Saunderson for 1 stirk from the feast of the Translation of St John of Bridlington [11 May], 4d. Total, 30s. 5d.

25   Bailiff's memorandum of receipts from Lackford, 1444–45

A crudely written and compiled memorandum, probably by the bailiff himself. No total is given, the scribe used abbreviations heavily, and the language employed is an odd mixture of Latin and English.

Suffolk Record Office, Bury St Edmunds, E3/15.12/5.3. Memorandum of receipts from the manor of Lackford (Suffolk), 1 September 1444 to 31 August 1445. Latin and English.

Memorandum of all maner of recetes recevyd be Willyam Yong, baly of the manor of Lakford and Flempton, the yere of kyng Herry the 6th the 23rd yer [1 September 1444 to 31 August 1445].

First, from Nicholas Dyer of Bury for one meadow called 11 roods, and half an acre of meadow, total value 5s. 6d. From John Rogers for one pasture called Dunnesyerd, 5s. From John Dunwych for one parcel of meadow in Sotherey, 4s. From William Wolman for one parcel in the same, 4s. From William Peyton for one parcel in the same, 20d.

From John Peyton for one orchard (*orto*) called Coweruys, 4s. From
John Brett for one pasture called Haddeswelle, 6s. From John Hammond
for a meadow called 6 acres, 21s. From Geoffrey Smyth for one parcel
of meadow, 8s. From John Dunwich for Cowesyerd, 3s. 4d. From
John Barry for 1 acre halme, 2d. From Robert Barry for half an acre
halme, 1d. From Adam Palleser for a parcel of meadow, 6s. 8d. From
John Goche jun. for one parcel of meadow, 3s. 4d. From Edmund Lucas
for divers parcels of meadow, 12s. 4d. From Thomas Bogy of Westley
for one parcel of meadow in le Pranglys, 10s. 6d. From Roger Mayner
for Prykmers, 5s. From John Braddeley for one rood of meadow in le
Erlesmedow, 6d. From John Barow jun. for le pettes, 16d. From John
Crowche for one parcel of meadow next to Lytelmor, 5s. 4d. From John
Hammond for one meadow called Lytelmor, 3s. 4d. From John Hyme
for le longrode [blank]. From John Tredegoolde for one parcel of hay,
2s. 6d. Geoffrey [blank] for 300 reeds, 4s. From the rector of Flempton
for reeds and thatch, 6d. From Thomas Dunwich and John Harrow
for one acre of thatch in le Brygefen, 3d.

26   List of reeve's debtors at Cuxham, 1347–48

Debts on the account were notionally charged to the reeve or the bailiff, even
though he himself may have been let down by a particularly recalcitrant or
troublesome debtor. Under such circumstances, the careful reeve kept an
itemised list of his debtors, which in this example includes some illustrious
names. By the fifteenth century, a time when arrears were particularly problematic, major debtors and their debts are identified separately at the foot of
the account.   ·

Harvey, ed., *Cuxham manorial records*, pp. 144–5. List of debtors, Cuxham
(Oxfordshire) 10 July 1347. Latin.

Debts which are owed to Robert le Oldeman, reeve of Cuxham, beyond
his account, 10 day of July of the 22 year [of the reign of Edward III,
1348].

Richard East owes 11s. 7½d. Robert Waleys, 9s. 11½d. Gilbert Bourdon,
3s. 1d. Robert atte Heycroft, 4s. 1d. Emma le Revelove, 6s. 5d. Richard
Miller, 10s. 9½d. Emma Aumoner, 3s. ½d. William Wauldrugg, 3s. 2d.
Hugo le Carter, 8s. 11d. Richard Alynot, 8s. 9½d. Joanna le Canon, 5s.
5d. Elias Bouech, 7s. Richard Croume, 12d. Alicia Aumoner, 12d. Henry
le Gardiner, 10d. Margery le Dryver, 9d. Robert Hayward, 18d. John
atte Beche, 14d. Thomas le Fouller, 3s. 4d. Christina atte Heycroft, of
old, 3s. 4d. Gilbert Bourdon, 3s. 4d. Robert Oldeman, 3s. 4d. The

bondmen of Cuxham for a communal payment of old, 3s. 4d. Richard
le Deyere of old, 23s. 3½d. by tally. The same Richard for the lease of
the fulling mill for two years, 26s. 8d. The same Richard for
maintenance of the same mill, 12s. 4½d. John le Fuller of Ascot.
Richard Eyst and Robert Waleys for the debt of Richard Miller of
Ascot. Amissia Okeslade, 6s. 6d. Robert Hayward, 3s. 11d. William le
Daie, 3s. 9¾d.

Respites on the back [of the parchment]

Lord Edward, king of England; Lady Phillipa, queen; Lord Edward,
Prince of Wales; John, earl of Cornwall, of old, £15 6s. 5d.

Lord Edward, king, for 9 quarters of oats in the 19th year [25
January 1345 to 24 January 1346]; lord Prince Edward for hay and
litter in the 20th year [25 January 1346 to 24 January 1347], 5s. 3d.
The same lord Prince Edward for 3 quarters of wheat in the 20th year
[25 January 1346 to 24 January 1347], 12s. The same lord Prince
Edward for 10 quarters of oats, 16s. 8d. Richard Cocus of Oxford for
assarted land, 12s. 2d. Richard Moton, 13s. Hugo de Berewyk, 8s.
John Sprewel, 8s. William Sprewel, 6s. Henry le Parker of Henley, 3s.

Grand total, £28 13 3¼d.

27 Collector's schedule and petition for allowances at Bury St Edmunds, 1400–1

These two small documents are sewn onto the manorial account of 1400–1
from the Grange, which served as the home farm to the convent of Bury St
Edmunds abbey. The 'warrener and collector' was responsible for collecting
certain categories of income within the account, which are detailed on the
'charge' schedule (the first document below). His 'petition' (the second
document) was presented at the audit, and detailed the items which he
regarded as uncollectable. The scribbled additions to the petition reveal that
the auditors worked through each claim, and judged which items were
allowed, respited (postponed) or chargeable. The discussion between Henry
Jorge and the auditors was presumably livelier than revealed by the dry
document.

Suffolk Record Office, Bury St Edmunds, A6/1/9. Schedule and petition for
allowances, the Grange manor of Bury St Edmunds abbey (Suffolk),
Michaelmas 1400 to Michaelmas 1401. Latin.

Charge (*onus*) of Henry Jorge, warrener and collector in the year above.

From arrears of the last account, 46s. 6½d. From ploughing works of the vill, £4 2s. 9¼d. From the court this year, 45s. From the lease of the land of the same Henry, 4s. 8d.

Grand total [of receipts], £8 18s. 11¾d.

Of which, in decays 38s. 11¾d. In wages of the warrener, 48s. In clothes this year, nothing. Item, given to the bailiff, 37s. 8½d. Item, given to the bailiff to pay various people for mowing and making hay from the regrowth (*relucratio*) in Nomansmedow, 41s. 10½d. Item, given to the bailiff to pay Walter Chapman for part of his sown land and part of his stipend, 10s. Total, £8 16s. 6¾d.

And thus he owes 2s. 5d. Afterwards, he is allowed by the lord 4s. 2d. as appears in a bill annexed hereto [printed below]. And thus he exceeds by 20d., which the bailiff is held to pay him.

[Second document] The petition of Henry Jeorge, warrener, in the 2nd year of the reign of king Henry IV.

First, he petitions for allowance of 20d. from the amercement of Simon Jeriaunt for pannage of his pigs, [superscript] allowed by the lord. Item, for [16d. deleted] for the amercement of Robert Smith, for the same. Item, for 12d. for the amercement of John Skynner, servant of the lord sacrist, [superscript] allowed. Item, for 6d. for the amercement of Roger Frampton for damage caused in the lord's pasture, [superscript] allowed. Item, for 6d. for the amercement of Adam Watirward for causing damage in the lord's barley, [superscript] allowed. Item, for [12d. deleted] for the amercement of Richard Hethe for damage caused in Nomansmedow. Item, 18d. for the amercement of John Wade, respited by the lord. Item, for 6d. for the amercement of Alexander the shepherd of the lord, because not possible to levy, [superscript] allowed. Total allowed, 4s. 2d.

28   Instructions to manorial officials of Walkern, 1324–25

Reeves/bailiffs were often allowed considerable flexibility in the day-to-day exploitation of the manor, but were constrained by their lord's general requirements for cash or produce from the manor. The steward would have communicated such requirements to the local official verbally, although occasionally specific instructions were issued. The following examples of written instructions issued by higher authorities to lesser officials, detailing precise actions to be taken on the manor, are exceptionally rare and highly revealing. Note that the 'personal' letter from the lord is written in French, while the 'legal' schedule is in Latin. Both have survived because the officials felt some unstated need to preserve the record of authorisation for their actions.

Hertfordshire Record Office, Roll 9325, two schedules attached to *compotus* of Walkern (Hertfordshire), 1324–5. Latin and French.

[Latin] This schedule sealed under the seal of Thomas atte Pole, steward of lord Robert de Morle, and made at Walkern on the third day of November in the 18th year of Edward [II, 1324], witnesses that Richard atte Holme, the reeve of the said lord Robert in his manor of Walkern aforesaid, paid to the said Thomas for divers things bought in London for the benefit of the lord by the same Thomas, 52s. 6d. Item, to the same Thomas for his expenses in London to buy the said things, and elsewhere on the lord's business, 6s. 8d. Item, to John Daunteryne, the servant and park-keeper of Walkern, for seeking the said things in London and staying there for two days to collect the said things, with the expenses of one horse during the same time, 18d.

[French] Robert de Morle to the serjeant and steward of Walkern. We order you to raise 24s. from the wheat or other corn that you have and take it to our steward to pay the aforesaid 24s. to Richard Mayner, taverner of le Newmarket, in full satisfaction of a debt which we owe him. And keep this letter for your guarantee of the sale of the said corn and for the payment of the above debt upon your account. Written at Walkern the 26th day of January in the 18th year [of the reign of Edward II, 1325].

Extracts from accounts

29 Cropping patterns on the demesne arable at Brandon, 1386–87

Most grange (grain) accounts within the *compoti* merely record the flows of grain during the accounting year [e.g. **19**, **20**], but some provide detailed information about the acreage sown and its location. Such additional detail permits calculations of both grain yields and land productivity, and the reconstruction of both cropping patterns and systems of fallowing. This extract from the bishop of Ely's manor of Brandon presents an unusually informative summary of the way in which the demesne arable was exploited that year. The area lying fallow is high, reflecting the onset of a depression in grain farming and the thin nature of the local soils, and the manor is leasing some parcels of the demesne piecemeal to local tenants.

Public Record Office, SC6/1304/36. *Compotus* of Brandon (Suffolk), Michaelmas 1386 to Michaelmas 1387. Latin.

Brandon. Grange account. As shown by the terrier, there are 564 acres 1 rood of demesne arable land in nine fields, including 64 acres 2 roods in Northfeld; 52 acres 3 roods in Estfeld; 54 acres in Oxwikfeld; 50 acres 1 rood in Drovefeld; 59 acres 3 roods in Midilfeld; 65 acres 1 rood in Cotefeld; 81 acres 2 roods in Bridhithefeld; 59 acres 2 roods in Wommanlodefeld; and 76 acres 3 roods in Fourhowefeld.

Of which, sown with the lord's grain upon 149 acres. And lying fallow and common until the following year, 89 acres. Lying *frisce* as pasture for sheep and rabbits, 264 acres 1 rood. And leased, as recorded overleaf, 62 acres.

There are also 79 acres 1 rood of demesne meadow and pasture. Of which, 6 acres mown for hay for the use of the manor. Depastured by the carthorses and lambs of the manor, 28 acres 2 roods. And leased, as recorded overleaf, 44 acres 3 roods.

30   Exploitation of woodland at Hundon, 1370–71

Manors located in areas of substantial woodland, or endowed with a large and productive park, often produce detailed and impressive information about medieval woodland management when the wood or park remained under direct exploitation, as evidenced by this extract from an account of the large manor of Hundon. The manor was part of the inheritance of the Clare earls of Gloucester, but many of its mature oaks were destined for use on the estates of ecclesiastical landlords, such as the bishop of Ely's manor at Walsoken (Cambridgeshire). This, together with the high prices fetched by the sale of many of the oaks, reflects the scarcity of mature hardwood in medieval England.

Public Record Office, SC6/999/26. *Compotus* of Hundon (Suffolk), Michaelmas 1370 to Michaelmas 1371. Latin.

[receipts section] *Sales of large wood.* And he answers for 16s. from one oak sold in the park to the prior of Chipley for the axle of a mill. And for 3s. from two crops of fallen oak, for work at the bishop's mill at Wals[oken]. And for 15s. from 36 [field] maples in the coppice of the park sold to Roger Thon. And for 13s. 4d. from 37 maples sold to Elizabeth Whelere at 5d. each. And for 4s. from two crops of fallen oak for the work on Pysenendebrygge at Clare, sold to John Debenham.

And for 3s. from the sale of one poplar at Poynteles. And 2s. from one peartree in the garden sold. And for 3s. 8d. from one oak sold to mend the post of the bishop's mill at Wals[oken]. And £6 16s. for 8 oaks in Hundon park sold to the constable of Clare, Richard [illegible], each oak 17s. And for 9s. from one poor quality oak sold to John Chapman. And for 10s. from one fallen oak with other trees sold there to the same John. And 16s. from one oak sold to the same John. And 16s. from one oak for the constable sold to William Clonyere. And 2s. 6d. from the croppings of one oak cut for the work at Clare castle, sold to William Carloo. And 2s. 6d. for the crop of two fallen oaks sold to John le Smith of Chilton for work on the castle. And for 12d. from one crop of oak sold to Richard Cliter. And for 13d. from branches of oak sold to John Herfete. And 5s. from three crops of oak sold to John Peytt, including carriage, 8d. per cartload. Total, £13 0s. 1d.

31   A works account from Thaxted, 1377–78

Many phase 2, and a few phase 3, accounts include a full statement of the labour services due and expended during the course of the year, presented as a 'works account' on the dorse of the roll after the grange and stock sections of the account. This example from Thaxted is not untypical of a works section of an account dating from the late fourteenth century, when labour services were in decline and customary tenants were increasingly reluctant to perform them. The individual categories of labour services, and the number of works due, are carefully identified, an exercise which must have drawn upon a detailed survey. The discharge of these works at Thaxted is particularly interesting, including time off for major religious holidays. Some works were uncollectable because a few customary holdings had been converted to lease-hold tenure, and consequently the labour services attached to them had lapsed.

K. C. Newton, ed., *Thaxted in the fourteenth century* (Chelmsford, 1960), pp. 86–8. *Compotus* of Thaxted (Essex), Michaelmas 1377 to Michaelmas 1378. Latin.

Works account

Malt making. And for making 23 quarters 2 bushels of barley into malt, arising from the rent of 7¾ virgates of land at Christmas, whereby each virgate will make 3 quarters of barley into malt or render 3d. per quarter in lieu by custom. Total, of making 23 quarters 2 bushels.

Of which, in deduction of 4 virgates of the above land because they are in the hands of the lord and leased as recorded elsewhere, 12 quarters of barley into malt. And sold [i.e. commuted] as recorded elsewhere, 11 quarter 2 bushels of barley into malt. Total, as above, and balances.

Customary ploughing, the value of ploughing one acre, 4d. And for the ploughing of 186 acres of land arising from 7¾ virgates of land at the seasons of winter, Lent and fallow, whereby each virgate will plough 8 acres of land at each season. Total customary ploughing, 186 acres.

Of which, in deduction of the ploughing [services] of the aforesaid 4 virgates because they are in the hands of the lord and leased as recorded elsewhere, 96 acres. And sold as recorded elsewhere the ploughing of 90 acres. Total, as above, and balances.

Winter works, valued at ½d. each work. And for 1,472½ works arising by custom from the customary tenants holding 7¾ virgates of land between Michaelmas [29 September] and the feast of the Nativity of St John the Baptist [24 June], for 38 weeks, whereby each virgate of land will perform each week during that time 5 works: namely, on Monday, Tuesday, Wednesday, Thursday and Friday, unless feast days shall fall on those days. And thus, due from each virgate, 190 works. And for 684 works arising from 9 akermen during the same time, whereby each holds 10 acres of land and will perform weekly 2 works. And thus from each of them, 76 works. And for 418 works arising from 11 coterells [cottars] during the same time, whereby each will perform weekly 1 work. And thus from each of them, 38 works. Total, 2,574½ works.

Of which, in deduction of the aforesaid 4 virgates because they are in the hands of the lord and leased as recorded elsewhere, 760 works. And in the allowance of the works of the remaining 3¾ virgates of land for the ploughing of 90 acres of land as above at the three seasons by the custom called 'Gavelerthe', 225 works, namely for the ploughing of each acre 2½ works. And in allowance of the works of the same for four feast weeks during the same period, namely the fortnight of Christmas, and the weeks of Pentecost and Easter, 75 works. And in allowance of the works of the same for 14 feast days which fell within the said time, namely the apostles Sts Simon and Jude on a Wednesday [28 October], All Souls on a Monday [2 November], St Katherine the virgin on a Wednesday [25 November], St Andrew the apostle on a Monday [30 November], the Conception of the Blessed Virgin Mary on a Tuesday [8 December], St Thomas the apostle on a Monday [21 December], the Conversion of St Paul on a Monday [25 January], the Purification of the Blessed Virgin Mary on a Tuesday

[2 February], St Peter in Cathedra on a Monday [22 February], St Matthias the apostle on a Wednesday [24 February], the Annunciation of the Blessed Virgin Mary on a Thursday [25 March], the Invention of the Cross on a Monday [3 May], and the Ascension of the Lord [27 May] and Corpus Christi on a Thursday [17 June], total 52½ works, namely for each virgate each day, 1 work. And in deduction of the works of 3½ akermen, namely John Peyt 1, John Cook 1, John Grene 1, and Matilda Haftere ½, because these holdings are in the hands of the lord and leased as recorded elsewhere, 266 works, for each akerman 76 works. And in deduction of the works of the tenement of John Yongy, ½ akerman, in the hands of the lord for shortage of tenants, this being the second year, 38 works. And in allowance of the works of 5 akermen working during the four weeks abovesaid, 40 works, for each akerman 8 works. And in deduction of the works of 2 coterells, namely one called Bretonneslond and one formerly of William Helder, because in the hands of the lord and leased as recorded elsewhere, 76 works. And in deduction of the works of one coterell's land called Rammes, formerly of Matilda Fischere, because in the lands of the lord and leased as recorded elsewhere to William Tyle, 38 works. And in allowance of the works of 8 coterells working during the 4 feast weeks abovesaid by custom, 32 works. And in making 267 perches of new hedging around Southfrith, 534 works, namely 2 works per perch. And sold as recorded elsewhere, 438 works.

Summer works, valued at 1d. per work. And for 418½ summer works arising by custom from the customary tenants holding 7¾ virgates of land between the feast of the Nativity of St John the Baptist [24 June] and Lammas day [1 August], thus for 5 weeks and 2 days working this year: they will perform for each virgate of land 10 works weekly on the aforesaid 5 [week]days, unless feast days shall fall on those days. And thus for each virgate, 54 works. And for 99 works arising from the 9 akermen during the same period, whereby each will perform weekly 2 works. And for 55 works arising from 11 coterells during the same period, whereby each will perform weekly 1 work. And for 30 works arising from 6 cotmen during the same time, whereby each will do weekly 1 work, and they will not work except in the harvest. And 1 work arising from Richard Ailmer for making the lord's hay. Total, 603½ works.

Of which, in deduction of the works of the aforesaid 4 virgates of land for the reason stated above, 216 works. And in allowance of the works of the remaining 3¾ virgates of land for 3 feast days which fell during

the working days within the said period, namely the apostles Sts
Peter and Paul on a Tuesday [29 June], the Translation of St Thomas
the martyr on a Wednesday [3 July], and St Mary Magdalene on a
Thursday [22 July], 22½ works. And in deduction of the works of the
aforesaid 3½ akermen in the hands of the lord for the reason above,
38½ works. And in deduction of the works of the tenement of John
Yonge, ½ akerman, in the hands of the lord for shortage of tenants,
this being the second year, 5¼ works. And in deduction of the works
of 3 coterells abovesaid for the aforesaid reason, 15 works. And in
allowance of the works of the aforesaid 3¾ virgates of land for
mowing 17 acres of meadow in Parkmad, 34 works, namely 2 works
per acre: nevertheless, each virgater will mow 9 acres, if it be needed,
by custom. And in allowance of the works for the same for making,
collecting and making into cocks the hay of the said meadow with the
help of the cotmen as recorded elsewhere, 30 works, namely for each
virgater by custom 8 works. And in allowance of the works of the
aforesaid 5 akermen, 8 coterells, and 6 cotmen working to make the
said hay and make it into cocks by custom, 76 works, for each of them
4 works. And in allowance of the works of divers customary tenants
for turning, removing and making the hay of 4 acres of meadow in
Pamphilonnesmede, because it is not of the demesne of the manor,
namely from each of them 2 works daily, nothing this year because
sold as grass within. And sold as recorded elsewhere, 166¼ works. It
is examined [added in the margin]. Total, as above, and balances.

Harvest works, valued at 1d. per work. And for 651 works arising by
custom from the customary tenants holding 7¾ virgates of land between
Lammas day [1 August] and Michaelmas [29 September], which fell
on a Tuesday this year, thus for 8 weeks and 2 days for working: they
will perform for each virgate of land 10 works weekly during the
aforesaid 5 working days, unless feast days shall fall on those days.
And thus for each virgate, 84 works. And for 144 works arising from
9 akermen during the same period, whereby each will perform 2 works
weekly. And for 88 works arising from 11 coterells during the same
time, whereby each will perform 1 work weekly. And for 48 works
arising from 6 cotmen during the same, whereby each will perform 1
work weekly. Total, 931 works.

Of which, in deduction of the works of the 4 virgates of land for the
above reason, 336 works, namely 84 works per virgate. And in allowance
of the works of the remaining 3¾ virgates of land for the five feast
days which fell on their working days during this period, namely St

Lawrence on a Tuesday [10 August], St Bartholomew the apostle on a Tuesday [24 August], the Nativity of the Blessed Virgin May on a Wednesday [8 September], the Exaltation of the Holy Cross on a Tuesday [14 September], and St Matthew the apostle on a Tuesday [21 September], 37½ works. And in deduction of the works of the 4 akermen abovesaid, becuase in the hands of the lord as above, 64 works. And in deduction of the works of 3 coterells as above for the reason abovesaid, 24 works. And sold as recorded elsewhere, 469½ works. Total, as above, and balances.

32   Details of haymaking at Wisbech Barton, 1340–41

The following extracts include all references in the cash and works' accounts relating to haymaking on the demesne of the bishop of Ely's manor of Wisbech Barton. The exceptional detail contained therein permits the calculation of labour productivity from a run of sequential accounts, and in particular the difference between the productivity of hired labour and customary labour services.[68]

Cambridge University Library, EDR D8/1/14. *Compotus* of Wisbech Barton (Cambridgeshire), Michaelmas 1340 to Michaelmas 1341. Latin.

[receipts section] *Expenses of mowing and haymaking.* In mowing 40 acres of meadow, at 5d. per acre plus 12d., in total 17s. 8d. In turning and spreading hay, 12d. Given to customary tenants from Elm at haymaking, by custom, 12d. Total, 19s. 8d.

[…]

[works' account] *Customary mowing works.* The reeve answers for 46 works for mowing the lord's meadows, owed by customary tenants of 46 homesteads in Wisbech, and for 61 works for the same task owed by customary tenants of 61 homesteads in Leverington. Total, 107 works.

Of which, 4 works allowed for 4 manorial officials, and 103 works were sold at 2d. each. Total, 107 works, and equals.

Customary haymaking works. The reeve answers for 46 works for preparing the lord's hay, owed by customary tenants of 61 homesteads in Wisbech, and for 61 works for the same task owed by customary tenants of 61 homesteads in Leverington. Total, 107 works.

68 See D. Stone, 'The productivity of hired and customary labour: evidence from Wisbech Barton in the fourteenth century', *Economic History Review*, 50 (1997), 640–56.

Of which, 4 works allowed for 4 manorial officials, and 103 works without food were used for preparing hay in the meadow. Total, 107 works, and equals.

Hay. And there remain 80 cartloads of hay by estimation. From the yield of 40 acres of meadow this year, 90 cartloads of hay by estimation. Total, 170 cartloads.

Of which, 48 cartloads of hay by estimation were given to the lord's carthorses and sheep this year, 32 cartloads were sent to the reeve of Wisbech castle for the constable's horses (10 cartloads of which were new hay), and 40 cartloads by estimation were sold. Total, 120 cartloads, and 50 remain.

33   The management of sheep flocks around Bury St Edmunds, 1480–81

Accounts contain considerable information about the management and exploitation of sheep, one of the major resources of medieval agriculture. However, the entries are not always immediately transparent, and the cross-references between the receipts, expenses and stock sections of the account require careful deciphering if the management of the sheep is to be properly understood. This extract usefully exemplifies two common practices. First, the physical transfer of sheep from the lord's home farm to his own kitchen is recorded in the stock account, and a valuation of those sheep covers the transaction as a 'sale' under receipts from stock. However, this is a *notional* sale for accounting purposes, because the lord does not actually pay money to himself for his own sheep, and consequently has to be counterbalanced by an entry for the equivalent sum in the expenses section, under 'transfers of money'. Note, however, that the fleeces and pelts were genuine sales. Second, the transfers of sheep recorded in the stock account reveal that this manor was not run as a self-contained sheep farm, but was integrated into a wider operation involving other manors on Bury St Edmunds abbey's conventual estates. Two flocks are mentioned at Elveden, one a breeding flock of ewes and the other a wether flock, and another at Ingham: both were demesne manors of the abbey.

Suffolk Record Office, Bury St Edmunds, A6/1/13. *Compotus* of the Grange of Bury St Edmunds abbey, Michaelmas 1480 to Michaelmas 1481. Latin.

[Receipts section] *Stock sold by the lord.* He answers for 109s. as payment for 109 wethers sold from the Grange to the abbey kitchen this year, price 12d. per head. And 7s. 4d. as payment for 11 rams sold to the flock of Monkshall in Elveden this year, 8d. per head. And £4 3s. 0d. as payment for 83 wethers sold from the Hardwick flock to the

abbey kitchen this year, 12d. per head. And 4s. 0d. as payment for 6
rams sold to the ewe flock of Stavys in Elveden, 8d. per head. Total,
£10 3s. 4d.

Fleeces and pelts sold by the lord. He answers for 21d. as payment for 14
pelts from the murrain of the grange this year, 1½d. each. And for
24s. 2½d. for 83 fleeces sold, 3½d. each. And for 3s. 1½d. as payment
for 25 pelts sold from the Hardwick flock at 1½d. each. And for 47s.
10d. for 164 fleeces sold from the Hardwick flock. Total, 76s. 11d.

[...]

[Expenses section] *Stock bought by the lord.* For 21 ewes, wethers, and
hoggs bought by the lord, as appears in the account of John Bott of
Elveden, for the stock of the Grange, 21s. For 50 wethers bought, as
in the account of John Hemgrave of Ingham, for the stock of
Hardwick, 50s. Total, 71s.

[...]

Transfers of monies ... given to the lord for 209 wethers, ewes and
hoggs sold to the abbey kitchen, £10 3s. 4d. Given to the lord in
payment for 39 pelts and 247 fleeces sold this year, £3 16s. 11d.

[...]

[stock account] *Wethers.* And 253 remain from the previous year.
Item, bought from the flock of John Bott of Elveden, as appears in his
account this year, 21. Total, 274.

Of which, 14 died of murrain. Item, 109 sold to the abbey kitchen by
tally. Also 11 rams sold to the ewe flock of Monkshalle in Elveden, as
above. Total, 134. And thus there remain 140 wethers.

Hardwick [flock]. And 272 remain from last year. Bought from the
flock of John Hemgrave of Ingham, 50 wethers. Total, 322.

Of which, 37 died in murrain, of which 2 produced pelts. Item, 83 sold
to the abbey kitchen, by tally. Also 6 sold to the Stavys flock in
Elveden. Total, 116. Thus there remain 206 wethers.

Fleeces. Issues of all sheep, except those taken in tithe, 249. Given to
the shepherds as contracted, 2 called 'bellewether fleeces'.[69] Sold as
above by the lord, 247. None remain.

---

69 The bellewether fleece was the pick of the crop, customarily given to the shepherd
in medieval East Anglia.

Pelts. And in murrain before and after shearing, 39 pelts and 2 pelts.
Total, 41. And sold by the lord as above. And equals.

34 The construction of a new barn at Kinsbourne, 1397–98

Occasionally, the compilation of an account coincided with the construction
of a substantial building on the manor, and consequently the costs of the
project are recorded in illuminating detail. This example is taken from a
compotus of Kinsbourne and records the erection of a large grange for the
hefty sum of £67. The insights which it provides into the medieval building
trade are varied and valuable: the differential wage rates for skilled and
unskilled workers, the sources of raw material, the various types of material
used, construction techniques and so on. The dependence upon Aldenham,
Amwell and Wheathampstead for carts is instructive, because they were also
demesne manors of Westminster abbey. The carters were paid, so their labour
was not rendered as part of their labour service, but the abbey probably
regarded them as reliable workers. The cash-flow for the project would have
required careful planning, involving advances from central authorities, and
John Thurlad clearly carried considerable responsibility in this regard.

Westminster Abbey Muniments, 8862 Dean and Chapter of Westminster.
Compotus of Kinsbourne (Hertfordshire), Michaelmas 1397 to Michaelmas
1398. Latin.

Costs of a new barn (*grangia*)

Paid to Robert Brid, carpenter, and his men for scappling various
pieces of timber at Aldenham and sawing 1000 feet of boards for one
new barn to be constructed at Kinsbourne, 53s. 4d. And for one cart
hired to carry axes and other carpenter's tools from Amwell to Aldenham and Kinsbourne,[70] 3s. 4d. And paid to John Waltham, carpenter,
and two other carpenters hired for 20 weeks to work on the barn, £8
6s. 8d., receiving between them 8s. 4d. per week. And paid to the same
John Waltham and three other carpenters hired for the same purpose
for 17 weeks £9 4s. 2d., receiving weekly between them 10s. 10d. And
for collecting timbers in one place, and carting them from time to
time, 8s. 8d. And for sawing 700 feet of oak boards for boarding the
walls of the barn, 8s. 9d., at 15d. for 100 feet. And paid to sawyers
hired for 45 days to saw sundry pieces of timber for uprights, braces
and other things necessary for the barn, 52s. 6d., receiving between
them per day 14d. And for splitting heart-wood laths (*hert latthes*) for

---

70 These are demesne manors of Westminster abbey: see Harvey, *Westminster abbey*,
for a history of their management.

the same barn, 10,000 at 20d. per thousand, 16s. 8d. And for one cart hired about 54 times for carrying timber and boards for the barn from Aldenham to Kinsbourne £6 15s., at 2s. 6d. on each occasion, that is Richard Edrich's cart 17 times, Thomas Porter's cart 9 times, Thomas Brewer's 7 times, Thomas Attehil's 7 times, William Sleigh's 12 times, Geoffrey Skippe's twice. And for carts of the manor of Aldenham hired to carry both timber and boards and laths to Kinsbourne on 31 occasions, 77s. 6d. at 2s. 6d. per occasion.

And for 43 men hired for the equivalent of one day for dismantling the old barn and collecting the timber therefrom, and clearing and levelling the site of the new barn and raising the new barn, 14s. 4d., at 4d. each per day, of which 12s. 4d. was paid by John Thurlad the lessee. And for 21 men hired for the equivalent of 4 days to help lift and erect the barn, 28s., each one receiving the same as above, of which 13s. 10d. was paid by Thurlad. For 3 rods of iron bought for making *dryvelles*, 6d. Item paid to 4 carpenters for 10 weeks, hired to erect the barn and board its walls, 108s. 4d., taking between them 10s. 10d. per week, of which 13s. 4d. paid by Thurlad. For 1,000 nails bought for the barn, 5s at 6d. per hundred. For 1,000 other nails bought for the barn, 5s. at 6d. per hundred. For 1,000 other nails bought for the barn, 4s. 2d. at 5d. per hundred. And for 800 other nails bought, 2s. 8d. at 4d. per hundred. Item for 19,000 roofnails bought, 23s. 9d. at 15d. per thousand. For 25,000 flat tiles bought from John Meldrope of Ridge (*Regge*), 108s. 4d. at 4s. 4d. per thousand with burnt lime for the laying of them. For 300 ridge tiles and corner tiles bought from the same, 15s. at 5s. per hundred. For 11 quarters of burnt lime bought for priming the walls from the same John, 8s. 4d at 9d. per quarter. For one quarter and one bushel of tile pins, 4s. 6d. at 6d. per bushel. For 5 cartloads of stone bought for the foundations of the barn with carriage to Kinsbourne, 33s. 4d. at 6s. 8d. per load with carriage. For 5 cartloads of stone bought for the same purpose at Dunstable, 25s. at 5s. per load with carriage, of which [blank] loads by the carts of Wheathampstead, two by the cart of Richard Clark, one load by W. Balle, one load by the hired cart of W. Balle, and one load by Aldenham.

For 6 quarters and 4 bushels of burnt lime bought at Dunstable for the barn, 8s. 1½d. at 15d. per quarter. For carrying the said lime to Kinsbourne on two occasions, 2s. 8d. by J. Dich and J. Thurlad. For digging sand and carrying it on occasions, with expenses of horses carrying the sand, 11s. by John Thurlad. For 7,000 flat tiles bought at Luton, 42s. at 6s. per thousand. For 50 ridge and corner tiles bought

3s., of which 15d. by W. Balle. For 7,000 flat tiles bought afterwards at Hatfield, 38s. 6d. at 5s. 6d. per thousand by W. Balle. For carrying these tiles to Kinsbourne, 14s. at 2s. per thousand, of which 2,000 in Aldenham carts, a thousand in J. Thurlad's cart, and 4,000 in Wheathampstead carts. For 2,000 roofnails bought by J. Shorefoot, 2s. 4d. at 14d. per thousand. And paid to J. Shorefoot, tiler, with his mate, hired for 76 days pointing the footings and walls of the barn, and also for tiling part of the barn, 69s. 8d. at 11d. per day. And paid to one other tiler, with his mate, hired for the same purpose for 14 days, 14s. at 12d. per day. And for the wages of one labourer for helping the aforesaid carpenters and tilers for 11 weeks in constructing and tiling the barn, 18s. 4d. at 20d. per week. For one pair of T-hinges, 4 pairs of hooks, 2 pairs of hinges for two small doors, 2 pairs of hooks and 4 eyes of iron for the large door, weighing in total 70lbs of iron, and costing, with work, 1¾d. per pound, 10s. 2½d. For two locks with keys bought, 12d. For one iron bolt for the large door, one *rynge* with one *stapel*, one latch and catch bought for the small door, 6d. Item for 5,000 sprig nails bought for cross-lathing, 3s. 9d. at 9d. per thousand. For collecting flints and carting them for strengthening (*pinnacione*) the walls of the barn, 3s. 4d. by John Dich. And for carriage to Kinsbourne of the aforesaid 7,000 tiles purchased at Luton, 14s. at 2s. per thousand, one thousand by J. Dich, one thousand by J. Thurlad, two thousand by Aldenham carts and three thousand by Wheathampstead carts.

Total, £67 4s. 2d., checked and found correct.

IV: MANOR AND LEET COURTS

Introduction

The abundant records of manor courts represent the single most important source for the study of English local society in the Middle Ages, and offer unique and highly detailed information relating to a wide range of subjects. Consequently, studies of court rolls have a long and distinguished pedigree, and in recent years the methods deployed by historians to analyse their contents have become increasingly sophisticated and innovative. The historiography of manorial court rolls is fully explored in Razi and Smith's monumental *Medieval society and the manor court*, to which the reader is referred for a thorough treatment of this subject.[1] This chapter aims to provide a general introduction to the manorial court, its format, procedures and business, and its usefulness to the historian, and to consider changes to its business in the fourteenth and fifteenth centuries.

The manor court

Surviving written records of the manor court (*curia manerii*) first appear in the 1230s, and proliferate after the 1260s.[2] For much of the later Middle Ages both the written format and the general business of these courts are remarkably consistent across the country, which partly reflects the use of widely distributed exemplars.[3] Records of this kind are exceptionally rare on the Continent, and so the explanation for their existence is peculiarly English.

Many historians doubt whether manor courts were held at all before the end of the twelfth century. The initial impetus to their creation was provided by the growth of royal justice and the development of

---

1 Z. Razi and R. M. Smith, eds, *Medieval society and the manor court* (Oxford, 1996), pp. 1–35.

2 Razi and Smith, *Medieval society*, pp. 39–40.

3 F. W. Maitland and W. P. Baildon, eds, *The court baron*, Selden Society, 4 (1890), pp. 3–4.

the common law, which generated both a precedent and a growing demand for judicial mechanisms to resolve disputes. Lords sought to distract their free tenants from using the emerging royal courts by developing their own manor courts along similar lines, thereby raising income from the curial profits and asserting their autonomy. The development and refinement of the common law of villeinage in the second quarter of the thirteenth century further encouraged them to record and collect assiduously exactions from their unfree peasants, and to use the manor court for this purpose.[4] Before the fifteenth century any lord could hold a manor court if he had sufficient tenants, or sufficient business, to make the exercise worthwhile.[5]

Thus manorial lords regarded manor courts as a medium to channel, satisfy and profit from the growing litigious behaviour of their free peasants, and to ensure that seigneurial rights over their dependent peasantry were properly enforced. In order to achieve these objectives, the manor court had to provide relatively cheap and efficient justice for both lord and peasant, and its procedures quickly came to reflect those of the royal courts. Improvements in their efficiency were especially apparent in the 1270s and 1280s when Edward I's legal reforms limited the power of lords to coerce their free peasantry into using manorial courts, thus forcing them to make their own courts more attractive in order to promote business. A clear indication of the growing popularity and sophistication of manor courts is the increasing tendency to document their activities. The earliest proceedings were probably not recorded, but during the thirteenth century a number of developments encouraged the shift to a written record: improvements in estate management, the desire of estate administrators to supervise local officials and procedures more closely, the spread of literacy, and the growing recognition of written precedents in law.[6]

---

4 Razi and Smith, *Medieval society,* pp. 45–6; R. H. Britnell, *The commercialisation of English society 1000–1500* (Manchester, 1996), pp. 134–47; and L. R. Poos and L. Bonfield, eds, *Select cases in manorial courts 1250–1550. Property and family law,* Selden Society, 114 (1997), p. xxi. Much is still unclear about the relative importance of the forces behind this process: 'the interrelation between legal and social change in mid thirteenth-century lordship and estate management remains a rich and exciting field for research'; P. R. Hyams, *King, lords, and peasants in medieval England: the common law of villeinage in the twelfth and thirteenth centuries* (Oxford, 1980), p. 268.

5 F. Pollock and F. W. Maitland, *The history of English law before the time of Edward I,* 2nd edn (Cambridge, 1911), p. 584; Maitland, ed., *Select pleas in manorial and other seigneurial courts,* Selden Society, 2 (1988), pp. xxxix, xli.

6 W. O. Ault, *Open-field farming in medieval England: a study of village by-laws* (1972), pp. 18–8; Razi and Smith, *Medieval society,* pp. 36–7, 48–9.

The manor court was a rapidly maturing institution by the end of the thirteenth century, and peaked between *c.* 1280 and *c.* 1400: the sheer quantity of extant court rolls, and their quality and length, are greatest from this period.

Manor courts were held in customary or designated places, sometimes outdoors or in the parish church, but normally in the hall of the manor house or, especially in later centuries, in a proper courthouse. The frequency with which they were held varied over time and place, but at their peak the busiest were held every three weeks. In the late thirteenth century this was certainly true of a large manor such as Gressenhall (Norfolk), although the volume of business on smaller manors may not have justified more than two or three meetings a year.[7] Elsewhere a single court might cover the activities of a number of manors. For example, one court covered the three contiguous manors of Oakington, Cottenham and Dry Drayton (Cambridgeshire) and met between three and five times each year, presumably because the volume of business in each individual manor did not justify regular meetings of a separate court, and because the arrangement proved administratively convenient for the distant lord who held all three manors.[8]

The earliest manorial courts dealt predominantly with civil litigation between free tenants, especially personal actions and land transactions. However, their function was soon extended to regulate many aspects of the relationship between lord and unfree peasants, and particularly the swearing of fealty to a new lord; recording land transactions and resolving disputes over property rights; prosecuting recalcitrant tenants, and damage and trespass against the lord's property; levying servile dues and incidents, such as heriot, chevage, merchet, and leyrwite; ensuring that tenants were found for empty holdings; electing manorial officials and regulating their performance; and upholding custom.[9] Similarly, personal plaints between peasants soon came to embrace the unfree peasantry, so that debt, trespass, damage and defamation

---

7 Z. Razi, 'Manorial court rolls and local population: an East Anglian case study', *Economic History Review*, 49 (1996), p. 760; R. Lock, ed., *The court rolls of Walsham-le-Willows*, Suffolk Record Society, 41 (1998), p. 6.

8 F. M. Page, *The estates of Crowland abbey: a study in manorial organisation* (Cambridge, 1934), p. 39.

9 Pollock and Maitland, *History of English law*, pp. 585–94. For a magisterial survey of the role of the manor court in dealing with issues of property and family at customary law, including many published examples, see Poos and Bonfield, *Select cases*. One of their objectives is to understand 'the quality of the manorial court's adjudicative role, and, indeed, the very meaning of customary law in the manor court', p. xvii.

cases abound. If the court belonged to the main manor in the village, it might also regulate local agricultural practices by issuing by-laws and punishing dissidents. The business of manorial courts, and by extension the range of detailed information their records convey to historians, were clearly significant and eclectic. 'The court was an administrative bureau as well as a judicial tribunal'.[10]

Attendance at the manor court was normally compulsory for all unfree tenants, and an occasional requirement (perhaps once a year, and whenever involved in a case) for free tenants, although local variations on this general rule can be found. Both free and unfree tenants of Chertsey abbey attended its manor courts without distinction, and Durham priory ran a separate 'great' court for its prominent free tenants (although lesser freemen were also expected to attend the local customary court).[11] The distances travelled to a court could be considerable for some tenants, and so it was a requirement on the same Durham estate that other tenants offered overnight accommodation.[12] A tenant who was unable to attend could apply at the court through a third party to be excused attendance, or 'essoined', and applications for essoins were invariably recorded at the top of the court roll before the main proceedings began. In some places, essoins could only be claimed by free tenants or were only relevant to those involved in active cases.[13] The reasons for non-attendance by individual tenants are rarely given, although sufficient grounds were required. Courts placed limits on the number of successive essoins each tenant could claim, and punished those who stayed away without due cause.

The lord of the manor nominally presided over the court, but only lesser lords actually did so. Most were represented by a senior estate official, normally a steward (or occasionally a bailiff), who controlled the proceedings, issued mandates, directed cases and fines, and assumed an influential role in defence of the lord's rights. Manor courts were governed closely by rules and regulations, which imply a strong working knowledge of legal procedures by both president and tenants. Indeed, those in late thirteenth-century Hinderclay display 'a careful regard for actions and processes of a kind almost identical to those

---

10 Page, *Crowland abbey*, p. 41.

11 E. Toms, ed., *Chertsey abbey court roll abstract*, Surrey Record Society, 31 (1954), p. ix; W. H. Longstaffe, ed., *Halmota prioratus Dunelmensis: containing extracts from the halmote court of the prior and convent of Durham 1296–1384*, Surtees Society, 82 (1889), p. xiv; Pollock and Maitland, *History of English law*, p. 586.

12 Longstaffe, ed., *Halmota*, p. xxxiv.

13 Page, *Crowland abbey*, p. 40.

found in the royal courts', where the conduct of pleading reveals an impressive respect for formal procedure.[14] In exceptional or sensitive cases, particularly those concerning seigneurial rights, the steward might defer a decision until the lord's counsel had been sought. In this regard, the abbots of Crowland and St Albans appear to have exerted an increasing influence over decisions taken in their manor courts in the later fourteenth century.[15]

The mechanism of the court was oiled by various manorial officials, who were active in presenting cases, implementing some of the curial directives, and collecting fines. Some of these officials were more directly involved in the operation of the court than others, and the manorial reeve and hayward (or messor as the office was alternatively known) were particularly prominent. At each session the court also elected (normally two) people, known as affeerers, from those attending to help determine in conjunction with the president the level of fines and fees to be levied in each case. All manorial officers were formally elected by the court, normally on an annual basis, irrespective of their involvement with the formal proceedings of the court: the exact form of these elections is not certain, but it seems likely that the court was simply invited to approve an appointment. The court was also required to monitor the performance of each official, and issue warnings and amercements for delinquencies if necessary.[16] As the majority of officers were themselves local tenants of the lord serving in an honorary capacity, they must have often struggled to balance the conflicting demands of the lord against the expectations of fellow peasants. This predicament was not lost upon Robert Dodd, bailiff of Walton (Suffolk) in 1389, who was fiercely assaulted and injured by another local peasant while conducting the business of his office.[17] Courts sought to uphold the authority of manorial officials by punishing severely any obstructive behaviour towards, or assaults upon, them: indeed, attacks on officials were held to be 'in contempt of the lord'.

Cases were brought to the court through either an individual action, for which a financial charge was levied, or a 'presentment' by an appropriate authority, such as the steward, manorial officers and

---

14 P. R. Schofield, 'Peasants and the manor court: gossip and litigation in a Suffolk village at the close of the thirteenth century', *Past and Present*, 159 (1998), 12; Poos and Bonfield, *Select cases*, pp. l–liii.

15 Page, *Crowland abbey*, pp. 44–5, 48; Poos and Bonfield, *Select cases*, p. lxxi.

16 Page, *Crowland abbey*, pp. 75–7.

17 Suffolk Record Office (Ipswich), HA119:50/3/17, m. 36.

appointed 'juries of presentment'. Once a case had been initiated, the named parties were expected to attend the relevant sessions of the court until some form of conclusion was reached. The plaintiff had to provide one or two 'pledges', and the defendant was summoned to respond to the plea. Pledges were local people who agreed to accept responsibility for ensuring that those involved in a case responded to the requests of the court and adhered to its procedures. An individual who remained absent would be 'attached' to attend the next court, which was effectively a verbal summons issued by a court official, and pledges might be appointed to act as surety for a reluctant defendant. An individual who still did not appear without a good essoin would then be 'distrained' to appear, which permitted the seizure and confiscation of goods or chattels until attendance. In some cases, orders were given to seize a recalcitrant tenant bodily to guarantee attendance at the next court, and in others pledges were fined or replaced for their ineffectiveness.[18] On occasions, the court might formally grant a delay in proceedings to both parties, known as a 'love day', in the hope that they would reach an informal settlement. Cases could therefore be delayed for some weeks or months, but the courts possessed a number of levers through which to compel attendance and guarantee some enforcement of its decisions: cases were probably concluded more quickly in manorial courts than many royal courts.

Cases were resolved in a number of ways, but the presiding lord or steward did not act as judge. Although the steward was an influential figure, judgements were the responsibility of 'suitors', i.e. those people who were required to attend the court. In principle those at court were required to provide a collective judgement, which explains why court rolls regularly contain references to pronouncements made by 'the whole homage' or in 'full court'. This was self-evidently a cumbersome process if followed rigidly or taken literally, and, in practice, cases were resolved in one of four ways.[19]

Disputes in the very earliest courts might be settled by old forms of trial, such as trial by fire or water, but these were scarcely appropriate

---

18 R. B. Pugh, ed., *Courts rolls of the Wiltshire manors of Adam de Stratton*, Wiltshire Records Society, 24 (1970), pp. 14–15, draws this firm distinction between the attachment and distraint, although in many manorial courts the distinction is not at all clear. A tenant who was physically seized by manorial officials must then have been incarcerated until the next court, presumably in an improvised gaol within the capital messuage. A few manors had gaols, see E. Miller, *The abbey and bishopric of Ely* (Cambridge, 1951), pp. 204–5.

19 Razi and Smith, *Medieval society*, pp. 50–4; Poos and Bonfield, *Select cases*, pp. lv–lviii.

for the types of petty cases that came before manor courts and the practice soon disappeared. Many thirteenth-century courts resolved cases by asking the defendant to 'wage law', known also as the 'common oath' or (especially in ecclesiastical courts) compurgation. Here the defendant would swear himself innocent of the accusation in front of the court, and then attempt to find a specified number (often either six or twelve) of other compurgators (which literally means 'oath-helpers') to swear to his good character and their belief in his word: if both plaintiff and defendant successfully waged law, then the defendant prevailed. Success or failure in this exercise would determine the outcome of the case, but clearly this method of resolving disputes did not depend upon the facts of a specific case and was essentially a test of good character. Given contemporary fears about the spiritual conse- quences of lying on oath, the assumption was that a person who swears innocence, and whose good character is sufficiently attested, is to be believed. Yet this was not a very satisfactory form of judgement: it was time-consuming, prone to delays, did not focus upon specific facts, and was already regarded as an inferior form of trial by the end of the thirteenth century.

The third, and in many ways most obvious, method of resolving actions was to agree an out-of-court settlement before a case moved to its denouement in full court. Manor court rolls commonly record the pay- ment of a few pence by one of the parties involved in a case 'for a licence to agree', an event which terminated the legal action and implied that an acceptable compromise had been struck. This proved a very common and popular form of settlement in Havering, where McIntosh suspects regular intervention and arbitration by other villagers in helping to settle cases without loss of esteem to either party. Other cases terminated without a formal agreement of this kind. A plaintiff might withdraw a case and formally acknowledge a false claim, or simply abandon a plea, in which case the court would impose an amercement and then perhaps award damages to the defendant. In other cases, a defendant might choose not to defend an initiated plea.[20]

The final way of deciding cases was through the use of one of two forms of jury, the presentment and the inquest jury. From the early fourteenth century the presentment jury became rapidly and increasingly important as the means of both presenting and deciding cases in the manor court. In essence, the court would appoint and swear in a jury

20 M. K. McIntosh, *Autonomy and community: the royal manor of Havering 1200–1550* (Cambridge, 1986), pp. 194–8; Schofield, 'Peasants and the manor court', pp. 14–15.

selected from the suitors, comprising anything from ten to twenty four men, to represent the whole court. Court rolls do not refer to them explicitly as presentment juries, but variously as 'the general inquiry made by …'; 'the inquisition by office under oath'; 'the homage'; and 'jurors who say on their oath'. By the fifteenth century the individual jurors are often named in the rolls.[21] Their collective responsibility as a presentment jury was simultaneously to report and judge a range of cases, so that each case they presented ('Adam Smith allowed his animals to trample the lord's corn') was taken as a true testimony, and the dissident fined. The guilt of the defendant was a basic presumption in this procedure, and, interestingly, it was exceptional for a defendant to challenge the verdict (literally 'true words') of the presentment jury.

The presentment jury had been used in thirteenth-century hundredal courts as an effective means of presenting offences against the community, and its subsequent spread to the manor court was intended to serve the same purpose.[22] Its benefits were soon apparent: it provided quick justice, based on a test of the facts rather than of good character, and spared manorial officials the time, effort and hassle of presenting 'public' offences. Consequently, the presentment jury became more common in manor courts, and its purview was gradually extended to include inter-peasant offences with 'public' implications (such as slander, crop destruction and animal trespass), seigneurial rights and manorial custom, although its extension into areas of manorial custom was often resisted by the peasantry.[23] By the end of the fourteenth century, presentment juries were a prominent feature of manor courts. The high volume of cases presented by them implies a considerable amount of preparatory work before the court sat, and one assumes they must have met beforehand to sift through the forthcoming business.

An inquest, or trial, jury was sworn in to accumulate evidence and pronounce judgement on a specific dispute, rather than to sift and then present a range of cases. The phraseology of court roll entries does not always allow the historian to distinguish immediately between an inquest and presentment jury, but with closer scrutiny the context of the case will reveal whether the jury has been formed specifically to

---

21 J. S. Beckerman, 'The articles of presentment of a court leet and court baron in English *c.* 1400', *Bulletin of the Institute of Historical Research*, 48 (1974), 230–4; J. S. Beckerman, 'Procedural innovation and institutional change in medieval English manorial courts', *Law and History Review*, 10 (1992), 197–252.

22 Razi and Smith, *Medieval society*, p. 52; F. J. C. Hearnshaw, *Leet jurisdiction in England* (Southampton, 1908), pp. 68–71.

23 Razi and Smith, *Medieval society*, p. 53.

investigate and pronounce upon a particular issue. The inquest jury is
certainly more common in thirteenth and early fourteenth century
manor courts, especially in disputes over titles to land: one of the
disputants would pay to have an inquest undertaken by a special jury to
decide upon the facts of the particular case.[24] This was an expensive but
effective form of justice, and in the thirteenth century was increasingly
used both to settle a wider range of personal plaints and to pronounce
judgement on more 'public' issues, such as manorial custom. Hence
between 1289 and 1304 around one third of all private suits at Hinderclay were concluded through judgements by inquest juries.[25] However,
the use of the inquest jury in the manor court had peaked by the early
fourteenth century. It was not uncommon thereafter, but the presentment jury was the dominant form in the fourteenth and fifteenth
centuries.

It is apparent from this discussion that 'proof' was often obtained
from the verbal testimony of jurors and compurgators, which implies
that potentially all suitors carried personal responsibility for 'justice'
and good order and that the details of many cases were public knowledge. The growth of written records and precedents during the
thirteenth century offered another form of proof, although manorial
courts did not routinely refer to them in order to resolve disputes.
However, from the early fourteenth century the practice of appealing
to manorial documents increased significantly, especially in disputes
over property. From this time the margins of court rolls are often
marked by a cross, a pointing finger, or special 'tags' sewn onto the
membrane, which served to remind the clerk or steward to pursue
certain cases or draw attention to important precedents, and the courts
themselves sometimes record a small fee paid by a suitor to 'search
the rolls', which implies that copies could be made accessible to all. Yet
the rolls were too voluminous to make searches easy, and consequently
some lords, such as St Albans and Chertsey abbeys, created abstracts of
important cases, precedents and land transfers in separate books.[26]

---

24 Razi and Smith, *Medieval society*, p. 51. The composition of the inquest jury in
   some land disputes was agreed by the two parties, Poos and Bonfield, *Select cases*,
   pp. 132–3.

25 Schofield, 'Peasants and the manor court', p. 13.

26 Poos and Bonfield, *Select cases*, pp. xxiii, lvi, lxvii; Toms, *Chertsey abbey*; A. E. Levett,
   'The courts and court rolls of St Albans abbey', *Transactions of the Royal Historical
   Society*, 4th series, 7 (1924), 52–76. Some of the marks and tags were inserted at a
   later date, sometimes centuries later, as users developed an interest in particular
   customs or land transactions.

The rise of first the inquest jury, and then in the fourteenth and fifteenth centuries the presentment jury, carried significant implications for the operation of the manor court, the business it conducted, and the quality of its justice. As juries became the preferred method of presenting and deciding cases, the power of the jurors who sat on them obviously increased while the power of the general body of suitors declined. Most presentment jurors were unfree tenants of the manor, because freemen could not be compelled to attend court regularly. The socio-economic background of these jurors, and the regularity with which they served, were clearly important influences on how the manor – and by extension local society – was regulated. Presentment juries unquestionably enjoyed the power to decide which cases and offenders came to court, and which might be referred to other courts, and so wielded real influence over the type and quality of justice that dissidents received. Equally, the juries had to be subject to certain checks and balances by the court to limit their power, and to promote disinterest in their presentments and veracity in their judgements. A good steward would keep a sensitive ear to the manorial grapevine, and court rolls occasionally record fines imposed on a jury for concealing certain cases, presenting information inaccurately, or not carrying cases through to their conclusion. Exceptionally, a steward might disband a jury if he doubted its verdict, or fine suitors for illicit conversations with jurors who were already under oath.[27]

Once a case had been decided, the court fixed a fee or punishment. A guilty individual was said to be in the mercy of the lord (*in misericordia*), and 'amerced' a sum of money determined by the steward and the affeerers. The size of the amercement reflected the nature of the offence, its severity, the custom of the manor on such matters, and the personal circumstances of the offender. Physical punishments were exceptional in manor courts, but were not unknown in leet courts (see below). Manor courts also levied 'fines' (essentially a fee) on those occasions when peasants required seigneurial permission to do something. Such occasions were prescribed by custom: for example, when entering a landholding (an 'entry fine' for unfree tenants, or a 'relief'(*gersuma*) for free tenants); raising a sheepfold on arable land; leaving the manor as a villein (chevage); and so on.[28] Amercements were normally small, amounting to a few pence, in contrast to fines and one-off capital payments (such as entry fines and merchets) which might run to a few

27 Page, *Crowland abbey*, p. 42.
28 Toms, *Chertsey abbey*, p. xii.

shillings. It is important to recognise that in medieval usage the word 'fine' meant a fee, or a licence, and did not carry its modern association with guilt and punishment; strictly speaking, fines and amercements were very different things in the medieval court. Occasionally an amercement or fine was charged but immediately waived by the steward, perhaps because of the poverty of the peasant or for tactical reasons. For example, good sense discouraged court officials from pursuing powerful manorial neighbours who had been amerced for a transgression, and so courts sometimes declined to enforce payments due from other lords. Similarly, a lord might explicitly pardon an amercement on grounds of charity, and courts commonly acknowledged the personal circumstances of tenants. However, if the offender was something of a recidivist, or if the offence was a source of general concern, the court would charge an amercement and also impose a greater financial penalty against any repetition of the offence.

Manor courts provided lords with a variable, but worthwhile, source of income. The court of a small lay manor probably generated a pound or so each year, and on most manors produced a few pounds. Yet the court of the large manor of Gressenhall (Norfolk) yielded between £30 and £47 annually between 1285 and 1295, more than all the standard assize rents of the manor. Razi partly ascribes this exceptional yield to the efficiency of the Gressenhall court, which dealt swiftly and firmly with defendants who failed either to appear or to honour their obligations by seizing their animals and chattels and amercing their pledges. By providing quick and effective resolution of personal plaints, the Gressenhall court attracted much business from non-tenants and drew more appearances from its own lesser tenants. The overall contribution of court perquisites to total seigneurial income obviously varied, but, for example, remained steady at around 5 per cent of the bishop of Worcester's annual estate revenue.[29]

The majority of the features described above are generic to all manor court rolls, such is the degree of consistency and standardisation in their construction and form. However, within these broad parameters 'manor court rolls varied a great deal (from manor to manor, court session to court session, and individual case to individual case) in the extent to which they recorded the details of each case … the introduction

---

29 Razi, 'East Anglian case study', pp. 759–62; C. C. Dyer, *Lords and peasants in a changing society: the estates of the bishopric of Worcester 680–1500* (Cambridge, 1980), pp. 174–5.

of evidence, and the basis for resolution of contested cases'.[30] Like-wise, the terminology used to describe curial procedures, and the forms of expression deployed in legal actions, varied considerably, so that it would be unwise to read too much into the use of different phrases and terms to describe similar activities: the differences may convey procedural nuances or may not. This variety in expressing and handling the basic types of curial business is evident in the examples given below [**36** to **40**], and owes much to the habits or preferences of the countless stewards and clerks who ran and recorded the manor court.

The leet court

The discussion so far has concentrated exclusively upon the ordinary manor court, which every manorial lord had the right to hold and which in later periods is sometimes termed the court baron. Some manors also held a leet court, or, to give it its proper name, a view of frankpledge (*visus francplegii*), which followed many of the same procedures as the manor court and was attended by many of the same people, but was a distinct and discrete jurisdiction.[31] The leet was held once, and at most twice, a year; its core business was significantly different from the court baron; and not all manorial lords possessed the right to hold a leet court, so that the leet could cover more than one manor. In fact the leet was not originally a jurisdiction associated with the manor, for it was essentially concerned with regulating the vill and the right to hold it was a privilege granted by the Crown. The court baron, to put it crudely, was the lowest court of seigneurial (i.e. feudal) jurisdiction based on the manor, while the leet was the lowest court of royal jurisdiction based on the vill.[32] Inevitably, such a tidy theoretical distinction was seldom apparent on the ground, because the administration of leets by manorial authorities tended to erode the differences between the two courts.

The leet court is best understood by sketching its origins in the organ-isation of local government and justice by the Crown. By the late Anglo-Saxon period the local enforcement of law and order was essentially conducted through a system variously called the 'frankpledge' or 'tithing'

---

30 Poos and Bonfield, *Select cases*, pp. xvii, xxxix.

31 Pollock and Maitland, *History of English law*, pp. 560–71.

32 Hearnshaw, *Leet jurisdiction*, pp. 77–8.

system, which itself belonged to an administrative structure based on the county, hundred (or wapentake), and vill. The vill was responsible locally for organising a range of fiscal, military and policing duties, and all adult males from the lower ranks of local society were held responsible for each other's behaviour. This was effectively 'a body of collective guarantors for the conduct of each member' who were required to report all misdeeds and produce the miscreants for justice.[33] All males over the age of twelve years and resident in the vill for more than a year and a day were required to be part of this system, with the exception of the clergy, wealthier freemen, and upper ranks of society, whose status was deemed sufficient surety for their behaviour. Women, servants and minors were exempt because they were assumed to be the responsibility of their head of household who was answerable for their behaviour.

In many parts of England, the vill discharged these civil responsibilities through the frankpledge system. Each vill was regarded as one frank-pledge unit, and in eastern, midland and southern England the frankpledge was often divided into several subgroups, known variously as tithings (*decenna*) or 'dozens', to make its administration more manageable: the frankpledge at Kempsey (Worcestershire) comprised ten separate tithings, each based on the ten major settlements within the vill.[34] As the etymology of these words suggests, each tithing theoretically comprised ten, and each 'dozen', twelve men, although in practice arrangements could be rather different. For example, in 1291 the vill of Messing (Essex) comprised five tithings of 16, 13, 14, 16, and 9 men. However, the use of subgroups within the frankpledge was unknown in parts of south-west England, where all eligible males were simply grouped in a single unit.[35] Similarly, in other parts of the country the use of separate tithings diminished with demographic decline in the late fourteenth and fifteenth centuries. Clearly, there were local variations in the internal organisation of the frankpledge.

It is worth reasserting explicitly that many vills in England, and espe-cially those in eastern, southern and midland areas, used the device of the frankpledge to discharge their civil obligations, and that such vills held leet courts. However, the frankpledge system was not used in

33 H. M. Cam, *The Hundred and the Hundred Rolls* (1930), p. 124. D. A. Crowley, 'The later history of frankpledge', *Bulletin of the Institute of Historical Research*, 48 (1975), 1–15.

34 Dyer, *Lords and peasants*, p. 356.

35 W. A. Morris, *The Frankpledge System* (1910), p. 90.

Herefordshire, Shropshire, Cheshire, Lancashire, Yorkshire and the far north, and consequently leet courts as such were not held in these areas. Instead, local civil administration on behalf of the Crown was vested in powerful landlords, who either held special courts for a number of vills or used their own courts for this purpose (see below, p. 182): for example, in County Durham the prior and bishop of Durham were empowered to deal with a range of petty criminal matters in their own manorial courts.[36]

Each frankpledge had a number of responsibilities. It was responsible for ensuring that its members attended royal courts as and when required: to offer testimonies at commissions and inquisitions; to provide witnesses on questions of fact; to collect information about, and to hand over to royal officials, the abandoned belongings of fugitives from justice (which were legally forfeit to the Crown); to respond to the hue and cry, raised when a suspected crime had been committed, and so pursue and capture suspects; and to send representatives (provide 'suit') to the hundred court.[37] In particular, the frankpledge was expected to present to the hundred court all major public nuisances and criminal misdeeds occurring within its bounds, such as felony, homicide, assault, poaching, breach of the peace, trading offences, counterfeiting, and obstruction of the King's highway [**43**]. Minor offences could be handled locally, but serious offences would be passed upwards to the appropriate judicial authority for further action.[38] The hundred courts, and each frankpledge unit within the hundred, were also responsible for processing and implementing attachments and distraints passed down from higher royal courts and justices, and ensuring attendance of jurors and witnesses where necessary and the delivery of fugitives.[39]

Thus the frankpledge unit was closely integrated through the hundred court into the wider structures of centralised royal justice. The hundred court itself was responsible to the county sheriff for ensuring that each of its constituent vills was properly administered, and twice yearly – at what was known as 'the sheriff's tourn' – was required to perform the 'view of frankpledge', in which each frankpledge was inspected and required to swear that all eligible males were bound into the

---

36 Morris, *Frankpledge*, pp. 44–5; Pollock and Maitland, *History of English law*, p. 569; R. A. Lomas, *North-east England in the Middle Ages* (Edinburgh, 1992), pp. 82–4.

37 Morris, *Frankpledge*, pp. 90–9; Cam, *Hundred*, p. 126.

38 Pollock and Maitland, *History of English law*, p. 564; Hearnshaw, *Leet jurisdiction*, pp. 43–6.

39 See Cam, *Hundred*, pp. 180–4, for hundred courts.

system.[40] At one of these annual views, each frankpledge unit had to pay a sum of money for the privilege of its inspection, an arrangement originally designed to offset the sheriff's operating expenses.[41] However, this procedure gradually became privatised in many vills, especially between the 1160s and 1260s, so that the right to undertake the view of frankpledge in a given vill became vested in one manorial lord. By the end of the thirteenth century the vast majority of views had been privatised, although in many cases lords appear simply to have assumed these rights, an arrangement which was acceptable to the Crown as long as the view was conducted properly and its obligations to the hundred court were still fulfilled.[42] The privatised view conducted its business through the leet court, and its existence created a potential conflict of interest with the hundred courts, many of which continued to be administered directly on behalf of the Crown, because it appears that the leets themselves decided what constituted a 'minor', and what a 'major', offence. The distinction was blurred between what constituted a 'minor' offence, to be handled by the leet, and what exactly was sufficiently serious to warrant forwarding to the hundred court or royal justices for action. An essential or definitive distinction between the jurisdictions of the hundred court and the leet was not even evident to contemporary lawyers.[43]

The benefits to a manorial lord in acquiring the annual, or twice annual, view of frankpledge in the vill were financial as well as jurisdictional. The annual payment by the frankpledge to the sheriff was now the prerogative of the lord, and could generate anything from a few shillings to a few pounds. For administrative convenience it was often a fixed sum [44], known as the 'common fine', but in a few places it continued to be levied at the rate of a penny or halfpenny for every male in the frankpledge, called 'tithingpenny' payments.[44] Furthermore, lords acquired the right to administer all of the minor misdeeds associated with the process and to profit from the amercements it generated, because the view of frankpledge had traditionally been the

40 Cam, *Hundred*, pp. 186–7; Page, *Crowland abbey*, p. 32.

41 Morris, *Frankpledge*, p. 102.

42 Morris, *Frankpledge*, pp. 133–40. Hearnshaw, *Leet jurisdiction*, pp. 148–55, suggests ways in which historians can discover who held the view in each vill, and highlights the Hundred Rolls of the 1270s and the *Quo Warranto* proceedings of the 1280s as useful sources.

43 Hearnshaw, *Leet jurisdiction*, pp. 65–6.

44 L. Poos, 'The rural population of Essex in the later Middle Ages', *Economic History Review*, 38 (1985), 515–20.

occasion for presenting criminal and nuisance offences to the hundred court.[45] In particular, after the 1260s the administration of the assize of bread and ale was added to the issues to be considered at the view, thus permitting lords to regulate the price, quality and measures used by local bakers and brewers and to punish dissidents: in practice, lords used this right to charge commercial retailers a small licence fee to operate.[46] Hence the annual, or biannual, meetings of the privatised frankpledge became a court held by a manorial lord, usually at Easter and/or Michaelmas, which dealt with an interesting range of petty activities and minor misdeeds: local brawls, retail infringements, minor obstructions of ditches, encroachments on highways, and so on. By the end of the thirteenth century contemporaries were in the habit of calling this court 'the leet', and its emergence was paralleled by the decline of the hundred court.[47]

The local arrangements for dealing with petty misdeeds were varied in those areas of northern England and the Marches where the frankpledge system did not exist. In places where the administration of the hundred/wapentake had been franchised into the hands of a private lord, such as County Durham, responsibility – and profits – lay with the lord. In the early fourteenth century the manor of Wakefield was held by the powerful Warennes, earls of Surrey, who possessed the right to deal with local criminal jurisdiction there, including the execution of felons. Certain townships within the manor (known as graveships) were expected to report all criminal activity to special 'tourns' held immediately after the manorial court. Hence the manor court rolls of Wakefield contain supplementary information about a wider range of criminal activity than that ordinarily contained within leet courts, especially petty burglaries and larcenies [46].[48]

Attendance at the leet was compulsory for all eligible males within the vill, and, in many respects, the court's format closely resembled that of the manor. A presentment jury normally presented cases,

45 Pollock and Maitland, *History of English law*, pp. 558–9; Page, *Crowland abbey*, pp. 33–4.

46 Pollock and Maitland, *History of English law*, pp. 581–2. For an excellent study of brewing which draws upon this type of material, see J. M. Bennett, *Ale, beer and brewsters in England 1300–1600* (Oxford, 1996).

47 Morris, *Frankpledge*, p. 132.

48 J. Lister, ed., *Court rolls of the manor of Wakefield, vol. iv, 1315–1317*, Yorkshire Archaeological Society, 78 (1930), pp. xi–xiii; K. Emsley and C. M. Fraser, *The courts of the county Palatine of Durham from earliest times to 1971* (Durham, 1984), pp. 7–8.

although the leet jury was comprised of 'capital pledges'. The latter were elected as chief representatives at the view of frankpledge, originally one for each tithing, and by the thirteenth century were required to represent the frankpledge at the monthly meetings of the hundred court. The practice in many fourteenth-century leets was to elect at least twelve capital pledges for the purpose of presentments, and in 1405 this became a statutory requirement. In many respects the capital pledges were acting as *de facto* constables by *c.* 1300, and this principle was extended in later leets when a constable for the vill was elected annually with specific responsibilities for keeping the peace and good order.[49] The office of constable becomes increasingly common from the fourteenth century, and, as a standing officer, was more effective in arresting felons, stopping fights and so on, than the attempts of sundry tithingmen who may or may not have responded promptly to the raising of the hue and cry.[50]

Most punishments in the leet took the form of petty financial amercements, although some offences were punished by committal to the stocks, pillory or tumbrell. Unfortunately such occasions are not always explicitly recorded in the rolls, but these instruments were regarded in law as the proper instruments of leet jurisdiction, and theoretically a lord who failed to provide and maintain them faced seizure of his right to view frankpledge.[51]

The frankpledge unit continued to send representatives to the hundred court and to report serious offences to, and receive summonses and instructions from, royal courts and commissions, but none of this activity was recorded in the leet court rolls which concentrated solely on the jurisdictional interests of the lord.[52] Like the records of the manor court, those of the leet simply recorded its decisions rather than the background to each case or detailed evidence. The business of the leet and the manor courts was theoretically separate, and in the thirteenth and fourteenth centuries was normally recorded separately too (although they were often enrolled together, and sometimes the record of the leet followed on from that of the manor court on the same roll of vellum). However, local practice could vary. Some business associated with the leet, such as the assize of bread and ale, could find its way into the manor court, and some manors maintained no rigid

49 Hearnshaw, *Leet jurisdiction*, p. 91; Morris, *Frankpledge*, pp. 102–6.

50 McIntosh, *Autonomy and community*, p. 204.

51 Morris, *Frankpledge*, p. 146; Pollock and Maitland, *History of English law*, p. 582.

52 Morris, *Frankpledge*, p. 100.

distinction between the types of offences which belonged to one court or the other.[53] By the fifteenth century it was increasingly common for both leet and manor courts to be amalgamated into one *magna curia*, a move which partly reflects the decline of the frankpledge system. The disappearance of separate tithings within some frankpledge units became commonplace in the fifteenth century, and difficulties finding capital pledges in some Essex vills forced the adoption of a new system in which landholders were appointed in rotation. By 1400 the system at Birdbrook (Essex) was maintained largely by the strenuous efforts of the lord in the face of indifference among the residents.[54]

Manor and leet courts after *c.* 1400

The decline of the frankpledge system, and by extension the declining powers of the leet court, is mirrored by a fall in the business conducted in manor courts during the fifteenth century. Continued demographic and economic decline after the 1370s certainly reduced the number of suitors, which in turn reduced the volume of personal plaints. For example, the numbers of inter-peasant suits peaked at the turn of the thirteenth and fourteenth centuries in courts held on the bishop of Worcester's estate, and dropped dramatically during the fifteenth century until they disappeared completely on some manors.[55] Furthermore, the withering of serfdom and the transformation of villein tenure into contractual tenures reduced the range and volume of seigneurial business conducted in manor courts, which in turn may have resulted in more lax administration and a greater slippage of cases. Most trappings of serfdom had disappeared by the end of the fourteenth century on some estates, but in many places they remained until the first half of the fifteenth century. The court of Wilburton (Cambridgeshire) remained highly active, including many presentments relating to labour services and serfdom, until the demesne was leased in the 1420s when seigneurial interest in the court declined rapidly.[56] Collective servile obligations disappeared from many courts in the early fifteenth century, such as labour services, mill-suit, recognition and tallage, although some

---

53 Page, *Crowland abbey*, 36–7.

54 Crowley, 'Later history of frankpledge', pp. 1–15; P. R. Schofield, 'The late medieval view of frankpledge and the tithing system: an Essex case study', in Razi and Smith, *Medieval society*, p. 439.

55 Dyer, *Lords and peasants*, p. 266–7.

56 Razi and Smith, *Medieval society*, p. 7.

individual elements – mainly heriot, merchet and chevage – proved resilient for much longer, mainly because collective obligations were much easier for the peasantry to resist than individual ones.

The timing, extent and causes of the declining business of courts are varied, but their effects are apparent in falling revenues. In the 1460s and 1470s annual income from the manor courts of Standon (Hertford-shire) was less than half the average received in the fourteenth century. In the 1420s curial income on the bishop of Worcester's estate was broadly similar to that received in the 1290s, but had halved by the middle of the fifteenth century and scarcely recovered thereafter.[57] Other factors contributed to the general decline in court income during the fifteenth century. The general level of fines and amercements fell, and lords were increasingly inclined to waive capital payments as land values dropped and tenants became harder to find.[58] Offenders became bolder in their refusals to pay their dues, and officials regu-larly complained that some court payments were difficult to collect, such as the amercement owed in 1490 by Alice Stapleton of Walberswick (Suffolk) for keeping a brothel.[59] On some fifteenth-century manors, lords agreed that half the revenues levied from certain communal trangressions should be diverted to the parish church, an initiative which reflected trends in lay piety and perhaps the difficulties faced by lords in collecting payments for their own purposes.[60]

As the power and importance of the court declined in the fifteenth century, so the enforcement of its decisions became more problematic. Repeated requests to implement earlier orders become more common, and distraints and bodily seizures were not effectively pursued. The lord's ultimate sanction against a recalcitrant suitor was to seize his landholding, but the shortage of tenants and abundance of land dimin-ished both the threat of this sanction and the seigneurial willingness to exercise it. In addition, the system of personal pledging, which had helped to enforce curial decisions in the thirteenth and fourteenth centuries, declined from the late fourteenth century, as revealed by the amercements levied on ineffective pledges and the repeated orders

57 M. Bailey, 'A tale of two towns: Buntingford and Standon in the later Middle Ages', *Journal of Medieval History*, 19 (1993), 368; Dyer, *Lords and peasants*, pp. 174–5.

58 Harvey, *Westminster abbey and its estate in the Middle Ages* (Oxford, 1977), pp. 271–3.

59 C. Richmond, *John Hopton: a fifteenth-century Suffolk gentleman* (Cambridge, 1981), p. 47.

60 W. O. Ault, 'Manor court and parish church in fifteenth-century England', *Speculum*, 42 (1967), 53–67.

that the court 'appoint better'. Hence by the 1460s the system of personal pledging had virtually died out on the bishop of Worcester's estates.[61] Some courts may have tried to bolster their declining powers of enforcement in the fifteenth century by increasing the use of the stocks and tumbrell as punishments.[62]

All of these developments mean that fifteenth-century courts are shorter, less frequent and less informative than those from the fourteenth century, but they can still contain valuable information about land transactions (especially leasehold, customary and copyhold), village by-laws, agricultural arrangements, peasant migration, and economic activity. Indeed, the use of the by-law increased in many courts during the fifteenth century in an attempt to benchmark standards of behaviour and counter identified threats to local orderliness, at a time when other methods of enforcing the court's will were losing their effectiveness.[63]

By-laws are easily identifed by their distinctive preambles and the stipulation of a financial penalty for any subsequent transgression: for example, 'it is ordained by all the inhabitants of the vill that …', or 'it is ordered by common consent that … under penalty of 3s. 4d.'. By-laws had been commonly used in thirteenth- and fourteenth-century courts to regulate communal farming arrangements, particularly the harvest, and to maintain footpaths and rights of way: for example, thirteen were passed in a July court in 1290 at Newton Longville (Buckinghamshire), where wardens were appointed to enforce them.[64] However, as the general usage of by-laws increased in the fifteenth century, so their application was extended to a range of public order issues, and in particular scolding (i.e. quarrelsome behaviour or backbiting), bad governance (i.e. unruly houses, especially ale-houses), immigration and eavesdropping.[65] By-laws were effectively local statutes, established with little or no supervision from external bodies or even the lord, which were directed towards those problems and disruptions that were deemed to threaten the smooth operation of local society.[66]

---

61 Dyer, *Lords and peasants*, pp. 267–8.

62 McIntosh, *Autonomy and community*, p. 250.

63 Dyer, *Lords and peasants*, pp. 329, 368; M. K. McIntosh, *Controlling misbehaviour in England, 1370–1600* (Cambridge, 1998), pp. 38–9.

64 Ault, *Open fields*, pp. 82–3.

65 McIntosh, *Controlling misbehaviour*, pp. 60–1. See D. Hall, *The open fields of Northamptonshire* (Northampton, 1995), pp. 29–33, for a discussion of by-laws regulating farming after *c.* 1500.

66 McIntosh, *Controlling misbehaviour*, p. 39.

They were theoretically drawn up by the common consent of the suitors, although small committees were formed on the Durham priory estates to draft by-laws which were then ratified at the main halmote meetings.[67] By the fifteenth century many by-laws were drafted by the presentment jurors, who were now drawn primarily from the principal landholding tenants of the manor. In other words, the by-law was increasingly deployed by the emerging village elite to promote their notions of harmony and to exercise local social control.

Records of manor courts remain plentiful after 1500, but the range and volume of cases, and the amount of detail relating to them, continue to decline gradually. Of course, the pace and extent of the decline depended upon the disposition and power of both the lord and the court, but even an active and efficient court with wide-ranging powers such as Havering (Essex) exhibits a significant diminution in business. Here the number of suitors fell from an average of 350 per annum in the 1460s to 120 per annum in the 1580s, and the volume of private and public suits also fell appreciably. Furthermore, the Havering presentment jury, which in the fifteenth century was still drawn from a relatively large number, and wide socio-economic range, of suitors, by the late sixteenth century had become dominated by fewer jurors drawn from the wealthy elite.[68] Exceptionally, the business of a court could dwindle to the point that it ceased to be held, as at Shrewton (Wiltshire) by the late sixteenth century.[69]

From the seventeenth century the range of cases recorded in courts baron tends to narrow quickly, until the business is largely confined to recording land transactions, mainly leaseholds and copyholds.[70] They therefore remain a valuable source for the local history of land tenures and landholding patterns until the eighteenth and early nineteenth centuries, but offer little else to the historian. Thereafter, the gradual but inexorable decline of copyhold tenure, and the growing preference among estate officials for processing land transfers through solicitors, further diminished the importance of the manor court as a form of jurisdiction and an historical source. In 1922 copyhold was abolished by the Property Act, which in 1936 was extended to any

---

67 Ault, *Open fields*, p. 59.

68 McIntosh, *Autonomy and community*, pp. 199, 249; M. K. McIntosh, *A community transformed: the manor and liberty of Havering 1500–1620* (Cambridge, 1991), pp. 298–313.

69 Ault, *Open fields*, p. 67.

70 S. and B. Webb, *English local government: the manor and the borough, part 1* (1908), pp. 116–8, 124–5.

surviving manorial customs or incidents. A few manor courts survived into the twentieth century, such as Cockfield (Suffolk) which continued to regulate small pieces of common land until the late 1940s. Potentially, the leet remains the more interesting and varied court after 1500. In the early modern period many of the civil and criminal cases handled by the medieval leet gradually shifted either to church courts or the petty and quarter sessions of the Justices of the Peace (JPs), a process which was particularly apparent in parts of midland and south-east England. However, some leets continued to record minor nuisance, trade and inter-personal offences, and minor behavioural misdemeanours, especially in the south, south-west and the north of England, and so remained an important medium for dealing with a variety of local offences. Leets almost everywhere continued to record some enclosures, encroachments, boundary destruction, neglect of buildings and ditches, and the sub-division of tenements. Indeed, historians of the sixteenth and seventeenth centuries have argued that leet courts were closer to the local community than quarter sessions (run by JPs) or church courts, and hence were actively exploited by the village elites who dominated the juries to regulate social behaviour in their locality and to exert pressure on miscreants. McIntosh detects a bust of energy in leets during the 1520s and 1530s, and a continued interest in public order issues throughout the sixteenth century.[71]

Thus the mechanism of the leet was used as a means of setting a social agenda for the locality, and issuing low-key warnings to selected individuals, without regular recourse to higher courts. Indeed, it provided village elites with a relatively autonomous means of exercising control within their own communities at a time when such measures were regarded as essential: 'problems with social harmony, good order and poverty were obviously still acute in the eyes of many local jurors at the end of Elizabeth I's reign, and in many sections of the country they continued to use their local courts to address those issues'.[72] Thereafter, the leet declined as local elites increasingly used other means, and institutions, to address their concerns, such as parochial structures, quarter sessions and church courts.[73] The leet was increasingly regarded as a relatively inflexible, negative and punitive institu-

---

71 McIntosh, *Controlling misbehaviour*, p. 43.
72 McIntosh, *Controlling misbehaviour*, p. 45.
73 Hearnshaw, *Leet jurisdiction*, pp. 242–4.

tion for imposing order, and lacking the power to bind people over or properly enforce its decisions.[74]

Leet courts continued to assume a greater importance in thriving market towns which lacked incorporated status and consequently the power to regulate trading activities as a corporate body.[75] At Braintree (Essex) the leet was active until the early nineteenth century in appointing constables and aletasters, and regulating the fish, flesh and leather trades in the market. At both unincorporated Birmingham (Warwickshire) and Manchester (Lancashire) the manorial lord had effectively relinquished control of the leet to prominent tenants, who used the court to regulate public trading, nuisance and order issues until their formal incorporation following the 1835 Act.[76] The leet courts of early nineteenth-century Manchester are lengthy and informative, and provide a fascinating account of the attempts to administer a rapidly industrialising city through an archaic medieval institution. At a stroke the Municipal Incorporation Act of 1835 displaced the remaining active, but creaking, leets.

Historical uses of court rolls

The great strengths of medieval manor court rolls will be apparent from the discussion so far: their survival in large quantities, the eclectic range of their business, and the remarkable insights they provide into the activities of the lower orders of society. Yet their usefulness as an historical source is constrained by weaknesses and inadequacies. A major weakness is that manor courts only focus upon specific aspects of medieval life, and certain players upon its stage. Inevitably, they are only concerned with the manor, which is not necessarily conterminous with the village or parish, and consequently certain activities and people in local society are not recorded in the rolls. Furthermore, they do not even focus upon all manorial activities, for their subject matter is largely confined to the administrative priorities and jurisdictional rights of the lords who held them, and to those private actions between peasants which happened to find their way into this court. And – like any court – they tend to record exceptional events and dysfunctional

74 M. K. McIntosh, 'Social change and Tudor manorial leets', in J. A. Guy and H. G. Beale, eds, *The law and social change* (1984), pp. 77–8, 85.

75 For example, F. J. C. Hearnshaw, ed., *Court leet records 1550–1624*, 2 vols (Southampton, 1905 and 1907).

76 S. and B. Webb, *Government*, pp. 72–4, 157–9.

behaviour rather than workaday life. Court rolls also tend to record the decisions reached rather than the processes which shaped, and the information which informed, those decisions. The most informative rolls for the historian are those where the clerk or steward chose to include some background details to a case systematically.

Clearly, the omissions from manorial courts are not inconsiderable, and many issues and social groups are either under-represented or absent entirely. Most obviously, women are under-represented and free tenants, minors, and other non-tenants feature occasionally, if at all. The lower ranks of local society – cottagers, smallholders, sub-tenants and the landless – seldom appear in court rolls, and almost a quarter of all smallholders never appear in the rolls of even a well-run court such as Gressenhall.[77] Concerns about the proportion of local people not recorded in court rolls, allied with difficulties in positively identifying individuals who existed under a number of aliases, has fuelled a lively debate on the potential for reconstructing kinship and local populations from manor courts.[78]

Another major weakness is that manor courts do not even record the business which they did transact with unerring consistency over time. The closeness of fit between what was happening and what was recorded varied according to the administrative efficiency of the court, the disposition of lord and peasants, and the prevailing concerns and *mores* of presentment juries. Does a sudden increase in the volume of business transacted reflect a genuine rise in activity or merely a tighter management of the court? The sudden surge of activity which invariably accompanied the accession of a new lord to the manor, or the appointment of a new steward, is a powerful reminder of fluctuations in managerial rigour and their influence upon the business of the court [40].[79] Does a growth in the number of debt cases over a given period of time reflect greater economic distress and indebtedness, or merely a change in court procedures relating to debt? Similarly, does a wave of presentments against, for example, the playing of games reflect a genuine growth of recreational pursuits or simply a decision to clamp down on such activity by a jury pursing a particular social

---

77 Razi, 'East Anglian case study', p. 759. See also Razi's seminal *Life, marriage and death in a medieval parish: economy, society and demography in Halesowen, 1280–1400* (Cambridge, 1980) for an exploration of the potential of court rolls for the detailed reconstruction of local society; and the work of the 'Toronto school' cited in the select bibliography, p. 252.

78 See the debate in Razi and Smith, *Medieval society*, pp. 298–368.

79 See, for example, Dyer, *Lords and peasants*, pp. 277–9.

agenda? One also senses that the details contained in fifteenth-century courts are increasingly a reflection of what certain tenants, not lords, wished to have recorded, not least because presentment juries were becoming more powerful and dominated by a social elite within the village (see p. 187). Certainly, the waning of serfdom, the growing assertiveness of the peasantry, and the fall in tenant numbers meant that fifteenth-century courts were invariably less informative, and more partial, in the activities they recorded than courts from the early fourteenth century. Absenteeism by suitors increased, while the frank-pledge system and the device of using personal pledges declined, all of which reduced the reporting and enforcement capability of the court.

Utilising the information contained in manor courts requires sensitivity to their weaknesses as a source, an awareness which extends to an understanding of the circumstances under which lords and peasants chose to use the manor court, why they chose this medium in prefer-ence to others, and the quality of justice they expected to receive there. A lively debate has recently emanated from this very issue between those historians who believe that medieval manor courts often provided flexible justice based on local social expectations and norms, and those who argue that their judgements were less flexible and based on substantive legal principles.[80] As Paul Hyams has written, 'each [court] constituted in some sense its own localised legal system catering for its own clients and customers. Yet no court stood alone; in varying degrees each was linked to others in its lordship or area, even within the same village. To use court rolls, one should understand first the system of law they recorded, and then the way the mini-system fitted into some larger, much larger, legal and cultural context'.[81]

Notwithstanding these limitations, medieval manor court rolls have sustained research into an extraordinary range of subjects, at a level of detail which is the envy of historians of other periods and places. The sheer quantity of extant court rolls in record offices and other repositories offers vast, but still largely unexploited, opportunities for research on medieval England. The majority of rolls survive from the fourteenth and fifteenth centuries, and are biased towards the estates of the greater, especially ecclesiastical, landlords. However, in contrast

80 See the discussion in L. Bonfield, 'What did English villagers mean by "customary law"?', in Razi and Smith, *Medieval society*, pp. 103–16, and Schofield, 'Peasants and the manor court', pp. 6–9; Poos and Bonfield, *Select cases*, pp. xxvi–xxxv.

81 P. R. Hyams, 'What did Edwardian villagers understand by law?', in Razi and Smith, *Medieval society*, pp. 69–70.

to manorial accounts, the geographical spread of survivals is more even, and greater numbers survive from the estates of lesser lords. The explanation for this is presumably that all landlords placed a higher premium on the preservation of court rolls, because they contained important information about manorial custom, landholdings and seigneurial jurisdiction.

The most revealing historical studies have drawn upon relatively complete series of courts surviving over a long period, relating to large manors that were virtually conterminous with the vill. Inevitably, such manors and documentary survivals are often associated with conservative lordship, but they do offer the best chances of reconstructing the activities of a representative cross-section of local society. The finest series of extant court rolls from such manors are catalogued as an appendix to Razi and Smith's *Medieval society.*

It is scarcely possible to do justice here to the range of subjects that have been explored through medieval court rolls, and, in any event, others have recently undertaken this exercise with distinction.[82] Major themes include the nature, evolution and dissolution of serfdom, and the changing – perhaps conflicting – relations between lord and peasant; the nature and operation of the 'village community'; local agricultural arrangements and field-systems, and the spread of enclosures in the open fields; land tenures, the land market and landholding structures in peasant society; the nature of kinship and family structures, and the links between families and village community; family reconstitution, population trends, and the causes of demographic change; peasant culture and material life; the leisure and recreational behaviour of peasants, and arrangements for welfare and charity; local socio-economic responses to crises such as famine or epidemic disease; commercial activities, such as petty craftwork and retailing, and the operation of local money markets; and the status and contribution of women to local society. This hardly exhausts the extent of historical research into court rolls, but conveys a good sense of the rich pickings to be gained from these documents which represent an extraordinary and exceptional resource.

82 Razi and Smith, *Medieval society,* pp. 2–33.

35   The manner of holding courts, 1342

A few tracts on how to hold a manor court survive from the thirteenth and
fourteenth centuries, and were compiled primarily for the stewards and clerks
who directed and recorded proceedings. They offered little advice on either
matters of procedure or the broad scope of curial business, concentrating
mainly on the regulation of villeinage by officials, but provide a good indication
of those issues which the lord regarded as central to the administration of the
manorial court.

F. W. Maitland and W. P. Baildon, eds, *The Court Baron*, Selden Society, 4
(1890), p. 102. Extract from manor court of Middleton (Essex), 1342. French.

[The steward shall enquire] whether the bailiff, reeve, hayward or
any other manorial officer performs badly in office, and in each case
how and in what.

Whether there be any vacant free or bond tenements, and what the
lord shall receive by their death by way of heriot or otherwise.

Whether any bondman be unable to hold the tenement which he holds,
and the reason.

Whether any bondman alienates his land or any part of it to any free
or other man without licence.

Whether any bondman has taken himself outside the domain [manor]
with his goods and family, and where to.

Whether any bondman's unmarried daughter has committed fornication and been convened in chapter, and what she has given the dean
for her correction.[83]

Whether any bondman or bondwoman has been charged in the chapter
regarding anything other than marriage or testament.

Whether any bondman's daughter has been married without licence,
and to whom, and what her father has given with her in the way of goods.

Whether any bondman has been ordained clerk without licence.

Whether any bondman has cut down oak or ash in his garden, unless
it be to repair the house, cart or plough, and how much he has taken.

---

83 This requirement is unusual, and likely to be found only on manors held by some
   monastic landlords. The manorial lord (in this case, the dean and chapter of St
   Paul's, London) requires any 'moral' offences committed by his peasants to be
   reported at the daily gathering of the canons (the 'chapter') where the business of
   the house is discussed. The dean is the head of the chapter.

36 Some early court rolls of Tooting and Ruislip, 1247–48

These court rolls represent some of the earliest records of the manor court to have survived in England. The vast majority of English court rolls record the curial activities of a single manor, but, unusually, the following extracts from a single roll document the business of a number of separate manorial courts held on the English estates of the abbey of Bec.[84] In these examples, the settling of disputes by compurgation and juries of inquiry is strongly evident. The volume of business conducted by the court is not very high, and the range of 'communal' offences is relatively narrow. However, the lord is already using the court as a medium for exercising control over the unfree peasantry.

F. W. Maitland, ed., *Select pleas in manorial and other seigneurial courts*, Selden Society, 2 (1888), pp. 12–15. Manor courts of the abbey of Bec, Tooting (Surrey) and Ruislip (Middlesex), 1247–48. Latin.

Tooting. Tuesday after the feast of St Dennis [15 October 1247].

The whole vill gives 2½ marks for the abbot's tallage.

William Jordan in mercy, 6d., for bad ploughing on the lord's land. John Shepherd in mercy, 6d., for encroaching beyond the boundary of his land, pledge Walter Reeve.

Lucy Rede in mercy, condoned, for her beasts caught in the lord's pasture when ward had been made, pledge Hame of Hageldon.

Elias of Streatham in mercy, 6d., for default of labour service at harvest.

Bartholomew Chaloner, who was at his law against Reginald Swain's son, has made default in his law. Therefore in mercy, 6 hens, and let him make satisfaction to Reginald for his damage and dishonour, 6s., pledges William Cobbler and William Spendlove.[85]

Ralph of Morville gives half a mark on the security of Jordan of Streatham and William Spendlove to have a jury to inquire whether he is the next heir to the land which William of Morville holds. And the 12 jurors come and say that he has no right in the said land, but that William Scot has greater right in the said land than anyone else. And the said William Scot gives one mark on the security of Hame of Hagelton, William of Morville, Reginald Swain and Richard Leaware that he may have seisin of the said land after the death of William of Morville in case he [Scot] shall survive him [Morville]. Afterwards

---

84 For the general background to the management of this estate, see M. Morgan, *The English lands of the abbey of Bec* (Oxford, 1946).

85 A good example of a failure to progress an initiated private plea by the plaintiff, with expensive consequences.

came the said William Scot and with the lord's agreement quitclaimed all the right that he had in the said land with its appurtenances to a certain William son of William of Morville, who gives 20s. to have seisin of the said land, and is put in seisin of it and swears fealty. Walter the serjeant is to receive the pledges.

Ruislip. Tuesday after the Purification of the Blessed Virgin [4 February 1248].

Robert Coke in mercy, 6d., for the lord's wood; pledge William Baldwin. John Brasdefer for the same, 6d.; pledges William Coke and Arthur Gardener.

Richard Maleville gives 2s. for licence to agree with William of Pinner in a plea of trepass; pledges Robert Maureward and William Field.

Robert King in mercy, 12d., for the lord's wood; pledges, Richard Maleville and Robert Maureward. Richard Brown in mercy, 12d., for the same; pledges, William Slipper and Gilbert Lamb. Ailwin Bithewood in mercy, 6d., for the same; pledges William Baldwin and William Cook.

Ragenilda of Bec gives 2s. for having married without licence; pledge, William of Pinner. The same Ragenilda demands against Roger Loft and Juliana his wife a certain messuage which belonged to Robert le Beck, and a jury of twelve lawful men is granted her in consideration of the said fine, and if she recovers seisin she will give in all 5s. And twelve jurors are elected, namely John of Hulle, William Maureward, Robert Hale, Walter But, Walter Sigar, William Brithwin, Richard Horseman, Richard Leofred, William John's son, Hugh Cross, Richard Ponfret and Rober Croyser, [added to the list] John Bisuthe and Gilbert Bisuthe, who are sworn. And they say that the said Ragenilda has the greater right, therefore let her have seisin.

William But in mercy, 6d., for his pigs causing damage to the lord; pledges Robert Maureward and Walter Reaper's son.

Alvena Leofred is at her law six-handed against Isabella of Hayes to prove that she did not take from her a certain knife on the Friday after last Midsummer's Day to damages and dishonour of 3s.; pledges for her law, William Blund and William Shepherd. Afterwards they have licence to agree with the court's consent, and Alvena pays 6d. on the security of the two pledges.[86]

---

86 The reference to 'six hands' signifies an initial intention to solve this case by waging law (see p. 173), but the parties then settled out of court.

Isabella Jonant demands a certain messuage with a croft which Arthur Gardener holds, and she gives 12d. to have the jury of the twelve said men, and if she recovers [seisin] she will give 2s.; pledges Robert Fountain and John Gery. And the twelve jurors aforenamed come and say that the said Isabella has the greater right.

Ruislip. Saturday after the Purification of the Blessed Virgin [same court as above, adjourned for four days].

Richard Guest gives 12d., and if he recovers [the land] will give 2s., to have a jury of twelve lawful men to decide whether he has the greater right to a certain headland at Eastcot which Ragenilda, widow of William Andrews, holds; pledges for the fine, John Brook and Richard of Pinner. And the said Ragenilda comes and says that she has no power to bring that land into judgement because she has no right in it save by reason of the wardship of the son and heir of her husband, who is under age. And Richard is not able to deny this, therefore let him wait until the heir reaches majority.

Agnes Street pays 12d. for licence to agree with Alice Street; pledges, Arthur Swineherd and Christian Leofred.

Walter Hulle pays 13s. 4d. for licence to dwell on the land of the prior of Harmondsworth so long as he shall live, and as a condition finds pledges namely William Slipper, John Bisuthe, Gilbert Bisuthe, Hugh Tree, William John's son and John Hulle, who undertake that the said Walter shall render all services and customs which he would do if he lived on the lord's land and that his heriot shall be secured to the lord in case he dies there.

William White pays 6s. 8d. to have seisin of the land which was that of Richard his father; pledges, Arthur Swineherd and Richard of Pinner.

37   Court rolls of Walsham-le-Willows, 1340

This extract translates the whole of two courts held at Walsham-le-Willows in 1340. Unusually, the court rolls of Walsham include the records of two separate manors, Walsham and Walsham High Hall. Both were held by different gentry lords, although considerable overlap is apparent between the suitors of each court. In contrast to the examples from the 1240s [**36**], these are lengthy, varied and detailed, containing many of the features and much of the business one expects to find in an active manor court at its peak. The layout of the court roll has become standardised, beginning with essoins, outstanding cases, and private plaints between peasants, and followed by the swearing in of the presentment jury. This jury dominates the proceedings of the June court, presenting a large number of communal and seigneurial cases. No presentment jury is formally recorded for the October court of High Hall, although the form and nature of the entries are very similar and one suspects that a jury sworn at a previous court was simply continuing its work. A very active land market in small parcels of customary land exists, and the transfers are recorded in a precise but repetitive manner: it seems unlikely that many transfers of free land were being recorded by the court by this date. Neither lord had the right to hold a leet court in Walsham, but, interestingly, some business associated with the leet (a few petty assaults, encroachments and presentments under the assize of ale) was being handled by this court. Again, this was not uncommon, and reflected both the judgement of local elites on which specific cases went before which courts and, presumably, indifference to the 'leakage' by the holder of the leet franchise (in this case the abbot of Bury St Edmunds).

Suffolk Record Office, Bury St Edmunds, HA504/1/4.22 and 4.23. Manor courts of Walsham, held 19 June 1340, and Walsham High Hall (Suffolk), held 23 October 1340. Latin. See Lock, *Court rolls of Walsham*.

Walsham [19 June 1340]

Adam Craske, defendant against William the bailiff of Alexander de Walsham, in a plea of trespass, essoin by Walter Craske; he pledges faith; William is present.[87] The same Adam, defendant against William Wyther in a like plea, essoin by John Craske; he pledges faith; William is present; and defendant against William Hawys in a like plea, essoin by John Margery, he pledges faith; William is present.

Walter Hawys amerced 3d. for licence to agree with Walter Hereward in a plea of land, pledge the hayward. The same Walter amerced 3d. for licence to agree with William Hawys in a like plea, pledge as above. The agreement is such that Walter says that he is content under this form: that Walter shall have as his share of all the lands, tenements, meadows, pastures and their appurtenances, following the death of Robert Hawys, their father, and the deaths of their brothers, Peter, Ralph, John and Nicholas, namely 4 acres 2 roods 10 perches of land, meadow and pasture, of which 3 roods of land lie at the Rowesend, next to the land of Robert Sare to the east, 3½ roods in Hatchmere, between the land of Peter Tailor and that of Robert Sare, 1 rood of land at Saresgate and 1 acre 2½ roods at Boynhawe, next to the land of Hugh de Saxham to the east, 3½ roods at Strondeswood, between

---

87 Adam is clearly a busy defendant in a number of ongoing private pleas, but is not present in court. Walter presents his essoin and, at the same time, pledges that Adam is acting in good faith.

the land of William of Cranmer and that of Robert Sare, ½ rood of meadow at Cocksbusk, and 10 perches of meadow at the Harwe in the Turfpits. Furthermore, William grants to Walter that he shall have [a routeway] next to his house in their late father's messuage, from the door of that house on the west side towards the tenement formerly of Gilbert Doo as far as the road, 7ft. wide; to hold this way for Walter's lifetime. After Walter's death the way shall revert to William and his heirs, quit of Walter and his heirs. Walter says that he is content with his portion of the said lands, and with ingress to, and egress from, the said way for the said term in the said form. And for this grant he remits to William all actions, complaints and demands whatsoever, from the begining of this world until the present day. In return William remits and quitclaims to Walter all actions etc. in the same form. They pay 3d. fine for the enrolment of this agreement, pledge the hayward.

John Man amerced 6d. for trespass against Walter Noreys, demolishing parts of a house to his loss of 3d.; ordered to raise, pledge the hayward; and 3d. for unlawful detention of five ells of linen cloth worth 7½d. from the said Walter, to his loss of 1d., which is ordered to be raised; and 3d. for the unlawful detention of a goat, worth 3d., for which the loss is remitted, pledges William the Smith and William Patel.

Adam of Cringleford amerced 3d. for licence to agree with Cristina Smith in a plea of trespass, pledge Walter the Smith. And Walter Goos 3d. for the same with Peter Neve in a plea of debt, pledge Robert Lene.

Richard of Wortham surrenders to Walter the Smith and his heirs ½ rood of land in the Millfield, granted to him to hold in villeinage, by services and works etc. Entry fine 6d., pledge the hayward.

Robert Tailor amerced 3d. for licence to agree with William the bailiff of Alexander de Walsham in a plea of trespass, and Alice Helewys 3d. for the same in a like plea, pledge for both the hayward.

Adam Craske amerced 6d. for damage with his sheep in the lord's oats and herbage at Currescroft, and in his oats at Blunteslond, pledges William Hawys and John Terwald.

William and Robert Cook pay 8d. fine [for licence] to rebuild the tenement Galyones by next Easter, pledge the hayward; and a day is given to them until that feast, pledges William of Cranmer and Thomas Fuller.

Thomas of the Beck amerced 18d. for trespass against the lord, felling and removing willows from the lord's bondage, namely from the tenement formerly of Thomas at the Lee.

Robert of Walpole amerced 6d. for trespass in the lord's herbage at Allwood with his sheep and pigs, pledge John Syre.

Walter Payn the shoemaker amerced 1d. for unlawful detention of 1d. from Walter Cooper; Walter Cooper amerced 1d. for unlawful detention of 1d. from Walter Payn, as found by the inquiry, damages remitted in each instance; ordered to raise.

William Hawys surrenders to John Noble, Alice his wife and their heirs 1 rood of land in the Millfield, granted to them to hold in villeinage by services and works etc. Entry fine 12d., pledge William Wyther.

Manser of Shucford amerced 6d. for trespass against William Rampolye, the reeve, defaming him, the damages to William being assesssed at 6d; ordered to raise.

William Hawys surrenders to John Noble, Alice his wife and their heirs a garden containing 1 rood 17 perches of land called Mayhewesyerd, granted to them in the same form as above. Entry fine 4s., pledge William Wyther.

Walter Noreys in mercy for his false claim against John Man in a plea of debt, pardoned because poor.[88]

General inquiry [the presentment jury] by William of Cranmer, John Terwald, Nicholas Goche, John Syre, Matthew Hereward, William Wyther, Walter the smith, Walter Payn, Simon Peyntour, Robert Tailor, Robert Lene, Nicholas Spileman, William Payn, Thomas Hereward, Robert Hereward, Richard Qualm, John of Stonham and John Tailor.

Edmund Patel held from the lord when he died a messuage and 7½ acres of customary land. The lord had as a heriot a cow after calving, at the feast of the Invention of the Holy Cross [3 May 1340], worth 7s. John and Richard, Edmund's sons, are his nearest heirs, and they have entry by the heriot. They swore fealty.

Agnes the widow of Robert Godefrey, villein, who following her husband's death holds half a garden and 2 acres of customary land in dower, amerced 6d. because she leased this tenement to William

---

88 The president of the court and affeerers may judge a guilty party to be too poor to pay an amercement: see A. May, 'An index of thirteenth-century peasant impoverishment? Manorial court fines', *Economic History Review*, 26 (1973), 389–402.

Rampolye and Walter the Smith for her lifetime without licence; ordered to take it into the lord's hands, and to answer for the profits.[89] The same Agnes gave birth outside wedlock, childwyte 2s. 8d.; pledges, William Rampolye and Walter the Smith.

Rose Stronde amerced 12d. because she leased to Robert Sare, freeman, without licence 5 acres of customary land for a term of years; ordered to take it into the lord's hands, and to answer for the profits.[90]

Peter Margery amerced 6d. because he ploughed over the lord's land at Cocksdrit, 4ft. wide and 4 perches long, pledge the hayward; ordered to make amends.

William Wauncy in mercy for cutting and taking away dry willow wood from Ladyswood, pardoned because poor.

John Man amerced 3d. because he milled his corn away from the lord's mill.

Thomas at the Lee sold by charter to Thomas of the Beck 3½ acres of customary land, without licence; ordered to take into the lord's hands, and to answer for the profits. Thomas of the Beck purchased from Thomas at the Lee [blank] of the lord's fee; ordered to distrain him to show [his title to] entry and for fealty.

William Rampolye the reeve amerced 3s. 4d. because he had straw worth 3d. carted from the lord's mill to his own house. William Wyther amerced 12d. because he carted this straw to William Rampolye's house in his own cart. William Rampolye amerced 3s. 4d. because he took a vat, a haircloth and a brass bowl out of the manor and had them carried to his house for his use.

Ordered to raise 4s. from Richard Qualm, John Man and William Patel the younger to the benefit of Richard of Wortham, which they undertook to pay through William Clevehog, as shown in the court of St Valentine's day, 11 Edward III [14 February 1339].

John Tailor amerced 12d. because he occupied and cultivated a sixth part of a messuage and 3 acres of customary land, of the right of Walter the son of William Springold, for four years without licence, pledge the hayward; ordered to take into the lord's hands, and to answer for the profits.

---

89 For a further development in this case, see the final entry of this court.

90 The seized assets were expected to raise some revenue for the lord, hence the order 'to answer for issues/profits': see p. 36.

Walter Pye amerced 12d., and Walter Rampolye and Amice the daughter of William Patel 6d. each, because they brewed and sold ale in breach of the assize; Robert Lenne 3d. for regrating bread. Manser of Shucford and William the Smith the ale-tasters each amerced 2d., because they did not perform their duties.

Walter Craske the miller amerced 3d. for trespass against John Man, assessed at 1½d., ordered to raise, pledge the hayward.

William Hawys pays 2s. for having a fold of 5 score sheep until Michaelmas, and no more because he is allowed 20, pledge the hayward.[91]

William Rampolye and Walter the smith were elected to the office of reeve; Nicholas Fraunceys and Walter Fuller to the office of hayward; and William Cook and Ralph Echeman to the office of woodward.

Ordered to execute the orders of the last court, marked with a cross, and not acted upon.

Agnes the widow of Robert Godefrey pays 6s. 8d. fine for licence to marry William Cook, pledges William Rampolye and Walter the Smith. Agnes surrendered and remitted to Walter the Smith all the right she had in 1 acre of land, with half a garden, held in dower after her husband's death; and in the other 1 acre held in dower to William Rampolye; granted to them to hold in villeinage, by services and works. Entry fines, 12d. and 6d. respectively, pledge for both the hayward.

Total 31s., except a cow, worth 7s., as a heriot, and the reeve's amercements. Affeerers: Nicholas Goche and Walter Payn.

High Hall. General court of Nicholas de Walsham [23 October 1340]

William Elys, essoins of common suit, [presented] by William Deneys; Walter Cristmesse of the same by Henry Trusse; and William of Cranmer of the same, by Robert Sare [superscript, 'he came']; John Wodebite, defendant against John Man in a plea of debt, essoins by Richard Patel; they pledge faith on summons.

The profits from 1 rood of free land which was taken into the lord's hands after the death of Richard Shepherd because the heir did not come for relief and fealty, and several defaults [amount to] 3d.; ordered to retain etc. And upon this Adam Shepherd comes and pays a fine for repossessing this land. He is pardoned [payment of the fine] and swears fealty.

91 The right to keep a flock of 100 sheep folded, by the use of mobile wattle hurdles, on an unspecified area of land: he has a standing right to keep a fold of 20 sheep.

Ordered as elsewhere to attach William Kembald for trespass in the lord's wood, corn and meadow; and Matthew the son of Richard Patel, carter of Robert Hovel, because he drove a cart over the lord's land at Angerhale several times.

John Helpe amerced 1d. because he did not execute an order of the court; and ordered as elsewhere to attach Walter Payn for damage in the lord's wheat at Hamstale with his horses and beasts to the value of 4 sheaves, worth 4d.

John Pynfoul amerced 1d. for damage in the lord's wood, cutting and taking away branches, pledges John Packard and the hayward.

William Deneys amerced 1d. for damage in the lord's peas at Hamstale, pledge the hayward.

Nicholas Fraunceys amerced 6d. because he did not make recompense for a cow taken from Robert Hereward, as he undertook, and Robert for damage with his beasts in the lord's newly sown wheat at Gothelardsyerd. Ordered to attach Robert for the same.

Ordered as elsewhere to attach Thomas Thurbern of Cotton, Richard of Depham and Edmund of Ipswich for homage, relief and fealty.

The first pledges of Agnes Fitte amerced 3d. because they did not have her reply to John Helpe in a plea of trespass; ordered to appoint better pledges.

Olivia Isabel amerced 2s. for trespass against the lord, and defaming Agnes and not paying for her services, pledge the hayward.

John of Angerhale amerced 3d. for his false claim against Peter Stag in a plea of trespass, pledge the hayward.

William Wodebite amerced 6d. because he did not rebuild a house in the tenement called Aprilles, for which he had a day at the last court; again ordered to rebuild.

Agnes Fitte gave birth outside wedlock, childwyte 2s.8d.

Robert Banlone amerced 3d. for damage in the lord's wood with the oxen of the manor, pledge John Packard; and 1d. for damage in the lord's peas to the value of 1 sheaf.

Ordered to attach Walter the Smith for damage in the lord's wood at Lenerithsdel with cows and bullocks; and Walter Payn for damage in the lord's oats at Ulversrowe with cows and calves to the value of 1 sheaf; and William Hawys for the same with sheep, 1 sheaf; and Alice, farmer of the cows of the Easthouse, for damage in the lord's wheat at the Hulver, 1 sheaf. John the son of John Packard amerced 1d. for damage in the lord's barley below the wood with cows and bullocks, pledge John Packard. The swineherd of the manor amerced 2d. and Robert Banlone 1d. for damage in the lord's peas at Doucedeux, pledge the hayward; ordered to attach John Syre and William Hawys for the same, 1 sheaf. Ordered to attach William of Cranmer, William Hawys, John Syre, Walter Payn, William Kembald, William Deneys, William Clevehog, Simon Peyntour and John Man for damage in the lord's peas at Hordeshawe with beasts, 4 sheaves.

Ordered to attach Robert Hereward for damage in the lord's garden, taking away the fruits of the garden [and] dung, and breaking and taking away hedges, and depasturing the herbage with his pigs; also for damage at the Newerowe with a cow; and to attach William Kembald, William of Cranmer and William Hawys for damage in the lord's wood; and William of Cranmer, William Hawys and the shepherd of the prior for damage in the lord's peas at Dousedewes; the swineherd and shepherd of the manor each amerced 1d. for the same.

Ordered to attach Robert Tybetot because he drove a stot worth 10s. so that it died. Ordered to attach William Blunte because a stot worth 4s. died as a result of his defective custody.

William Wodebite amerced 3d. because he did not bundle enough of the lord's straw for the men, as he was ordered; and 6d. because he was summoned for harvest work and did not come; John Goche 3d. and William and Olivia Isabel 3d. for the same.

Ordered to attach Nicholas Fraunceys, Avice Deneys and Agnes Fitte for damage with their beasts in the lord's newly sown wheat at Sheephouse.

John of Angerhale leased 3 acres of customary land to Henry the rector of Westhorpe without licence; ordered to take into the lord's hands, and to answer for the profits.

John Packard was elected to the office of reeve, and took the oath; Peter Goche was elected to the office of collector, and took the oath.

John Packard amerced 6s. 8d. for breaking the agreement, made in the court, between Alice, John's wife, and Margery the wife of William Wodebite, under penalty of 13s. 4d., concerning which the inquiry found that Alice struck Margery and drew blood, pledge the hayward. William Wodebite amerced 2s. for trespass against John Packard and Alice his wife by Margery, William's wife, as found by the inquiry. Damages assessed at 6d., ordered to raise. Ordered to attach John and

Alice Packard to reply to William and Margery Wodebite in a plea of debt.

[Total not stated]

38   Court rolls of Walsham-le-Willows, 1389

This extract complements the previous one by reproducing a court for Walsham held in 1389. The business is still lengthy and varied, indicating that the court remains active, although no court for High Hall manor was held this year. However, since 1340 there are subtle signs of a fall in the demand for arable land and changes in the balance of power between lord and peasants. Entry fines for customary land are generally lower, and are waived in some cases in order to attract tenants, and the lord is shedding some demesne land on to the local land market rather than exploit it directly. The number of presentments for damage caused by stray animals also implies a shift from arable towards pastoral pursuits. The court is also becoming concerned about the migration of serfs from an already depopulated manor, and deals more aggressively than in the previous example with a tenant who declines to hold a major manorial office. The pledging system also exhibits signs of decay, with fewer employed and regular calls to appoint better, the dilapidation of housing is causing concern, and non-performance of labour services is a problem.

Suffolk Record Office, Bury St Edmunds, HA504/1/9 m.2. Manor court of Walsham (Suffolk), 19 January 1389. Latin.

Walsham. General court held on Tuesday after the feast of St Hilary in the twelfth year of the reign of Richard II [19 January 1389].

Simon Sadlere, essoins of common suit by Nicholas Typtot; John Bradmere of the same by John Hereward; John Manncel of the same by John Fraunceys; John Fuller of the same by Thomas Fuller; Adam Fraunceys of the same by Robert Payn.

John Boman who was elected by virtue of his tenement at the last court to the office of reeve for this year pays 40s. fine for being discharged from the office.

John Mauncer amerced 3d., John Frebern 3d., and Richard Rampolye, afterwards he came, because they did not warrant their essoin for the last court.

The eight pledges of Robert Spylman amerced 3d. because they did not have him to reply to Robert Spryngold in a plea of debt. Ordered to appoint better. The eight pledges of the said Robert amerced 3d.

because they did not have him to reply to the said Robert in a plea of trespass. Ordered to appoint better. Order to distrain Thomas Crane to reply to John Grocer, chaplain, in a plea of debt. Order to distrain Robert Salman to reply to John Roman in a plea of trespass.

The eight pledges of Robert Spylman amerced 3d. because they did not have him to reply to Roger Sprener in a plea of debt. Ordered to appoint better.

Order to distrain Roger Prede, holding 16 acres 1 rood of land, 1 acre of wood and 2 acres 1 rood of meadow of the tenement formerly of Robert Hawys, which John Rampolye, chaplain, occupies holding 5 acres of land, 1 acre of meadow and ½ acre of wood of the same tenement, which William Hawys and Robert Hawys occupy; and John Cooper, John Frebern, Edmund Patil, Almory Grym and William Springman to show their charters at the next court to establish by what right they entered into the fee of the lord, namely into the tenement formerly of Robert Hawys.

Order to seize into the lord's hands a messuage and 3 acres of villein land which William Godefrey leased to William Grocer for a term of 3 years without licence; and now he comes and pays a fine for licence to lease until the feast of St Michael next.

Inquiry by Robert Paye, Thomas Fuller, William Hawys, John Armyte, John Spileman, Adam Hecheman, John Warde, Nicholas Fuller, Robert Man, Walter Fraunceys and Robert Spryngold.

Elianora Pach surrenders a messuage and 7½ acres of land of the lord's bondage to William Man, who came and received the said land to hold by the rod. Entry fine, 4s. and made fealty.

Order. At the last court Nicholas Fuller had a day to make good waste on the lord's bondage in the tenement called Brokes, and in mercy because he had not made good. Ordered to make good by the next under penalty of 40d.

At the last court it was ordered to take into the lord's hands all the tenements which Nicholas Typetot held in bondage, which consist of a messuage with various closes and 28 acres of 'werklond', because he disposed of them to William Blount of Westhorp without licence. Because it was found that the disposition was made fraudulently and in prejudice to the lord it is annulled, and the said Nicholas shall remain tenant of them. Therefore profits nil.

A day was given to Peter Robhod to make good the waste on the tenement formerly of William Tippetot by the feast of St Michael next under penalty of 40s., pledge John Hawys.

It was ordered elsewhere to take into the lord's hands a pasture measuring 14 perches long by 2 perches wide of the lord's bondage, which is a parcel of the tenement of John Spilman senior, because Robert Spilman sold it to Robert Spryngold without licence. Because it was attested by the bailiff that it is to the loss of the lord if the said Robert Springold holds it separately from the said tenement, then the lord granted the said tenement to the said Robert Springold to hold by the rod. Entry fine 4d., and made fealty.

Robert Spylman surrenders outside the court into the hands of John Hereward and others of the homage 1 rood of villein land to Alice Gilberd, who came and received the said land to hold by the rod. Entry fine 4d., and made fealty.

Margery Rampolye surrenders whatsoever she has in the name of dower in the tenement Rampolyes, which was of Robert Rampolye, to Walter Rampolye. She remitted it to him and his heirs, for which surrender and remission the said Walter gives a fine, 4s., to the lord.

Simon Sadler and Joanna his wife claim concerning 12 acres of land, 2 acres of meadow, 1 acre of wood and half a messuage of the lord's bondage against William Hawys and Robert Hawys in a plea of land. Because they did not proceed against them, they are in mercy. The said Simon and Joanna formerly surrendered the said tenements here in court because they regularly defaulted, and afterwards to this complaint made a plea to prosecute in the nature of a writ of right and many times afterwards appeared in court as appears in the rolls etc. And also because the lord sent this letter to his steward, as appears sewn in with this same roll, to give judgement on it in accordance with law and custom. It was decided by the court that the aforesaid tenants shall retain the aforesaid tenements to hold to them and their heirs by the rod in peace from the said claimants and their heirs in future.

[The text of the letter from the lord to his steward is sewn into the court roll at this point, and is written in Anglo-French][92]

William Amham, knight and lord of Walsham, to his very dear and well-beloved steward of his lands. Greetings. With regard to a certain dispute concerning 12 acres of land, 2 acres of meadow, 1 acre of wood and half a messuage of my bondage between William Hawys

92 The inclusion of such correspondence in the rolls is very unusual.

and Robert Hawys claimants, and Simon Haver [*sic*] and Joanna his
wife defendants, as fully appears in the rolls of my court held at
Walsham on the feast of the nativity of St John the Baptist in the 7th
year of the reign of King Richard the Second after the Conquest [24
June 1383]. And so from one court to another the said Simon and
Joanna were summoned by the officers of the court and did not come
to defend themselves but made default. And at the last court held
there on Tuesday next after the feast of the Exaltation of the Holy
Cross in the year following [20 September 1384], the said Simon and
Joanna were summoned and did not come but made default, so that
the right to the said land, meadow, wood and half the messuage was
determined and judged to the said William and Robert by their right of
inheritance, and orders were given to the bailiff to deliver seisin and to
take a fixed fine for the same. And I understand that the said Simon and
Joanna have renewed their claim in the same land, meadow, wood and
half the messuage. Therefore I request and charge that you try and
judge the right between them according to the ancient custom of the
vill as you will answer before God, so that no further dispute shall arise
in this matter. Written the 15th day of January the 12th year of R.

Elias Tippetot, who lately died, held from the lord a messuage and 14
acres of land, ½ acre and 20 feet of meadow by estimation and 1½ rod
of pasture of the lord's bondage. They say that following the custom
of the manor, bond land is partible between males and that John and
William his sons are his nearest heirs. They came and received the said
tenements from the Lord to hold by the rod etc. They pay an entry fine
and made fealty. Pledges for services etc. are Nicholas Tippetot and
John Ermyte. And they say that the lord shall have a heriot, his best
beast which is a cow priced 10s., which was delivered to the dairyman
of the manor. Entry fine, nothing, because entry by the heriot.

The same Elias surrendered outside the court, into the hands of Nicholas
Tippetot in the presence of John Ermyte and Robert Man and others
of the homage, a messuage which was his capital messuage to Hillary
his wife to hold for the term of her life. And after the death of the said
Hillary the said messuage shall return to the heirs of the said Elias.
She came and received the said messuage to hold in the said form.
Entry fine, 6s. 8d., and made fealty.

Robert Margary and Hillary his wife sold to Katerina Spilman and her
heirs a third part of a messuage and 8 acres of land formerly of the
tenement called Bolles of the lord's bondage, and the same Robert and
Hillary, duly examined, surrendered the said tenement to the use of

the said Katerina whom came and received the said land from the lord to hold by the rod. Entry fine, 4d, and made fealty.

Robert Spylman son of John Spylman sold 5 roods of pasture lying in a close of the lord's bondage without licence, amerced 4d. Ordered to take into the lord's hands and to answer for profits.

Adam Pydlake surrenders outside the court into the hands of the bailiff, in the presence of William Hawys, William Swyther and others of the homage, and into the hands of the lord half a pightle and 2½ roods of land of the lord's bondage formerly of Walter Osborn for the use of William Swyft, who comes into court and receives the said land from the lord to hold by the rod. Entry fine 12d. and made fealty.

William Grocer surrenders into the hands of the lord 2 acres of villein land of Hollond for the use of John Rampoly, chaplain, who receives the land from the lord by the rod and gives 4s. entry fine.

John Bradle, bailiff of the lord for the past year, did not have the lord's oats reaped at the appropriate time, as a result of which the said oats deteriorated to the loss of the lord assessed by the jury as 1 quarter of oats; ordered to raise.

By default of the said bailiff a servant to the lord's plough-team absented himself from the lord's service for half a year to the lord's loss, amerced 6d.

John Wauncy, amerced 3d., and John Bradmere, 3d., did damage in the lord's wood at Ladyswood with their beasts.

The prior of Ixworth, amerced 2d., Thomas Fuller 1d., Peter Robhod 2d., John Cooper 1d., Robert Margery the younger 1d., and Robert Lester 1d., made pits on the common to the general nuisance and to the loss of the lord; ordered to make good under penalty of 40d. each.

Adam Blakewell took away 1 sheaf of oats without licence, amerced 3d.; the said Adam took away sticks out of the wood called Ladyswode without licence, 3d.

John Jay did not come at the order of the bailiff to perform ploughing works at various seasons in the past year with half a plough-team, amerced 2s. 6d.

Simon Sadelere did not repair his villein tenement, amerced 6d.; ordered to make good by the next court under penalty of 2s.

John Baxster, amerced 4d., John Marler 2d., baked and sold bread contrary to the assize.

John Lester, amerced 6d., John Fraunceys 4d., Thomas Bonde 2d., and Richard Qualm 4d., brewed and sold ale contrary to the assize. John Frost 3d., Robert Lens 3d., ale-tasters, did not do their duty.

Edmund Patel, serf by blood, purchased certain tenements of the lord's bondage making Nicholas Patel his father take the said tenements here in court and Edmund himself occupies the said tenements without licence, amerced 12d.; ordered to seize and answer for the profits. And afterwards the said Edmund came and found pledges, namely Nicholas Tiptot and John Frost, that he show at the next court that he occupies the said tenement by licence of the court and not otherwise.

A day was given to the inquiry to certify by the next court concerning 1 rood of land, lately of Ayla Wedewe who owed suit of the last court, which William Pye now holds, and to scrutinise the rolls and the terrier meanwhile by the next court. And a day was given to the same William to produce his evidence.

Adam Sire felled a certain ash tree at Heyehall, priced [blank], on the lord's ground, amerced 12d.

Ordered to distrain John Hawys to satisfy the lord for withholding one reaping work; and the supervisor and the bailiff ordered to survey all the tenements wasted on the lord's bondage by the next court.

John Jay found pledges, Robert Margery and Robert Bare, for the good behaviour of him and his wife towards John Ward, under penalty of 40s. And the same John Ward found as pledges Adam Ebell and Robert Margary for the good behaviour of him and his wife towards John Jay, under penalty of 40s.

A day was given to Robert Spryngold, plaintiff, and Robert Bakewell, defendant, in a plea of debt to come to the next court.

A day was given to Adam Blakwell, plaintiff, and Robert Spryngold, defendant, in a plea of trespass to come to the next court.

A day was given to Peter Robhod plaintiff, and Nicholas Tipptot, defendant, in a plea of trespass, and also between Nicholas Tipptot, plaintiff, and Peter Robhod in a plea of detaining chattels.

John Jay and Margaret his wife had a day in a preceding court that they behave well towards John Ward and his wife, under penalty of 20s. And it was attested by the homage that they are guilty, and therefore liable to the aforesaid penalty which is now incurred.

[Total not stated]

39   Court roll of Downham, 1311

Downham is located in the heart of the Cambridgeshire fens, and the importance of sedges (reeds used in thatching and bedding) and turves (peat
cuttings for fuel) to the local economy is strongly apparent from this court.
The other points of note are the acquisition of a house and garden in two
separate transactions by John Daepersonnes, and the classic example of a
reversionary gift of land from parent to child, whereby Agnes Bridge grants
land to her son William but William agrees that she should continue to occupy
it until her death.

Cambridge University Library, EDR C11/1. Court roll of Downham
(Cambridgeshire), held 26 February 1311. Latin.

Downham. Court held here on Thursday the day after Ash
Wednesday in the fourth year of the the the reign of king Edward and the
first year of the episcopate of John of Ketene [26 February 1311].

Essoins. William Bunting against Peter Gille in a plea of trespass,
pledge Clement the Brewer. For the first time. Affeerer.

Adam the son of Philip, 3d., for licence to come to an agreement with
Geoffrey Stout in a plea of trespass, pledge the hayward.

Simon Cardinal junior, 3d., for licence to come to an agreement with
Javyn Daipersones in a plea of trespass, pledge the hayward.

John Man, 3d., for licence to come to an agreement with Robert Carter
in a plea of debt, pledge the hayward.

Adam the Chaplain, 6d., for his great offence against the wife of Robert
Allen and for false complaint against the said Robert, etc.

Adam the son of Philip admitted withholding one thousand sedges from
Ralph Bolay, which he unlawfully held for one year. The damages were
12d. which the court acknowledges. And he is in mercy, 3d. Pledge,
Philip Lovechild, to be paid at the feast of St John the Baptist [24 June].

Adam the son of Philip admitted withholding from Nicholas Prat 12s.
10d. which Nicholas had paid for him because he was pledge to the
said Adam for his damages, assessed at 2s. which the court considered
that he should repay etc. And Adam is in mercy, 3d. Pledge for Adam,
Philip Lovechild, and he is given a day for paying before Easter.

Agnes Bridge and her son John came and surrendered into the lord's
hand a half-land in Downham for the benefit of William Bridge the
son of the said Agnes, who came and took it from the lord to hold by
villein tenure and the services that belonged to that land. And he gave

to the lord half a mark for the entry fine, pledges the hayward and Simon Pope. And for this surrender, William agreed that the afore-said Agnes his mother should recover the said land and hold it for the whole of her life. And after her death the land was to revert to the said William to hold as aforesaid etc. And he was given a day to pay, one half at the feast of the Annunication [25 March] and the other half at the feast of St John the Baptist [24 June] etc. And he made his oath and fealty.

John Man admitted withholding from Ralph Bolay a thousand sedges and 3d. which he unlawfully kept, to his damage assessed at 12d. which the court etc. And he is in mercy, 3d. Pledges, Philip Lovechild and Geoffrey Scot, payment to be made at the feast of St John the Baptist, etc.

Richard the Butcher came and surrendered a house (*placeam edificatam*) for the benefit of John Daepersonnes who came and received the same from the lord to hold for himself and his heirs by villein tenure for the rent of 1d. per annum payable to the lord. And he paid 3s. entry fine and made his oath and fealty.

Simon Pope came and surrendered an empty plot of land, at the head of the aforesaid building, 3 roods long by a half wide for the benefit of the aforesaid John Daepersonnes who came and received it from the lord to hold by villein tenure for a half penny per annum payable to the lord, and he paid 12d. entry fine to the lord.

John Man admitted withholding from John Albyn of Littleport 500 sedges which he unlawfully held from him to his damage assessed at 3d., which the court considers etc., and he is in mercy, 3d. Pledges Philip Lovechild and Geoffrey Scot, and he was given a day to pay at the feast of St John the Baptist [24 June].

An action between Clement the Brewer and Alice his wife and Thomas Pope concerning a plea of trespass adjourned until the next court etc.

William Bunting gave Peter Gill 2s. for the offence he had committed against him by beating and ill-treating him, and for this offence is in mercy, 4d. Pledges, John Fox and Simon Cardinal etc.

Twelve jurors present that Alice the daughter of Amicia committed adultery and is therefore in mercy, pledge S. Pope.

Simon Cardinal sold 4,000 sedges outside the vill contrary to the regulation, therefore etc., 2s. Nicholas Dunfrey sold 1,000 sedges 6d., Simon Starling 1,000 sedges 6d., Maurice Attehethe 500 sedges 3d.,

Reginald Smerles 1,000 sedges 6d., John Smerles 500 sedges 3d., John Bridge, keeper of the sedges, 300 sedges 2d. Maurice Atteheth sold 3,000 turves, 9d., Nicholas Eastheth 500 turves 1½d., Reginald Smerles 1,000 turves 3d., Thomas, servant of Robert, 500 turves 1½d., John Bridge 500 turves 1½d.

An oath was taken by the twelve jurors that the bailiffs would make known at the next court who were the people who had cut the sedges inside the park boundary at Downham, and that this would not happen again etc.

Total of this court, 18s. 9d.

40   Court rolls of Yeadon, 1449, 1452 and 1459

Between 1449 and 1455 the court for this large manor, covering a number of settlements, was held annually. The court for 1449 begins with the presentment of named transgressors under a standard range of offences, some of which reflect the wooded and pastoral nature of the local economy. Its activity also extends to a number of public order offences, which implies that the court also deals with business normally associated with the leet. The annual election of manorial officials remains a significant responsibility, even at this late date. Only one court was held between 1456 and 1458, followed by an especially vigorous session in 1459 when the sudden increase in presentments for allowing houses to become ruinous is more likely to indicate that the management of previous courts had been lax rather than a spate of house destruction. The tighter management of the court is indicative of a change of administrative regime. Indeed, Yeadon was held by Esholt priory, which suffered from poor management and financial distress in the 1440s and 1450s, until the election in 1459 of a new prioress.[93] Her influence upon the administration of Yeadon manor is immediately apparent.

G. R. Price, ed., *The court rolls of Yeadon 1361–1476* (Skipton, 1984). Court rolls of Yeadon (Yorkshire), held 29 December 1449, 3 January 1452, and 7 July 1459. Latin.

Yeadon. Court held in the same place on the Monday in the feast of St Thomas of Canterbury in the 28th year of the reign of King Henry the sixth after the conquest [29 December 1449].

It is presented that Robert Walker, 6d., cut elders and willows in le Dybbe without licence. The same Robert, 1d., cut withies and other wood in le Yedonynge without licence.

93 *VCH Yorkshire,* vol. 3 (London, 1913), pp. 161–3.

William Watson, 1d., he denies so to inquisition, found guilty by the jurors, cut an ash sapling in his croft without licence.[94] Richard Roudon, 2d., cut an aspen in le Dybbe without licence. Thomas Pykard, 3d., cut an ash tree in Bastanclytrod without licence. The same Thomas, 1d., cut a [field] maple in le Longcrottend without licence. The same Thomas, 2d., cut holly in his field and in other places within the domain without licence. He denies so to the inquisition, found guilty by the jurors.

Robert Walker senior, 1d., cut branches of ash without licence in his garden. John Marshall, 2d., cut an ash in le Calfall.

Attached for wood. William Jakson, 8d., is attached for trespass of wood, so is in mercy. John Rastrik, 4d., for trespass. Richard Couper, 3d. the same. John Miklowe, 1d., Robert Walker, 3d., William Marshall, 3d., John Snawdon, 3d., Robert Walker junior, 3d., William Watson, 3d., William Snawdon, 2d., John Watson, 2d., John Marshall, 3d., Richard Roudon, 2d., Thomas Pykard, 3d., William Yeadon, 4d., John Adynett, 3d., William Wykars, 3d., William Roudon, 2d., Thomas Pyper, 4d., John Wryght, and William Sadyler, 2d.

Defaults of court. The tenant of the land [which was held] lately by Robert Mailserver for default of court, so in mercy, 4d. John Haukesworth, 4d., for the same. William Rodys, for the same. The tenant of the land lately William Wryght's, 4d., for the same. John Miklowe, 2d., for the same.

Verdict. Inquisition taken on oath by Richard Roudon, John Snawdon, Thomas Pykard, John Rastryk, William Watson, John Watson, Robert Walker, Robert Walker junior, John Marshall, William Snawdon, William Marshall and William Jakson, the jurors, who say that Joanna the wife of Richard Couper, 12d., has scolded and quarrelled with Margaret the wife of Thomas Piper, 12d., in contravention of a penalty imposed for this, and so they are in mercy.

They say that Sibell the wife of John Watson, 12d., has scolded and quarrelled with Margaret the wife of Thomas Piper, 12d., against a penalty imposed for this, and levied.

They say that Joanna the wife of Richard Couper, 12d., equally has scolded and quarrelled with Sibell the wife of John Watson, 12d., against a penalty and good order.

---

94 An uncommon instance of a suitor challenging the presentment of the jury.

They say that John Snawdon made one ditch and encroached upon the soil of the lady at his freeholding in le Southcroftes in Yeadon, by estimation in length [blank] and in width [blank] and penalty is placed on him to amend it before the next court, under penalty of 6s. 8d. payable to and assessed by the lady.

They say that Richard Yeadon encroached on the soil of the lady in making one hedge in Midynkarres between the freeholdings of the prioress and the said Richard in Yeadon, by estimation in length 60 feet and in width three feet, and a penalty is placed on him to amend it before the next court: under penalty of 20d. payable to and assessed by the lady.

They say that the wife of Thomas Piper, 2d., brews and sells ale against the assize, and so in mercy. The wife of John Rastrik, 2d., for the same.

They say that Robert Rastrik, 1d., allowed one cow within the domain where it was not allowed. Richard Walker, 2d., allowed one heifer within the domain where it was not allowed. John Pykard, 2d., allowed one cow within the domain etc. Emma Pykard, 1d., allowed one heifer within the domain. They say that John Wryght, pardoned, allowed 2 cows in le Notegatefeld in Yeadon against ancient custom. They say that Robert Marshall, 2d., allowed a cow within the domain where it was not allowed. John Snawdon, 2d., cut one ash in his orchard without licence.

Election of officers. William Yeadon is elected reeve and sworn in. Richard Raudon, William Watson, John Wryght and John Marshall are elected guardians of the by-laws and sworn in. William Yeadon, John Rastrik, John Marshall and William Jakson are elected overseers of dwellings and sworn in. Affeerers of the court: John Rastrick, William Yeadon and William Watson.

John Rastrick came into the court and took from the lady one messuage with its appurtenances, formerly in his own tenure, to be held by him from the feast of St Martin in winter next [11 November] for the term of ten years, and to render each year the customary rent; and he gives to the lady for entry 13s. 4d., and he made a surety to the lady through pledges of William Yeadon and William Jakson.

John Snawdon came into the court and took from the lady one messuage with its appurtenances, formerly in his own tenure, to be held by him from the feast of St Martin in winter next [11 November] for the term of ten years, and to render each year the customary rent; and he gives to the lady for entry 13s. 4d., and he made surety to the lady through pledges of William Jakson and William Snawdon.

Richard Couper came into the court and took from the lady one messuage with 9 acres of land and meadow, lately in the tenure of William Skeldan, to be held by him from the feast of St Martin next [11 November] for the term of ten years, and to render each year 10s. at the two usual annual terms by equal portions; and he gives to the lady [blank] for entry through pledge of William Jakson.

William Snawdon came into the court and took from the lady one messuage with one bovate of land, lately in the tenure of William Snawdon his father, to be held from the feast of St Martin next [11 November] for the term of ten years, and to render each year the customary rent; and he gives to the lady for entry 6s. 8d. and he made a surety to the lady through pledges of William Yeadon and John Snawdon.

John Watson came into the court and took from the lady one messuage with one bovate of land, lately in the tenure of John Watson his father, to be held by him from the feast of St Martin next [11 November] for the term of ten years, and to render each year the customary rent; and he gives for it for entry 20s., and he made a surety to the lady through pledges of William Jakson, William Adamson and William Watson.

Total of this court [blank].

Court held in the same place on the Monday next after the feast of St Thomas of Canterbury in the 30th year of the aforesaid king [3 January 1452].

Defaults of court. The tenant of land lately of Robert Mailserver, 6d., for default of the court, and so in mercy. John Hawksworth, 6d., for the same. William Rodys, 6d., for the same. The tenant of the land lately William Wryght, 4d., for the same. John Marshall, 2d., for the same. Richard Rawdon, 2d., for the same. Thomas Pykard, 3d., for the same. William Yeadon, 3d., for the same. Robert Walker junior, 2d., for the same. William Marshall, 2d., for the same and John Snawdon, 2d., for the same.

Attached for wood. William Jakson, 2d., John Wykars, 4d., Thomas Gybton, 2d., Margaret Rastriks, 4d., Richard Couper, 2d., William Yeadon, 6d., Robert Walker, 3d., Thomas Pykard, 6d., Richard Roudan,

2d., William Watson, 2d., John Watson, 2d., John Snawdon, 2d., John Marshall, 3d., William Marshall. 2d., Robert Walker junior 3d., John Walker 2d., Richard Walker, 2d.

Attached for beasts. It is presented that William Turner of Guiseley allowed 2 heifers in the brushwood called Nunwod. John Wykars, 1d., allowed 1 stirk in the same place.

Verdict. Inquisition taken on oath by William Jakson, Robert Walker, William Watson, John Walker, John Watson, Robert Walker, Richard Couper and others, the jurors, who say that William Yeadon, 6d., and Richard Wryght, 6d., have not amended le Swynkerdyke against the penalty placed on them by the last court and so in mercy; and a penalty is placed on the same William and Richard that they amend the said ditch before the feast of St Michael [29 September] next under penalty of 6s. 8d., payable to and assessed by the lady.

They say that John Wryght, 2d., allowed oxen to run amok, called garthbreakers, to the damage of the crops of all the lady's tenants.

They say that William Yeadon, pardoned, keeps one greyhound which the tenants believe to be a sheep worrier, so he must destroy it.

Richard Rawdon keeps one dog called a sheep worrier and so he is placed under a penalty of 40d., payable to and assessed by the lady.

They say that John Wryght of Overyeadon, pardoned, kept one bullock and one heifer in the brushwood of the lady called Nunwod. Thomas Pykard, 4d., kept sheep, pigs and other beasts in the same place. Constantine Mahaut kept his draught animals there in the same place. William Yeadon, 1d., kept sheep and other cattle in the same place.

John Wryght, 2d., cut wood of the lady without licence. William Walker, 2d., did the same, Robert Wryght, 2d., William Wykars, 2d., William Rawdon, 2d., Thomas Marshall and his mother, 2d., and Robert Holynes, 2d.

They say that William Jakson, 2d., kept his geese in standing crops of the lady in divers places within the domain. Richard Couper, 2d., with his geese for the same. Margaret Rastryk, 2d., for the same with her geese. John Wykars, 2d., for trespass with his geese. They say that Margaret Rastrick keeps one unringed sow[95] within the domain to the damage of the crops of the lady and her tenants.

95 A pig whose snout has been ringed is unable to root: unringed pigs can cause considerable damage to crops.

They say that John Watson senior, 20d., made an affray with William Roudon against the peace of the lord king.

They say that Richard Roudon, 20d., made an affray with the said John Watson senior against the peace of the lord king.

They say that Richard Rawdon senior, 20d., made an affray with William Watson, 20d., against the peace of the lord king and good order equally.

They say that John Watson, 20d., made an affray with William Roudan, 20d., against the peace of the lord king and good order equally.

They say that Robert Walker senior, 20d., made an affray with Robert Roudon against the peace of the lord king.

William Watson, 20d., made an affray with Robert Rawdon, 20d., against the peace of the lord king and good order equally.

William Walker, 20d., made an affray with Robert Rawdon against the peace of the lord king.

They say that John Wykers, 1d., took and carried off clippings and cuttings of wood of the lady outside le Gill without licence.

They say that Robert Walker junior, 1d., does not wish to comply with the by-law against the peace.

They say that Margaret Rastrick, 2d., malts, brews and sells ale against the assize. The wife of Thomas Marshall, 2d., for trespass and so in mercy.

Election of officers. William Watson is elected reeve and sworn in. Richard Rawdon, John Marshall, William Watson and John Wryght are elected guardians of the by-laws and sworn in. William Yeadon, William Jaksan, Robert Walker senior and John Marshall are elected supervisors of dwellings and sworn in.

Sum of this court [blank in text].

Court of Lady Emma Burgh, prioress of Esholt, held in the same place on the Saturday in the feast of the translation of St Thomas Archbishop of Canterbury in the 37th year of the reign of King Henry the sixth [7 July 1459].

Defaults of court. The tenant of the land lately Robert Mailserver's, 6d., for default of the court, so in mercy. John Hawkesworth, 6d., for the same. The tenant of the land lately William Wryghte, 4d., for the same.

Election of officers. Thomas Marshall is elected constable and sworn in. John Wykares is elected reeve and sworn in. John Marshall and John Snawdon are elected tasters of bread and ale and sworn in. John Marshall, William Watson, Robert Rawdon and John Wright are elected guardians of the by-laws and sworn in. William Yeadon, John Marshall, William Watson and Stephen Rousse are elected supervisors of dwellings and sworn in.

Attached for wood. William Yeadon, 16d., Thomas Pykard, 12d., Robert Rawdon, 4d., John Marshall, 6d., John Watson, 3d., Thomas Hall, 5d., John Wryght, 2d., Robert Smyth, 2d., William Snawdon, 5d., William Watson, 6d., Robert Walker junior, 16d., John Snawdon, 4d., Richard Walker, 5d., William Wythie, 6d., Thomas Marshall, 4d., William Marshall, 4d., Robert Walker senior, 6d., Thomas Gibton, 4d., Margaret Rastrick, 3d., Richard Couper, 4d., William Jakson, 4d., John Wykarres, 6d., John Walker of Northcroft, 6d., John Holynes of Guiseley and Robert Brerretan, 6d. All these are pronounced guilty of cutting and carrying off the wood of the lady without licence.

The jurors say that the tenement in the tenure of William Watson is ruined, 2s. And a penalty is placed upon all tenants that anyone of them not repairing his tenement before the feast of St Martin next [11 November], under penalty for default of 6s. 8d., to be surrendered to the lady.

The jurors say that Robert Bryg, 12d., of the vill of Rawdon took clippings, namely from elders, [field] maples, birches and other wood of the lady by bushel-loads, to take and sell at Leeds etc.

The jurors say that John Pykard, 12d., allowed 40 sheep, 4 bullocks, 5 heifers and a horse within the domain where he was not permitted to do so before.

Inquisition taken on oath by William Yeadon, Thomas Pekard, John Wykarres, Stephen Rousse, William Watson, John Marshall, Robert Roudon, Robert Walker junior, John Snawdon, William Marshall, William Snawdon, Richard Crosed and John Watson, the jurors, who say that Robert Walker senior obstructed the course of water in le Kirkloyn of Nether Yeadon to the damage of property, and did not clear an alternative route in the same place. And a penalty is placed on him that he makes amends well and sufficiently before the feast of St Martin next [11 November], under penalty of 40d. to be surrendered to the lady.

The jurors say that the tenement in the tenure of Robert Walker has become dilapidated through neglect. And a penalty is placed on him that he rebuild the said tenement before next Christmas, under penalty of 20s. to be surrendered to the lady.

The jurors say that the tenement in the tenure of Robert Walker senior is ruined. And a penalty is placed on him that he make amends well and sufficiently before the feast of St Martin [11 November] next, under penalty of 20s. to be surrendered to the lady.

The jurors say that the tenement in the tenure of William Yeadon is ruinous. The jurors say that the tenement in the tenure of Thomas Pykard is ruinous. The jurors say that the tenement in the tenure of Robert Raudon is ruinous. The jurors say that the tenement in the tenure of John Marshall is ruinous. The jurors say that the tenement in the tenure of William Marshall is ruinous. The jurors say that the tenement in the tenure of John Watson is ruinous. The jurors say that the tenement in the tenure of William Snawdon is ruinous. The jurors say that the tenement in the tenure of John Snawdon is ruinous.

Richard Croaer came into the court and took from the lady one toft with a croft in Guiseley, lately in the tenure of John Holynes, to hold from the feast of St Martin in winter last passed [11 November] for a term of 10 years, and to render each year the customary rent at the two usual annual terms by equal portions. And he made a surety to the lady through pledges of William Yeadon and John Wikarres.

William Marshall came into the court and took from the lady one tenement previously in his tenure in Yeadon, to hold from the feast of St Martin in the winter last passed [11 November] for a term of 10 years, and to render each year the customary rent at the two usual annual terms by equal portions. And he gives to the lady for entry 8s., and he made a surety to the lady through pledges of William Yeadon and John Marshall.

Stephen Rousse came into the court and took from the lady one messuage with a garden and its appurtenances and the water-mill, lately in the tenure of William Jakson, with multure, and owes suit to the court as a tenant, just as was rendered formerly, to hold from the feast of St Martin in the winter last passed [11 November] for a term of 10 years, and to render each year the customary rent, namely 21s. at the two usual annual terms by equal portions. And he gives to the lady for entry 20s. through the pledges of William Yeadon and William Watson.

Thomas Pykard came into the court and took from the lady one messuage with its appurtenances formerly in his own tenure, to hold from the feast of St Martin in winter [11 November] next for a term of 10 years, and to render each year the customary rent at the two usual annual terms by equal portions. And he gives to the lady for entry 6s. 8d., and made a surety to the lady through pledges of Stephen Rousse and John Marshall.

Thomas Henryson came into the court and took from the lady one messuage with its appurtenances, lately in the tenure of Richard Couper, to hold from the feast of St Martin in winter [11 November] last passed for a term of 10 years, and to render each year the customary rent at the two usual annual terms by equal portions. And he gives to the lady for entry 6s. 8d. And he made a surety to the lady through pledges of John Snawdon and William Snawdon.

Sum of this court: [blank]. Affeerers of the court: John Wikarres and John Marshall.

41   Extract from a court roll of Great Bromley, 1382

Large quantities of manorial records in south-east England were burned by rebels during the Peasants' Revolt of 1381 in an attempt to destroy the record of the terms and conditions of tenure and to strike a blow against lordship. The accessibility of manorial records to the rebels implies that most were kept locally, probably within the manor house itself. Very few court rolls survive from the period when the Revolt was active (May–June), which reveals that, even in places where records were not destroyed, curial activity ceased temporarily. This extract from the first court held after the Revolt at Great Bromley provides a marvellous insight into the actions of the rebels, and their consequences: a formal and humbling reassertion of lordship over the customary holdings of the manor.

Essex Record Office, D/DU 40/1. Court of Great Bromley (Essex), held 20 March 1382.

Because all tenants in bondage of this manor, against the law and custom of the realm of England and in contempt of the lord king and his crown and to the disinheriting and contempt of this lordship, treacherously rebelled against the lord king and against Lady Anna, farmer of this manor, and also against Lord Thomas de Morley (to whom reversion of this manor belongs), and assaulted Lady Anna in her hall and threatened her, and illegally took all court rolls, all extents and all other muniments pertaining to this manor, concerning both

the said Anna and Lord Thomas de Morley, against the peace of the
lord king and against the will of the said Anna, and carried them away
in contempt of this lordship, and burned all the said rolls feloniously,
to the perpetual disinheritance of both lordships. Because of which it
was ordered that all tenements in bondage be seized into the lady's
lands as forfeit, during the said lady's lease, with all goods and
chattels within them, and that the issues be accounted for until then,
etc. ...

42   Matters for consideration by the frankpledge, 1285

Because the frankpledge was originally a royal jurisdiction, the central
records of the Crown contain a number of summaries of the business to be
considered by each unit (see pp. 180–2). The lesser offences would be handled
by the local court leet, and the more serious passed up to higher royal courts.
Consequently, these summaries provide a useful checklist of the types of
offences which might be found in the leet, and the other business which leets
discussed but did not record in their court rolls.

The Statute of Winchester, 1285, taken from the *Statutes of the Realm*, vol. I
(London, 1810), p. 246. Latin.

First, you shall say unto us[96] by the oath which you have made if all
   the suitors that owe suit in this court are present, and which not.
2. And if all the chief pledges be here, as they ought, and which are
   not.
3. And if all the deceners[97] be in the frankpledge of our lord the king
   and which not, and who received them.
4. And if there be any of the king's villeins fugitive, dwelling elsewhere than in the king's domain; and of such as be within the king's
   domain, and have not been resident for a year and a day.
5. And if there be any of the lord's villeins in frankpledge elsewhere
   than in this court.
6. Of customs and services due to this court withdrawn, how and by
   whom, and in what bailiffs' times.
7. Of purprestures made in lands, woods, and waters to annoyance.
8. Of walls, houses, dikes and hedges, set up or beaten down to
   annoyance.
9. Of bounds withdrawn and taken away.

96 I.e. the king (using the royal 'we').

97 The 'deceners' are those males over twelve years of age who are liable for entry
   into the frankpledge.

10. Of ways and paths opened or stopped.
11. Of waters turned or stopped, or diverted from their right course.
12. Of housebreakers, and of their receivers.
13. Of common thieves and their receivers.
14. Of petty larceny,[98] as of geese, hens, and corn sheafs.
15. Of thieves that steal cloths, or of thieves that do pilfer clothes through windows and walls.
16. Of such as go on messages for thieves.
17. Of [the hue and] cry[99] levied and not pursued.
18. Of bloodshed and of affrays made.
19. Of escapes of thieves and felons.
20. Of persons outlawed who have returned without the king's warrant.
21. Of women ravished and not presented before the coroners.
22. Of clippers and forgers of money.
23. Of treasure found.[100]
24. Of the assize of bread and ale broken.
25. Of false measures, as of bushels, gallons, yards, measures, and ells.
26. Of false balances and weights.
27. Of such as have double measure, and buy by the great, and sell by the less.
28. Of such as continually haunt taverns, and no man knows on what they live.
29. Of such as sleep by day, and watch by night, and have nothing.
30. Of cloth-sellers and curriers of leather dwelling outside merchant towns.
31. Of such as flee into church or churchyard, and afterwards depart without doing that which belongs there.[101]
32. Of persons imprisoned, and afterward let go without mainprise.
33. Of such as take doves in winter by engines.
34. And of all these things, you shall do under the oath you have taken.

---

98 Petty larceny is strictly defined as the theft of goods valued less than 12d.

99 A reference to the raising of the hue and cry to alert the vill to a suspected crime, see p. 180.

100 This requirement underlines the responsibility of the vill for a wider range of civil duties, such as informing the coroner of treasure trove.

101 Suspected felons could claim sanctuary at a designated church and then leave ('abjure') the realm under escort. They were not to return without a royal pardon. See p. 234.

43 The manner of holding leet courts, 1340

This example differs from that above [42] in three main ways: it includes an explicit statement of the oath made by the jurors at the beginning of the court, it contains greater detail, and the original copy is recorded in the court roll of a local leet rather than in the central archive of the Crown. It sketches the responsibilities and jurisdiction of the vill, and by extension the business which the view of frankpledge should consider. Not all of this business would be recorded in the rolls of the leet, because some cases and information would have been passed onto other courts and authorities. These guidelines were constructed for the benefit of the estate stewards who presided over the leet court, perhaps implying that even they were not entirely certain of the exact bounds of its jurisdiction.

F. W. Maitland and W. P. Baildon, eds, *The Court Baron*, Selden Society, 4 (1890), pp. 93–6. Extract from leet court of Weston (Hertfordshire), held 19 October 1340. French.

Here shall the steward charge the frankpledges with the articles which are to be presented at this court, and shall speak as follows to the presenters, and the beadle shall hold a book in his hand and the steward shall say: 'Hold [up] your hands. You shall loyally enquire among yourselves and loyally present all the articles of which you shall be charged on behalf of the king and the lord of this court to the best of your knowledge. So help you God in the day of judgment.'

First whether the presenters be all here as they should be; and if not, tell us of the defaults.

Whether all those who owe suit to this session be here; and if not, present the defaults.

Whether all those who are twelve years old and upwards be in a tithing; and, if not, tell us who has harboured them since [that age].

Whether hue and cry hath been levied among you in an affray of the peace, and if the parties were duly attached by the suit of the tithing-men.

Whether blood has been shed among you; how and by whom, and whether the parties have been attached.

Whether any purpresture has been made in the vill or the fields, as for instance a dung-heap placed in the high street to the nuisance of the locality, or a wall raised by one neighbour upon [the land of] another or on the king's highway, as for instance on roads or field-paths, that this day it may be abated; or whether in the fields one neighbour has ploughed upon [the land of] another or on the king's highway.

Whether any watercourse be stopped in its right course; how and by whom; that this day it may be set right.

Whether any paths to the church, the mill, or the common spring be destroyed; and by whom.

Whether there be among you any petty thieves, as of geese, ducks, and poultry; and who they be.

Whether there be among you any great thieves, as of horses, oxen, pigs and sheep; who they be, what their thefts, and what their goods and chattels.

Whether there be among you any who rob in the woods or on the king's highway; and who be their maintainers.

Whether there be among you any thieves who snatch cloths or other things from windows; what be their thefts and who their receivers.

Whether there be among you any who harbour folk contrary to the assize, for often it chances that such harbourers and receivers murder their guests by night.

Whether there be among you any ale-wives or regraters who brew and sell contrary to the assize, and that by false measures.

Whether there be among you any bakers or regraters who bake and sell bread contrary to the assize, and that by false weights.

Whether there be among you any tailors who know how to make, and do make, leggings and caps and the like out of a cloak.

Whether there be among you any goldsmiths who are wont by night to melt down cups or bells or other vessels of silver and to make out of them buckles, rings, and goods for wearing, such as brooch-pins and ear-rings.

Whether there be among you any smiths who know how to make out of a stolen plough-share or coulter, horse-shoes and chains, tongs and trivets.

Whether there be among you any who counterfeit the king's money or who clip the said money.

Whether there be among you any who have abjured the land and afterwards have returned and who hath since harboured or received them.[102]

___

102 See n. 101.

Whether there be among you any maid, widow or wife, or other woman who hath been ravished against her will.

Whether there be among you any man who goes around loafing by night, commonly haunting the tavern and who is no rich proprietor or rich merchant.[103]

Whether there be among you any who fish without licence with nets or baskets or any other thing in river, pond or preserve.

Whether there be among you any who without licence chase with dogs in the warren of the lord or of the king or take the deer called fallow, buck and doe or roebuck, or with a ferret take rabbit, hare, fox or badger.

Whether there be among you any fowler who with net, trap or other engine without licence takes crane, heron, wild goose, woodcock, snipe, thrush, lark, pigeon, goshawk or sparrow-hawk in the park or elsewhere.

Whether any treasure be found underground or elsewhere within the franchise of the lord; where and what it be.

Whether any waif be found in the vill or in the fields or in the woods, be it beast, clothes or other thing; has the lord been put in possession of this as is right.[104]

Whether there be among you any pilferer who at harvest-time by night steals the corn of others in small quantities or by handfuls or horse-loads or cart-loads.

Whether there be among you any usurer; present the facts.

Whether there be among you any butcher in the place who receives fat beasts stolen and makes delivery of them at market or at the tan-yard.

Whether there be any tanner who buys hides and skins which to his knowledge came from beasts thus stolen.

Whether there be any vagabond who goes to strange localities and by colour of his going as a merchant steals horses by the way and on his return into the country sells a mare or a foal for 10s. which is worth 20s.

---

103 This point recognises that much legitimate commercial activity took place in inns and taverns.

104 Abandoned stock or goods which remained unclaimed after proclamation and a specified time for recovery were forfeited to the holder of the leet.

Whether there be among you any who is used or accustomed to unshoe horses which he finds tied up and then sells the shoes.

Whether any rescue be made from the king's bailiffs or the lord's bailiff when distress or attachments have been made.

Whether any man be attached for suspicion of larceny and whether he has been delivered out by any; and by whom.

Whether there be any among you who has bought by one measure and sold by another, as some bakers and brewers do.

Whether there be any chandler who sells by false weight.

Whether there be among you any draper or clothier who uses false measures in buying or in selling.

And of those matters which are against the crown, inquire among yourselves and if you wish for a clerk you shall have one. And then when the dozeners have gone forth to inquire of the articles, the essoins of pleas shall be called on.

44 A leet court at Fifield, 1441

The records of many leets are segregated from the manor court, either on a separate roll, or as a separate court on the same roll, or as a separate section within a manor court. The activities of the leet at Fifield were still recorded separately in the mid-fifteenth century. The frankpledge unit appears to comprise three tithings, each based on a named settlement within the vill.

N. J. Hone, ed., *The manor and its records* (1925), pp. 154–7. Court leet of the manor of Fifield (Berkshire), 31 July 1441. Latin.

Fifield. View of frankpledge held there on the last day of July in the 19th year of Henry VI [31 July 1441].

The tithing man comes there and presents 7s. of certmoney[105] this day, and 4 quarters of fine wheat, valued at 2d. per bushel – sold, 5s. 4d. And they present that Robert Dodde 2d., John servant of John Gollofer 1d., Thomas servant of the said John 1d., William Hykkes 1d., John Huet [blank], William Symmys 1d., John Symkyns 2d., William Croftacre 1d., William Symkyns 1d., Richard Chapman 1d., Walter Banester 1d., John Ele 1d., John Wayfer 1d., William Levying 2d. have brewed ale and broken the assize, and therefore in mercy.

105 Certmoney is the local name for the common fine, see p. 181. The additional payment of grain as 'wardcorn' is a local peculiarity, and refers to some ancient military responsibilty upon the vill.

And they present that Bray the Miller has taken excessive toll, therefore in mercy. And they present a swarm of bees, valued at 9d., was forthcoming as stray (*extrahura*) about the feast of St John the Baptist [24 June] last past and has not been claimed, and therefore forfeited to the lord. And to the same court come Alice Strange and Thomas Bocher and give to the lord 10d. for licence to brew from the feast of Michaelmas [29 September] last past for one year, as appears in the margin and over their names.

The tithing man of Kingston comes into full court with his tithing and gives 20d. certmoney this day and a quarter of fine wheat, sold to John Newman for 16d. And that William Lord has brewed and broken the assize, and therefore is in mercy. And that all other things are well.

The tithing man of Dencheworth comes into full court with his whole tithing and gives 4d. certmoney this day. And they present that John Hesy, smith, 1d., and John Spycer, 1d., have brewed and broken the assize, and therefore are in mercy.

Verdict. 12 jurors, namely Thomas Symkyns and his fellows, come and present upon their oath that all the tithing men above have presented well and faithfully in all things, and all other things are well.

Affeerers: John Wybbyn and John Croftacre, sworn.

Sum. Of certmoney of this view, 9s. Of perquisites of court, 4s. 9d. Of wardcorn, 5 quarters.

45 A leet court at Brandon, 1385

The business of the leet at Brandon was recorded within the body of the manor court roll: the particular example of November 1385 begins with entries from the manor court and then switches without any formal break or distinction to the leet, which simply begins with the list of capital pledges. The extract starts at this point and continues until the end of the roll. Two points are worthy of special note: first, the business of Brandon's leet is varied and highly active, as befits a small but thriving market town, and, second, the core of regular bakers who are also active brewers, and who are thus identifiable as the main innkeepers of the town.

University of Chicago, Joseph Regenstein Library, Bacon Collection 292, m.11. Court leet of Brandon (Suffolk) extracted from the manor court, 30 November 1385. Latin.

Brandon. Court with leet held there on the Thursday in the feast of St Andrew the apostle in the 9th year of the reign of Richard II [30 November 1385].

Capital pledges. John Waterman, John Barker, Reginald Chapman, John Gebon, John Knyth, Thomas Hoggeson, Simon Talior, John Styward, Thomas Hobelot, John Notekyn, William at Mere, Richard Waterman, sworn upon oath. They present that they give 4s. to the lord of the leet court from ancient customary use, as is evident in past rolls.

Stephen Gebon drew blood maliciously from Richard Waterman, and so in mercy and amerced 6d. And the same Stephen made an affray upon the said Richard, and so in mercy and amerced 6d. Richard Cook made a breach of the peace upon Richard Waterman, amerced 6d. Richard Waterman drew blood from the said Richard in self-defence, and so in mercy and amerced 3d.

William Esteler drew blood from John Soutere maliciously, and so in mercy and amerced 6d. John Crowe did similarly upon John Dollingham, amerced 6d.

Robert Knyth assaulted John, servant of Richard Felys, amerced 6d. The said John raised the hue against the said Robert wrongfully, and so in mercy and amerced 6d.

Richard Cook made an affray upon Laurence Smith, and so in mercy and amerced 6d.

Stephen Gebon drew blood from John, servant of Richard Felys, maliciously, and so in mercy and amerced 12d.

Richard Swan assaulted Alice Swon maliciously, and so in mercy and amerced 6d.

John Folcham drew blood from John Brigge maliciously, and so in mercy and amerced 3d.

Agnes Brigge raised the hue against John Folsham wrongfully, and so in mercy and amerced 3d.

Richard Felys made an affray upon Thomas Elyot, amerced 6d.

Walter Fishchere made an affray upon John Honington maliciously, and so in mercy and amerced 12d. John Honington raised the hue against Walter Fishchere wrongfully, amerced 12d.

John Crowe made a trench in the common way to the harm of the neighbours, and so in mercy and amerced 3d. And he is ordered to repair it by the next court, under penalty of 2s.

Benedict Munk defamed Joan, wife of John Gebon, and so in mercy and amerced 3d.

John Brigge, 6d., and Matthew Peris, 6d., made an affray upon Simon Munk, and so in mercy and amerced.

Stephen Gebon caught a hare within the lord's warren. The lord's advice is sought.

Alice Lister amerced 3d. because she does not come to answer John Stracour of Weeting in a plea of debt. Ordered to attach her against the next court.[106]

They present that John Manys of Wangford, who is the abbot of Warden's man, commoned in the commons of Brandon with 20 cows but is not a commoner, and so in mercy and amerced 2s.

William Waterman made an affray upon Simon Cook, amerced 3d.

Agnes at Bregge 12d., Thomas son of Roger 6d., William Metfeld 6d., Richard Cook 5s., John Houghton 12d., John Barkere 12d., Alex Tailor 18d., Gilbert Clerk 10d., Richard Waterman 12d., John Knyth 18d., John Crowe 18d., Richard Felys 10d., Reginald Chapman 2s., Thomas Smith 12d., William at Mere 10d., Simon Tailor 18d., John Horsthe 12d., and John Gebon 3d. sold ale contrary to the assize. Benedict Munk did similarly, 2d. Total, 22s. 11d.

John Brigge 6d., William de Metfeld 2d., Richard Cook 2s., William Baxter 12d., Richard Waterman 3d., John Crowe 6d., Richard Felys 3d., and Reginald Chapman 18d. baked and sold bread against the assize. Total, 6s. 2d.

Agnes at Brigge 3d., the wife of Thomas son of Roger 3d., John Barker 3d., Alice Talior 3d., the wife of Gilbert Clerk 3d., the wife of Richard Waterman 3d., the wife of John Knyth 3d., the wife of John Crowe 3d., the wife of Richard Felys 3d., the wife of Reginald Chapman 3d., the wife of Thomas Smith 3d., the wife of William at Mere 3d., the wife of Simon Tailor 3d., the wife of John Horsthe 3d., the wife of John Gebon 3d. brewed but did not produce their measures. Total, 4s. 6d.

Agnes at Brigge 3d., the wife of Thomas son of Roger 3d., John Barker 3d., Alice Tailor 3d., the wife of Gilbert Clerk 3d., the wife of Richard Waterman 3d., the wife of John Knyth 3d., the wife of John Crowe 3d., the wife of Richard Felys 3d., the wife of Reginald Chapman 3d., the

---

106 This and the next case deal with matters which do not concern the leet, but have found their way into the record of its business.

wife of Thomas Smith 3d., the wife of William at Mere 3d., the wife of Simon Tailor 3d., the wife of John Horsthe 3d., the wife of John Gebon 3d. brewed but did not summon the ale-tasters to their brewing and did not come for approval of their ale. Total, 4s. 6d.

John Brigge 6d., William Baxstere 6d., and Reginald Chapman 6d. baked but did not produce their weights.

William Baxstere 4d., Richard Cook 4d., John de Bury 4d., John Dullingham 4d., Robert Knyth 4d., Thomas son of Roger 4d., John Barker 4d., William Coupere 4d. for respite from attending the court leet.

Simon Tailor 3d., and Thomas Smith 3d., because they did not fulfil their office as ale-tasters. Stephen Bate and Roger Sas chosen for the office of ale-taster for this year, and they are sworn.

John Lister amerced 3d. because he did not come when called, and order to attach him to answer John Benyt in a common plea.

The capital pledges have a day appointed before the next court to inquire about certain men who keep greyhounds to the damage of the lord and dogs causing damage in the warren ... [the manuscript is damaged] ... and not of right, and this to the value of 20s.

Deaths. The jurors present that 13 hoggs and 2 ewes died accidentally before Michaelmas and not due to negligence.

46   A tourn held on the manor of Wakefield, 1316

Wakefield lay outside the area covered by the frankpledge system, but the local jurisdiction over civil and criminal activites had been granted to the lord of the manor (the earl of Surrey). The manor was subdivided into 'graveships', based on the main settlements within the manorial territory, which were responsible for reporting cases to a special tourn in much the same way as individual tithing units reported to the frankpledge. In addition to the standard business of the leet, the tourn records cases of grand larceny within its jurisdiction for referral to higher courts for further action, and, on occasions, the outcome of those cases (see the fate of the Shepherd brothers). The preamble to the tourn indicates that Wakefield was in the grip of a crime wave, which necessitated the unusual step of swearing in a double presentment jury to clear all the accumulated business. Many were crimes of desperation, for the whole of western Europe was suffering the effects of a disastrous famine: the harvest of 1316 had failed catastrophically, compounding the severe distress caused by the appalling harvest of 1315. The attack by a father and son upon Thomas son of Peter while he harvested his corn, and all for just three puny sheaves of barley worth 3d., is symptomic of this tragic and devastating episode in which perhaps ten per cent of the population died.[107]

J. Lister, ed., *Court rolls of the manor of Wakefield, vol. iv, 1315–1317*, Yorkshire Archaeological Society, 78 (1930), pp. 153–6. Tourn of Wakefield (Yorkshire), held 16 November 1316. Latin.

Tourn held at Wakefield on Tuesday the feast of Edmund the archbishop, in the 10th year of the reign of Edward II [16 November 1316], by double juries on account of the frequent burglaries and the great number of thieves, as to which the truth cannot be ascertained.

Twenty-four jurors. Robert of Wyverumthorp, William of Dewsbury, Henry of Chivet, John Patryk, Robert of Stodley, John Pykard, John Aleyn of Eccleshill, Richard son of John of Osset, German Filcok, John Erl, Thomas son of Lawrence, and William of Castleford in the first inquisition. Richard of the Saltmarsh, Walter of Toftclyf, John of the More, Adam Sprigonel the younger, Thomas of the Bellehous, William Grenehod, Robert the Fuller, Robert of Heyrode, Thomas atte Kirke of Ardsley, William of the Okes, Robert the Drapur of Stanley, and Adam of Wodesom in the second.

[Order to the] bailiff. Adam Vapurnient of Wiveley and Agnes Spire to be taken for burgling the house of Robert Alayn of Bretton and stealing woollen and linen clothes, meat and other goods to the value of 5 marks. Margaret of the Wodhall of Wiveley to be attached for receiving them and the stolen goods.

Richard, son of Henry son of Roger of Drytker, to be attached for stealing 3 sheaves of barley worth 3d. in the harvest from Thomas son of Peter.

Henry son of Roger amerced 12d. for drawing blood from Thomas son of Peter.

Ellen daughter of Rochard Cosyn to be taken for stealing 2 bushels of oats worth 12d. from John Patrik's grange. Eva wife of William Cort to be attached for knowingly receiving the said 2 bushels, and amerced 12d. for violence and drawing the blood of a certain woman from outside [the manor].

John son of William of the Okes stole 2 thraves and 6 sheaves of oats worth 3d. in the harvest from the earl's crop at Sandal.

107 A fine introduction to the European famine of the 1310s is W. C. Jordan, *The great famine* (Princeton, 1996).

Thomas son of Agnes of Crigleston amerced 3d. for not coming to the tourn. John the Smith of Walton amerced 3d. for not coming. William Cokewald of Dewsbury to be attached for bloodshed upon Godfrey of Dewsbury.

John Maufesour to be taken for burgling the grange of Richard son of Hust of Ardsley and stealing one and a half bushels of oats worth 3s. William son of Richard of the Haghe to be attached for knowingly receiving the said oats. The said John to be taken for stealing a horse for the said Richard son of Hust.

Robert son of Ivo amerced 12d. for bloodshed upon John of the Haghe and 12d. upon Richard the Carpenter.

Hugh Virour and the said Richard the Carpenter 12d. each for bloodshed upon each other.

Thomas the Forester to be taken for stealing a dish worth 2s. from Robert the Walker's house, and a carpet worth 10d. from the same house.

Thomas the Hatter amerced 3d. for not coming to the tourn.

Robert Cheep 12d. for bloodshed upon Henry Calf.

John Damyas 12d. for diverting the watercourse in the Westgate, ordered to be rectified.

Walter the Spicer's wife justly raised the hue upon Richard Wythe-houndes for attacking the said Walter after breaking the windows of his house, and Richard amerced 6d.

Mauger the Turner to be attached for habitually receiving unknown thieves.

Peter Spink unjustly raised the hue upon Philip of the Hill and is therefore amerced 6d.

Adam son of Lawrence amerced 6d. for having a big hole in front of his door in the Northgate to the nuisance of his neighbours.

Henry Shepherd of Floketon and his brother Thomas, and Peter of Whitteley, stole a horse of John of Horbury worth 33s. 8d. and two oxen of Robert of Stodeley worth 20s., a heifer of William of Hewton worth 5s. and a mare of Robert of the Wro worth 8s., for which the said Henry and Thomas were hanged at Harewood and Peter is in prison at York.

Geoffrey Ruddock to be taken for stealing 12 sheaves of oats worth 12d. belonging to William of the Byrkenschaghe.

Osset. Eva daughter of William the White of Ossett, and Alice and Annabel, daughters of the said William, amerced 6d. each because they are deflowered. And because these lecherwytes have been concealed for several tourns by the graveship of Osset, the said graveship is amerced 40d.

Bailiff. Order to take Marjory, daughter of Richard Cosyn, for burgling the house of Marjory daughter of Hugh son of Emma of Emmeley, and stealing 6s. in money, a tunic and surcoat worth 9s. 6d. and a silver buckle worth 2s.

Adam Cosyn to be taken for stealing 5 half thraves of oats at Denby grange worth 6s. 8d.

Agnes, wife of Nicholas of Batley to be attached for stealing 12 sheaves of oats belonging to Robert of Wyverumthorpe worth 6d.

Alice daughter of Emma the Longe to be attached for furtively cropping the corn of the said Robert to the value of 1d.

Stanley. Alice the younger daughter of Beatrice Gunne amerced 12d. for bloodshed upon her sister Alice.

Philip son of of Philip the Sawyer 12d. for likewise upon Robert son of Richard of the Ker.

Maud daughter of Richard of the Ker to be attached for stealing flour and meat from Robert the Leper's house to the value of 6d.

Bailiff. A certain alien thief stole a shirt worth 4d. from the same house and another shirt worth 4d. from the house of Richard of the Ker, who caught the thief, took the shirts from him and suffered him to go; and concealed Robert's shirt until it was found in his possession. Richard to be attached.

Richard of Blakeburne and Eva his wife to be attached for suspicion of sheep-stealing and other petty larcenies.

Orders to attach: Elias the Saucer for stealing 40 herrings worth 4d. from John of Fery's shop; Richard of Batley for stealing half a sheaf of oats belonging to Robert of Fery; Simon Tyting for stopping up a path through his croft in Stanley to the nuisance of the neighbours; Richard of the Ker for continuing to keep Margaret daughter of Thomas in incest.[108]

---

108 The range of kinship covered by the medieval definition of incest was wider than that which applies in modern times.

William son of Richard of the Haghe is amerced 40d. because he lent 20s. to Alice the Stinter and takes 10d. per week in usury. Jordan of Idle gives 2s. for having aid, pledge William of Floketon. Richard Tylly and Thomas of Ceyvill, two of those elected, amerced 12d. each for not coming to the tourn. William of Floketon 6d. for contempt.

Grand total of this tourn, 25s. 5d., of which on the bailiff, 18s. 1d., on Stanley 2s., and Osset, 5s. 4d.

47   A case from a leet court of Walkern, 1337

This extract from a leet court hints at a complicated and difficult set of personal relationships. The jury's presentment self-consciously explains the failure of the frankpledge to capture either of the suspects, one of whom sought sanctuary in the local church before fleeing the village. The record of their forfeiture of goods and chattels, including land with standing crops, provides rare but valuable information about peasant agriculture and material culture.

Hertfordshire Record Office, Roll 9334. Walkern (Hertfordshire) court leet held 26 June 1337.

The jury say on oath that on the Saturday after Trinity Sunday in the eleventh year [21 June, 1337] William le Maners came with force and arms to the house of Isabel, formerly the wife of Robert le Gardyner, and there in the garden of the said Isabel, and with her assent, wounded and killed Thomas le Gardyner with bow and arrows, and escaped through the lane at the bottom of the garden which once belonged to Robert le Gardyner. And that the aforesaid Isabel was the guardian, harbourer and supporter of the same William, and after the said deed she fled to the church. And after this the said Isabel fled from the county.

As a consequence of this deed, 8 acres of *frisce* land are seized into the hands of the lord. Item 3 acres of land sown with wheat, and 3 acres sown with peas and oats. Item 3 roods of land sown with oats which the said William held from the lord, valued at [blank].

Item one messuage, 3 acres sown with wheat and half an acre sown with barley seized into the lord's hands which Isabel held.

Item seized from the chattels of the said William one horse valued at 3s., one cow valued at 6s. 8d., one bullock valued at 3s., six ewes, two hoggets, four lambs valued at 6s. And other chattels of cloth, valued at 12d.

Item from the goods and chattels of the said Isabel two old coverlets of tartarin ('coverlytes de Tyrteyn') valued at 12d., two over-tunics with one furred hood valued at 4s. Item one tablecloth, two and a half ells long, 3d. Item one brass, 12-pint, vessel, 12d., and one pan of four quarts, and one small basin, 6d. Item one plate, 10d., and one pewter vessel, 16d. Item 5lb. of wool, 6d. Item two chests, 18d. Item one large bowl, 4d., brushwood and old timber, 2d. Item hemp and flax soaked in oil, 6d.

Other manorial courts

48 A wreck court at Sizewell, 1378

Leiston abbey enjoyed the right to profit from all wreckage washed ashore on land pertaining to the vills of Sizewell and Thorpeness, a franchise acquired as a special privilege from the Crown. The abbey did not seek to collect wrecked material and valuable flotsam for its own use, but merely to charge those local people who did. Consequently, it administered its right through a special court held in December each year (known locally as the 'Hethewards moot'), whose procedures borrowed heavily from leet and manor courts. The boatmasters operating from the shore during the autumn fishing seasons were compelled to serve as jurors and ensure that all claims for wreckage were presented during the year. Those persons claiming wreck, often fishermen, were named, and the nature and value of their wreckage recorded and assessed by specially appointed court officials. The abbey would then have charged a percentage (normally fifty per cent) of the value of the claimed goods. The court was also used by the boatmasters to resolve disputes between themselves relating to the fish trade, and consequently provides a rare insight into an under-recorded but important local activity.

Suffolk Record Office, Ipswich HD 371/1. Wreck court of Sizewell and Thorpeness (Suffolk), held 6 December 1378.

Sizewell and Thorp. Court of the Hethewards Moot held on Monday on the feast of St Nicholas, the 2nd year of the reign of King Richard II [6 December 1378].

Names of the Masters of Thorp in all 'fares' [fishing seasons]: Simon Cote, Simon Hane, Stephen Drenge, John Packe, John Bras, William Plemm, Andrew Grey, Nicholas Hame.

The jury say that John Packe made a contract with Andrew Grey, Stephen Waite, Richard Hert, John Portman of Freston and Simon Rust to provide them with one boat for the duration of the Sparlingfare. And because the said John broke this contract, and did not provide them with a boat, he is in mercy.

Simon Baxter found [i.e. claims as wreck] planks to the value of 2s.

Nicholas Hane and Simon Hane senior found planks to the value of 12d.

Simon Hane junior found planks to the value of 12d.

Simon Cote and his crew found one weighbeam from a mast, to the value of 2s.

Stephen Drenge of Preston and his crew from Thorpe found planks floating on the sea during the Fishingfare, value 2s.

John Ukekyn found one barrel, value 2d.

Andrew Grey found one barrel, value 2d.

William Plem found horse shoes, value 2d.

Assessors (*vagantes*): John Packe and William Plenn are assessors this year.

John Packe found a barrel and a damaged barrel, value 6d.

Andrew Grey, plaintiff, versus John Packe in a plea of broken contract.

John Packe has licence to agree with Andrew Grey in a plea of broken contract.

Stephen Drenge, boat master, for default.

Sizewell. Names of masters in all fares: John Casel, Robert Francys, John Cowyn, Robert Legat, Walter Cos, jurors.

They present that John Walwyn and John Brok found one 'barmskyn' and one plank, value 6d.

Robert Francys found one 'bowk', value 2d.

John Bluere found 600 'astels' [splinters], value 4d.

John Cowyme and his crew found one plank, value 2d.

49   A market court at Newmarket, 1409

The right to hold a weekly market on a manor implied the right to hold a market court, although the volume of business would determine whether its work was recorded in separate market court rolls or merely subsumed within the rolls of the manor court. The survival rate of market court rolls is very low, but this example from Newmarket reveals that they followed the format of manor courts, complete with market bailiffs (one of whom presided over the court) and clerk. The court was held on market day, normally at the toll booth in the marketplace. A few cases were presented by the bailiffs of the market, but most were private actions between traders. Presentment juries were rarely employed and were drawn from the stallholders. Inquisition juries were even less common: the obvious difficulties in ensuring the simultaneous attendance of twelve itinerant merchants at some future court meant that inquisition juries offered a slow and frustrating form of justice.

Suffolk Record Office, Bury St Edmunds, 1476/1/20. Market court of Newmarket (Suffolk), held 8 January 1409. Latin.

Newmarket. Market court held there on the Tuesday next after Epiphany in the 10th year of the reign of Henry IV [8 January 1409].

Thomas Hancok, merchant, 4d., submits himself for licence to agree with William Coupere, merchant, pledged as above [i.e. in a previous court]. William Wryte, merchant, 4d., submits himself for licence to agree with Stephen Brasyere, merchant, pledged as above.

To this court comes John Lylys and takes from the lord one vacant place in Skynnersrowe next to the shop of Robert Gateward, containing in length twelve and a half feet and in breadth seven feet. To hold to him and his issue (*sequele*) by the rod at the will of the lord according to the custom of the manor, and rendering for this 2s. per annum to the lord at the usual terms, and owes suit of court. And makes fealty to the lord. And he gains seisin. And he gives a[n entry] fine, 24s.

It is found by the bailiff that Simon Bonere sold one shop next to the door of John Barbor to Simon Childerston without licence, thus it is ordered to seize the shop and answer for issues. And afterwards Simon Childerston is able to complete an agreement, and pays a fine of 20d. to hold in chief as his right for a term of eight years.

To this court comes William Howeson and takes from the lord one shop in 'le Bocherye', lately held by Richard Farewel, with the assent of the said Richard. To hold to him and his issue by the rod and at the will of the lord according to the custom of the manor. And makes fealty. And he gains seisin. And pays a fine, 5s.

John Wode, merchant, 6d., submits himself for licence to agree with John Taylor, merchant, pledge Thomas Sowcere.

50   Trade disputes recorded in market courts at Newmarket, 1403–10

The following extracts have been lifted from four different market courts at Newmarket to illustrate typical cases and procedures. The most common forms of business in the Newmarket courts were pleas of debt, pleas of trespass, breach of contract, concealment and detention of chattels, many of which provide colourful details of trading activity. The court readily attached goods and chattels from offenders to ensure compliance with its orders, and sought to provide swift resolution of disputes for itinerant traders. Goods and chattels for attachment were carefully selected for this purpose: deadstock and horses featured commonly in attachments, the former because it deteriorated rapidly so had to be claimed quickly, and the latter because they provided merchants with their means of departure. The unusual survival of compurgation in dispute resolution in the early fifteenth century is presumably a function of the desire to provide quick, at the possible expense of fair, justice.[109]

Suffolk Record Office, Bury St Edmunds, 1476/1/13, 1476/1/28, 1476/1/35. Extracts from various market courts of Newmarket (Suffolk), held between 1403 and 1410. Latin.

[Court held 6 November, 1403] Roger Smith of Soham, merchant, is plaintiff against Thomas Eustas, merchant, in a plea of debt, John Kyrkeby is pledge for the plaintiff. And Thomas was attached by a horse valued at 13s. 4d., which remains in the hands of John Roydon, barker, until trial by inquisition [*patria*].

[Court held 13 December, 1407] Richard Derlyng is plaintiff against Thomas atte Heel in a plea of trespass, because the aforesaid Richard bought a horse valued at 10s. from the aforesaid Thomas after bargaining. And the aforesaid Thomas warranted the aforesaid horse to be sound in wind and limb, and sold the horse fraudulently to Richard knowing it to be unsound in wind and limb, to the aforesaid Richard's damage. And Thomas denies any wrongdoing, and says he did not warrant the horse. And puts himself at mercy for a verdict by waging law, and is given days, to the next court, to come with six hands [i.e. people].

[20 December, 1407] Thomas atte Heel does not come with his law to answer Richard Derlyng on the given date. Therefore it was agreed

109 See pp. 173–5.

that Richard should recover his damages as declared above. And Thomas is in mercy.

[18 February, 1410] William Goddard and John Chaundeler, bailiffs, present that William Saman assaulted them while collecting their lord's dues, and he pulled his dagger on them to the lord's prejudice. Afterwards William places himself in mercy, 6d.

51   A fair court at Newmarket, 1408

Fair courts, like those of markets, follow the basic format of manor courts. A feature of the fair court at Newmarket is the wider use of presentment juries than in the market court: they comprised anything from three to twelve stallholders.

Suffolk Record Office, Bury St Edmunds, 1476/1/22. Fair court at Newmarket, held 29 October 1408. Latin.

Newmarket. Fair court held there on Monday next after the feast of Sts Simon and Jude the apostles in the 10th year of the reign of King Henry IV [29 October 1408].

The First Hour. 6d. from Stephen Vynter of South Elmham, merchant, because it is not possible to deny that he owes five marks and seven shillings to Richard Cauncellare, merchant, which were ordered to be levied to the benefit of the said Richard together with damages assessed by the court, and the same Stephen in mercy.

It is ordered to retain one horse and one saddle with bridle taken from Edmund Wykys, merchant, and to take more until he finds pledges to respond to Thomas West, merchant, in plea of debt.

6d. from Thomas Maleyn, merchant, for licence to agree with Nicholas Pertrych, merchant, in plea of debt.

4d. from the pledges of Thomas Teversham, merchant, who did not have him respond to Peter Wanton, merchant, in a plea of debt. And it is ordered etc., pledge Robert Dowale.

6d. from John Scot, merchant, because he does not proceed against John Gertmaker, merchant, in plea of debt.

6d. from Thomas de Wrottinge, merchant, for licence to agree with John Dalsham, merchant, in plea of debt, pledge Stephen Gille.

6d. From Thomas Vincent, merchant, for licence to agree with John Wylkyn in a plea of debt.

Inquisition by office, taken by Robert Gateward, John Odye, Robert Doushole, Richard Farewel, Thomas Prydyton, Richard Tornor, John Mordon, John Phelyp, John Aston, William Alewyn, Laurence atte Thorn, John Sturdy and William Tornor, jurors.

They present that John Wynde, 3d., allows the roofing of a shop lately held by Beatrix Feke to waste, and ordered to repair. Richard Farewel, 6d., does likewise in a shop in le Bocheryerowe, ordered to repair.

Robert Colyn sold John Prydyngton, linen draper, two shops in le Draprerowe without licence, and thus ordered to seize.

John Lacy, 3d., John Hogesson, 3d., William Sygo, 3d., Adam Buck, 3d., and John Peyte, 3d., fail to perform suit of court.

The Second Hour. It is ordered just as before to retain one horse and one saddle with bridle taken from Edmund Wykys, merchant, and to take more until he finds pledges to respond to Thomas West, merchant, in plea of debt.

3d. from the pledges of Thomas Teversham, merchant, because they do not have him respond to Peter Wanton, merchant, in plea of debt.

The Third Hour. Again ordered to retain one horse and one saddle with bridle taken from Edmund Wykys, merchant, and to take more until he finds pledges to respond to Thomas West, merchant, in plea of debt.

3d. from the pledges of Thomas Teversham, merchant, because they do not have him respond to Peter Wanton, merchant, in plea of debt.

At the third hour just past the bailiff was ordered to retain one horse, a saddle and bridle taken from Edmund Wykys, merchant, etc., and at the said third hour the same Edmund became liable for his debts as he had not appeared. Thus by the custom of the manor the aforesaid horse, saddle and bridle are valued at 3s. 4d. by the merchants there.

Affeerers: John Phelyp of Mildenhall, roper, and Thomas Prydyngton of Fordham.

GLOSSARY

This glossary is not exhaustive, but contains most of the technical terms that occur throughout the book. Fuller discussions in the text of some of these terms are identified by page number references.

advowson, the legal right to appoint a priest to a parish church or **benefice** (p. 5)

affeerer, a **suitor** appointed by a court to advise on the level of **amercements** (p. 171)

affer, a small, versatile, draught horse, *see also* **stot**

agistment, payment for grazing animals on someone else's land

aid, payment made by a **vassal** to his lord, normally on specific occasions (such as the marriage of the lord's eldest daughter)

ale-taster, court official appointed to monitor the **assize of ale** within the **vill** (p. 189)

alienate, to grant land to someone else or an institution

allowance, the cancellation of a charge upon an official by the auditors

amercement, a financial penalty levied by a court (pp. 176–7)

ancient (or royal) demesne, land that comprised the royal estate at the time of Edward the Confessor

appropriate, to transfer the endowment, or part of the endowment, of a parish church to a religious institution (p. 5)

appurtenances, the rights attached to a piece of land

assart, land recently cleared for cultivation

assize, a legal procedure

assize of bread and ale, a legal procedure that regulated the quality and price of bread and ale for sale

attachment, the order to, or seizure of, a person to comply with a directive issued by a court

bailiff, the local official responsible for the day-to-day management of the manor. The bailiff performed a similar job to the **reeve**, but the bailiff was salaried (pp. 99–100)

baulk, a grassy, unploughed, strip of land within an open arable field. *Cf.* **headland**

benefice, an ecclesiastical living (carrying income)

boonwork, a seasonal **labour service** owed on the lord's **demesne**, often attracting the provision of food and ale by the lord. It originated as a free will service, or 'boon', to the lord

bordar, a smallholder, holding land on **customary tenure**; similar to a **cottar**

borough, a town characterised by the presence of burgage tenure and some trading privileges for certain tenants. Many, but not all, **boroughs,** were endowed with a **charter** of liberties

bovate, measure of arable land, especially in eastern and northern areas, normally equivalent to *c.* 15 acres

burgage, a form of property within a **borough**

bushel, a dry measure of 8 gallons used for grain and fruit especially

cablish, windfallen wood

capital messuage, a **messuage** containing a high status dwelling house, often the manor house itself

carrying services, a form of **labour service** requiring a tenant to transport goods for the lord

cartulary, a book containing copies of deeds, charters, and other legal records

carucate, a unit of taxation in northern and eastern counties, equivalent to the **hide**, notionally comprising 120 acres

charter, legal document recording the grant of land or privileges

chattels, movable personal property

chevage, annual payment to the manorial lord permitting a **villein** to live outside the manor

childwyte, fine paid to the manorial lord when a **villein** gave birth outside wedlock

common fine, *see* **hundredpenny**

common land, land over which tenants and perhaps villagers possessed certain rights (such as to graze animals, collect fuel, etc.). *Cf.* **severalty**

common law, a body of laws that overrode local **custom**

commutation, money payment in lieu of (labour) services

compurgation, the process of swearing innocence or good character on oath in court by the accused, with the support of perhaps six or twelve other oathmakers; also known as **waging law** (p. 173)

cotland, a smallholding held on customary tenure

cottar, an **unfree** smallholder. *See* **bordar**

croft, an enclosed plot of land, often adjacent to a dwelling house. *See* **pightle**

curia, the Latin word for 'court', but sometimes used to describe the **curtilage** or **messuage**

curtilage, *see* **messuage**

custom, a framework of local practices, rules and/or expectations pertaining to various economic or social activities

customary tenure, defined in the courts of common law as **unfree tenure**, whose obligations and terms were determined and enforced in the manor court; also known as **villein tenure** (pp. 28–34)

default, failure to fulfill a requirement laid down by a court

demesne, the land within a manor allocated to the lord for his own use

disseisin, dispossession

distrain, **distraint**, temporary confiscation of land and/or goods to enforce a court's decision or recover a debt

domain, all the land pertaining to a manor (i.e. **demesne**, **commons**, tenant land, etc.)

dower, widow's right to hold a proportion (normally one third) of her deceased husband's land for the rest of her life

dowry, land or money handed over with the bride at marriage

dredge (also **drage**), an equal mixture of oats and barley sown together

encroachment, an addition to a plot of private land by enclosing an adjacent piece of (often common) land. *See* **purpresture**

enfeoff, to grant land as a **fief**

engross, to amalgamate holdings or farms

entry fine, a payment by a tenant on taking up a landholding (p. 30)

escheat, land that has reverted to its lord

escheator, a royal official responsible for upholding the king's feudal rights

essoin, an excuse for not attending court (p. 170)

famuli, the regular labourers employed by the lord to work on his **demesne** land

farm, (in medieval usage) a fixed sum paid for leasing land; a **farmer** is therefore a lessee

fealty, an oath of fidelity sworn by a new tenant to the lord in recognition of his obligations

fee, fief, hereditary land held from a superior lord in return for **homage** and (often military) service

felony, the most serious crimes, as opposed to trespass and misdemeanor, which carried the possibility of capital punishment

fine, money payment to the lord to obtain a specific concession (p. 176). *Cf.* **amercement**

fodder, a crop grown for cattle-feed

fold, a penned or enclosed area for keeping animals, often sheep, by night

fold, liberty of, the right to keep a fold or foldcourse

foldcourse, an area designated for sheep grazing, often including some fallow arable land

foldsuit, the requirement for tenants to graze their sheep within a seigneurial foldcourse

forestall, the practice of trading before the formal opening of a market with the expectation of selling later in the day at a higher price

frankpledge, a group of men bound together by mutual surety to bring criminals to justice and report on criminal activities and civil issues (pp. 178–82)

free boar, the right to have a boar run free among the village swine and on local pastures (p. 47)

free bull, the right to have a bull run free among the village cattle (p. 47)

free warren, a royal franchise granted to a manorial lord allowing the holder to hunt small game (especially rabbit, hare, pheasant and partridge) within a designated **vill** (pp. 4–5)

free tenure, tenure or status that denoted greater freedom of time and action than, say, **customary tenure** or status; a **freeman** was entitled to use the royal courts, and the title to free tenure was defensible there (pp. 27–8)

full age, the age at which heirs were able to inherit land. The age varied according to local custom, but was normally 18 or 21 years.

furlong, a subdivision of open arable fields

garderobe, a latrine

geld, an Anglo-Saxon levy, or tax, on property based on the **hide**

gersuma, a relief payable to the lord on the entry of a new tenant to a land-holding (p. 30)

glebe, the landed endowment of a parish church

hamsoke, aggravated burglary

hayward, manorial official responsible primarily for overseeing the harvest. Also known as **messor**

headland, a ridge of unploughed land at the head of arable strips in open fields providing access to each strip and a turning place for the plough. *See* baulk

herbage, permission to pasture animals on someone else's land

heriot, a death duty, normally the best beast, levied by the manorial lord on the estate of a deceased tenant

hide, hideage, Anglo-Saxon land measurement, notionally 120 acres, used for calculating liability for geld. *See* **carucate**

hocktide, the second Monday and Tuesday after Easter

hogg, hogget, castrated sheep in its second year

homage, act by which a **vassal** acknowledges a superior lord

hue and cry, raising the alarm after a suspected offence, followed by pursuit of the suspect by members of the **frankpledge**

hundred, the unit of local government between the county and the **vill**

hundredpenny, annual payment by members of the frankpledge, originally to the sheriff but latterly to the holder of the **leet**. Also known as the **common fine**. *See* p. 181

impartible inheritance, the custom of inheritance by only one heir, often the eldest son. *Cf.* **partible inheritance**

incumbent, the person holding a **benefice**

knight's fee, land held from a superior lord for the service of a knight

labour services, the duty to work for the lord, often on the **demesne** land, as part of the tenant's rent package

leet, the court of a vill whose view of frankpledge had been franchised to a local lord by the Crown (p. 181)

leyrwite (also **lecherwite**), fine paid to the manorial lord when a **villein** woman fornicated (p. 33)

mainpernor, mainprise, a guarantor nominated by a court to ensure that another person upholds its orders. *See also* **pledge, surety**

manumission, the formal release from **villein** status, often recorded in a **charter** and obtained from the lord through either purchase or service

mark, sum of money equivalent to two thirds of a pound, i.e. 13s. 4d.

maslin, an equal mixture of wheat and rye sown together

merchet, a fine paid by **villein** tenants to the lord for permission for one of their children to marry (normally a daughter but sometimes applied to non-inheriting sons too)

messor, *see* **hayward**

messuage, a plot of land containing a dwelling house and outbuildings; *see also* **curtilage**

metes and bounds, formal boundaries delimited by measures and markers

mill-suit, the requirement for **villeins** to grind their corn at the lord's mill

molmen, rent-paying tenants holding molland, which was land on which services had been anciently **commuted**

moot, a meeting

multure, a fee for grinding corn, normally paid in kind; multure can also refer to the corn thus rendered

murrain, a generic name for animal disease

neif, a hereditary serf by blood

pannage, the right to feed pigs in woodland

parcener, a tenant holding land jointly with others

parker, manorial officer responsible for custodianship of the lord's deer park, and sometimes for stray animals

partible inheritance, the custom of inheritance equally among heirs. *Cf.* **impartible inheritance**

patron, the person responsible for the appointment of a priest to a benefice

pecia, a piece or strip of unenclosed arable land. *See* **selion**

penny, a small sum of money (d.) equivalent to 1/240th of a pound (as opposed to one new penny (p.) which is equivalent to 1/100th of a pound: the new penny succeeded the old in 1971)

perch, a linear measure of 16½ feet and a square measure equivalent to one fortieth of a **rood**

perquisites, seigneurial income from rights, **fines** and **amercements**

pightle, an enclosed yard or **croft**, often adjoining a dwelling house

pledge, *see* **mainpernor**, **surety**

pound, animal pen for keeping strays and **distraints**

presentment, an accusation brought before a court by a body of men under oath (pp. 173–4)

purpresture, an illegal encroachment on to land. See **encroachment**

quarantena, the East Anglian word for **furlong**

quarter, a dry measure equivalent to 8 **bushels**

quitclaim, a **charter** formally renouncing a claim to land

recognisance, a bond agreed in court binding a person to undertake a stated action

recognition, a fine payable by the villein tenants of some ecclesiastical estates on the election of a new abbot/bishop

recovery, (in this context) taking **distrained** goods or impounded animals without seigneurial permission

rector, the person or institution entitled to the endowment (such as the **tithes** and **glebe**) of a parish church

reeve, the local official responsible for the day-to-day management of the manor. The reeve performed a similar job to the **bailiff**, but the reeve was elected from the manorial tenantry (pp. 98–9)

regrate, to buy goods, especially fish and corn, during market hours and resell them later in the day at a higher price. *Cf.* **forestall**

relief, payment made by a free tenant on entering a holding

respite, a postponement of a financial charge upon an individual

rod, a symbol of the lord's authority when ratifying land transfers. Land held 'by the rod' was held at the will of the lord (p. 38)

rood, measure of land equivalent to one quarter of an acre; and forty **perches**
sanctuary, a temporary place of safety for suspected criminals, normally a church
scutage, payment in lieu of military service
seisin, possession (of land)
selion, a strip of ploughed land in an openfield system. *See also* **pecia**
serf, an unfree peasant characterised by onerous personal servility. *See* **neif,**
    cf. **villein**
serjeant, manorial official with a status similar to that of **bailiff**
several, severalty, land that is not subject to common rights. *Cf.* **common**
    land
sheriff, official responsible for the administration of a county by the Crown
shilling, a sum of money (s.) comprising twelve pennies, and equivalent to
    1/20th of a pound
socage, a form of tenure of peasant land, normally free (p. 27)
springs, the new growth in a wood
steward, an estate administrator, often of gentry status
stot, a small, cheap, horse. *See* **affer**
subinfeudate, the grant of land by one lord to another to hold as a **fief**
suit of court, the right and obligation to attend a court; the individual so
    attending is a **suitor**
suit of mill, *see* **mill-suit**
surety, *see* **mainprise, pledge**
tallage, a seigneurial right to tax unfree peasants at will
tenant-in-chief, a tenant holding land directly from the king
tenement, tenementum, a landholding
thegn, an Anglo-Saxon freeman of high status
thrave, a bundle of corn sheaves, normally 24, standing in the field
tithe, a tenth of all issue and profit (mainly grain, fruit, livestock and game)
    owed by parishioners to their church. *Cf.* **rector**
tithing, *see* **frankpledge**
toft, an enclosure for a homestead
tourn, a biennial court held by the sheriff to ensure the operation of the
    frankpledge system
trespass, a wrong committed against another person or their property
tumbrel, a dung cart, in which miscreants were sometimes placed as a punish-
    ment by leet courts
turbary, the right to dig peat for fuel
turves, peat dug for fuel; sometimes sods used for roofing
unfree tenure, *see* **customary tenure, villeinage**
vassal, a tenant, often of lordly status
view of frankpledge, see **frankpledge**
vill, the local unit of civil administration (p. 7, n. 15)
villein, peasant whose freedom of time and action is constrained by his lord;
    a villein was not able to use the royal courts. *Cf.* **freeman**
villeinage, *see* **customary tenure, unfree tenure**
virgate, a quarter of a **hide**; a standardised **villein** holding of *c.* 30 acres. Also
    known as a **yardland**

waging law, *see* **compurgation**

wainage, a **labour service** involving carting goods for the lord. A wain is a
  light, two-wheeled, cart

warren, free, *see* **free warren**

week works, onerous **labour services** rendered weekly; often a test of **villein
  tenure**

wether, castrated sheep in or after its second year

withies, flexible twigs bound together; wickerwork, especially baskets

woodward, manorial official responsible for woodland and hedges

yardland, *see* **virgate**

Useful works of reference

J. L. Fisher, *A medieval farming glossary* (Standing Conference for Local
  History, 1968)

D. Hay, ed., *The Oxford Companion to local and family history* (Oxford, 1996)

R. E. Latham, *Revised medieval Latin word-list* (London, 1965)

SELECT BIBLIOGRAPHY

This bibliography is intended as a guide to the secondary works that are especially helpful as either a general introduction to, or a detailed discussion of, key aspects of manorial records. The place of publication is London unless otherwise stated.

Medieval manorial records

The best general introductions to manorial records are: M. Ellis, *Using manorial records*, Public Record Office, London, Guide to Sources, 6 (1994); P. D. A. Harvey, *Manorial records*, British Records Association, 5 (2nd edn, 2000); P. D. A. Harvey, ed., *Manorial records of Cuxham, Oxfordshire, c. 1200–1359*, Oxfordshire Record Society, 50 (1976). Harvey (1976) offers an excellent commentary on the major classes of medieval manorial records, and is required reading for anyone wishing to understand them in greater detail.

The original documents are, of course, handwritten in medieval Latin, and the following works provide a good introduction and source of reference for both the language and the palaeography: E. A. Gooder, *Latin for local history: an introduction* (1978); H. E. P. Grieve, *Examples of English handwriting 1150–1750* (Essex Education Committee, 1954); L. C. Hector, *The handwriting of English documents* (Dorking, 1980); R. E. Latham, *Revised medieval Latin wordlist from British and Irish sources* (1994); C. Trice-Martin, *The record interpreter* (reprinted, Chichester, 1982); D. Stuart, *Manorial records: an introduction to their transcription and translation* (Chichester, 1992); J. Thorley, *Documents in medieval Latin* (1998).

The medieval manor and its administration

A charming and reliable general introduction to the medieval English manor is H. S. Bennett, *Life on the English manor* (Cambridge, reissued 1971). A succinct definition of the manor is given in B. F. Harvey, 'The life of the manor', in A. Williams, ed., *Domesday Book Studies* (1987), pp. 39–42. More technical discussions are contained in F. Pollock and F. W. Maitland, *The history of English law before the time of Edward I* (2nd edn, Cambridge, 1911), pp. 594–633; and P. Vinogradoff, *The growth of the manor* (1911), although some of Vinogradoff's theories are outdated. The shift towards local lordship in the late Anglo-Saxon period, which provides the context to the emergence of the manor, is surveyed effectively in R. Faith, *The English peasantry and the growth of lordship* (Leicester, 1997); and C. Lewis, C. C. Dyer and P. Mitchell-Fox, *Village, hamlet and field: changing medieval settlements in central England* (Manchester, 1997). For a comprehensive discussion of manorial types and

SELECT BIBLIOGRAPHY 249

variations in late thirteenth-century England, see E. Miller and J. Hatcher, *Medieval England: rural society and economic change 1086–1348* (1978), pp. 9–22 and 184–8; S. R. Rigby, *English society in the later Middle Ages: class, status and gender* (1995), pp. 34–44; and E. A. Kosminsky, *Studies in the agrarian history of England in the thirteenth century* (Oxford, 1956), pp. 68–151. A excellent, detailed, case study is B. M. S. Campbell, 'The complexity of manorial structure in medieval Norfolk: a case study', *Norfolk Archaeology*, 39 (1986), 225–52. General surveys of manorial administration between *c.* 1100 and *c.* 1500 can be found in N. Denholm-Young, *Seignorial administration in England* (Oxford, 1937), pp. 151–4; Miller and Hatcher, *Medieval England*, pp. 213–39; J. L. Bolton, *The medieval English economy, 1150–1500* (1980); and F. M. Page, *The estates of Crowland abbey: a study in manorial organisation* (Cambridge, 1934). Useful, individual, case studies are listed below.

Surveys and extents

The survey is considered in detail in P. D. A. Harvey, ed., *Manorial records of Cuxham, Oxfordshire, c.1200–1359*, Oxfordshire Record Society, 50 (1976). See also R. A. Skelton and P. D. A. Harvey, ed., *Local maps and plans from medieval England* (Oxford, 1986). Extents are explored comprehensively in R. V. Lennard, 'What is an extent?', *English Historical Review*, 44 (1929), 256–62; E. A. Kosminsky, *Studies in the agrarian history of England in the thirteenth century* (Oxford, 1956), pp. 47–57; B. M. S. Campbell, J. A. Galloway, and M. Murphy, 'Rural land use in the metropolitan hinterland 1270–1339: the evidence of IPMs', *Agricultural History Review*, 40 (1992), 3–6; B. M. S. Campbell, *English seigniorial agriculture 1250–1450* (Cambridge, 2000), pp. 37–41; and R. F. Hunnisett, 'The reliability of inquisitions as historical evidence', in D. A. Bullough and R. L. Storey, eds, *The study of medieval records* (Oxford, 1971), pp. 206–35.

Accounts

Technical discussions of medieval accounts and accounting are provided in: F. B. Stitt, 'The medieval minister's account', *Society of Local Archivists' Bulletin*, 11 (1953), 2–8; P. D. A. Harvey, 'Agricultural treatises and manorial accounting in medieval England', *Agricultural History Review*, 20 (1972), 170–82; B. M. S. Campbell, *English seigniorial agriculture 1250–1450* (Cambridge, 2000), pp. 26–36; J. S. Drew, 'Manorial accounts of St Swithun's Priory, Winchester', in E. M. Carus-Wilson, ed., *Essays in economic history, vol. II* (1962), pp. 12–30; D. Oschinsky, ed., *Walter of Henley and other treatises on estate management and accounting* (Oxford, 1971); P. D. A. Harvey, 'Mid thirteenth-century accounts from Bury St Edmunds abbey', in A. Gransden, ed., *Bury St Edmunds: medieval art, architecture, archaeology and economy*, British Archaeological Association Conference Transactions, 20 (1998), pp. 128–39.

The evolution of accounts is closely related to the direct management of manors by landlords. For an introduction to this subject, see P. D. A. Harvey,

'The pipe rolls and the adoption of demesne farming in England', *Economic History Review*, 27 (1974), 345–59; E. Miller and J. Hatcher, *Medieval England: rural society and economic change 1086–1348* (1978), pp. 189–239. On the introduction of methods of profit and loss accounting, see E. Stone, 'Profit and loss accounting at Norwich Cathedral priory', *T.R.H.S.*, 5th series, 12 (1962), 28–36; and D. Postles, 'Perceptions of profit before the leasing of demesnes', *Agricultural History Review*, 34 (1986), 1–15.

Manor and leet court rolls

The development and procedures of manor and leet courts are considered in Z. Razi and R. M. Smith, 'The origins of the English manorial court rolls as a written record: a puzzle', in Razi and Smith, eds, *Medieval society*, pp. 36–68; F. W. Maitland and W. P. Baildon, eds, *The court baron*, Selden Society, 4 (1890); S. and B. Webb, *English local government: the manor and the borough, part 1* (1908); F. M. Page, *The estates of Crowland abbey: a study in manorial organisation* (Cambridge, 1934); R. B. Pugh, ed., *Court rolls of the Wiltshire manors of Adam de Stratton*, Wiltshire Record Society, 24 (1970); W. O. Ault, *Open-field farming in medieval England: a study of village by-laws* (1972); J. S. Beckerman, 'The articles of presentment of a court leet and court baron in English c. 1400', *Bulletin of the Institute of Historical Research*, 48 (1974), 230–4; J. S. Beckerman, 'Procedural innovation and institutional change in medieval English manorial courts', *Law and History Review*, 10 (1992), 97–252; F. J. C. Hearnshaw, *Leet jurisdiction in England* (Southampton, 1908); W. A. Morris, *The frankpledge system* (1910); D. Crowley, 'The later history of frankpledge', *Bulletin of the Institute of Historical Research*, 48 (1975), 1–15; P. R. Schofield, 'The late medieval view of frankpledge and the tithing system: an Essex case study', in Razi and Smith, *Medieval society*, pp. 408–49; L. R. Poos and L. Bonfield, eds, *Select cases in manorial courts 1250–1550: property and family law*, Selden Society, 114 (1997); W. O. Ault, 'Manor court and parish church in fifteenth-century England', *Speculum*, 42 (1967), 53–67; M. K. McIntosh, 'Social change and Tudor manorial leets', in J. A. Guy and H. G. Beale, eds, *The law and social change* (1984), pp. 73–85.

A debate upon the usefulness of court rolls as a source for demographic history is summarised in L. R. Poos, Z. Razi, and R. M. Smith, 'The population history of medieval English villages: a debate on the use of manor court rolls', in Razi and Smith, eds, *Medieval society*, pp. 298–368; and Z. Razi, 'Manorial court rolls and local population: an East Anglian case study', *Economic History Review*, 49 (1996), 758–63. The nature and 'quality' of law dispensed in manor courts is the subject of another active debate, which can be followed through: L. Bonfield, 'What did English villagers mean by "customary law"?', in Razi and Smith, eds, *Medieval society*, pp. 103–16; P. R. Hyams, 'What did Edwardian villagers understand by law?', in Razi and Smith, eds, *Medieval society*, pp. 69–102; Poos and Bonfield, *Select cases*, pp. xxvi–xxxv; and P. R. Schofield, 'Peasants and the manor court: gossip and litigation in a Suffolk village at the close of the thirteenth century', *Past and Present*, 159 (1998), 3–42.

Useful case studies

The study of estate management in the Middle Ages has a long pedigree, both for individual manors and whole estates. The classic studies, which provide many general pointers to the historian approaching the range of manorial records for the first time, are: F. G. Davenport, *The economic history of a Norfolk manor, 1086–1565 (Forncett)* (Cambridge, 1906); J. A. Raftis, *The estates of Ramsey abbey* (Toronto, 1957); P. D. A. Harvey, *A medieval Oxfordshire village: Cuxham 1240 to 1400* (Oxford, 1965); J. Hatcher, *Rural economy and society in the Duchy of Cornwall, 1300–1500* (Cambridge, 1970); E. Searle, *Lordship and community: Battle abbey and its banlieu* (Toronto, 1974); B. F. Harvey, *Westminster abbey and its estates in the Middle Ages* (Oxford, 1977); C. C. Dyer, *Lords and peasants in a changing society: the estates of the bishopric of Worcester 680–1500* (Cambridge, 1980). Although not a classic study, the potential for studying unchartered market towns through manorial records is summarised in M. Bailey, 'Trade and towns in medieval England: new insights from familiar sources', *The Local Historian*, 29 (1999), 194–211.

Studies of individual manors which draw upon a good series of one or more categories of manorial documents, or studies of a number of manors based on a single category of document, are as follows:

Surveys and extents. Surveys are used extensively in analysing regional differences in medieval landholding patterns in each of the medieval volumes of the *Agrarian History of England and Wales* series: H. E. Hallam, ed., *The agrarian history of England and Wales: vol. II, 1042–1350* (Cambridge, 1988), pp. 594–715, and E. Miller, ed., *The agrarian history of England and Wales, III: 1348–1500* (Cambridge, 1991), pp. 587–743. Hundreds of extents have been analysed to distinguish regional patterns of rural land use around *c.* 1300: the methodology and preliminary results are considered in B. M. S. Campbell, J. A. Galloway, and M. Murphy, 'Rural land use in the metropolitan hinterland 1270–1339: the evidence of IPMs', *Agricultural History Review*, 40 (1992), 1–22, and the evidence considered further in B. M. S. Campbell, *English seigniorial agriculture 1250–1450* (Cambridge, 2000). The importance of late-medieval surveys and terriers in reconstructing medieval field systems is discussed in D. Hall, *The open fields of Northamptonshire* (Northampton, 1995), especially at pp. 42–50.

Accounts. The construction and use of a national database of agricultural land use, based upon information contained in hundreds of medieval accounts, is charted in the evolving and hugely impressive work of Bruce Campbell: see B. M. S. Campbell, J. A. Galloway, D. Keene, and M. Murphy, *A medieval capital and its grain supply: agrarian production and distribution in the London region c. 1300*, Historical Geography Research Series, 30 (1993), 18–22; B. M. S. Campbell and J. P. Power, 'Mapping the agricultural geography of medieval England', *Journal of Historical Geography*, 15 (1989), 24–39; B. M. S. Campbell, 'Measuring the commercialisation of seigniorial agriculture *c.* 1300', in R. H. Britnell and B. M. S. Campbell, eds, *A commercialising economy; England 1086 to 1300* (Manchester, 1995), pp. 132–93; and, finally, B. M. S. Campbell,

English seigniorial agriculture 1250–1450 (Cambridge, 2000). For examples of detailed studies of individual manors, see R. H. Britnell, 'Production for the market on a small fourteenth-century estate', *Economic History Review*, 30 (1977), 53–66; M. Bailey, 'The prior and convent of Ely and their management of the manor of Lakenheath in the fourteenth century', in M. J. Franklin and C. Harper-Bill, eds, *Medieval ecclesiastical studies in honour of Dorothy M. Owen* (Woodbridge, 1995), pp. 1–19; C. Thornton, 'The determinants of land productivity on the bishop of Winchester's demesne of Rimpton, 1208–1403', in B. M. S. Campbell and M. Overton, eds, *Land, labour and livestock: historical studies in European agricultural productivity* (Manchester, 1991), pp. 183–210.

Court rolls. The essential and indispensable starting point for court roll studies is Z. Razi and R. M. Smith, eds, *Medieval society and the manor court* (Oxford, 1996), especially the historiographical survey at pp. 1–35. The specialist essays in this volume are complemented by an equally impressive study of the law relating to property and inheritance, which contains much invaluable technical analysis: L. R. Poos and L. Bonfield, eds, *Select cases in manorial courts 1250–1550: property and family law*, Selden Society, 114 (1997). Studies of individual villages through manorial court rolls include those from the 'Toronto school' of historians, led by J. A. Raftis, *Tenure and mobility: studies in the social history of the medieval village* (Toronto, 1957); E. B. DeWindt, *Land and people in Holywell-cum-Needingworth: structures of tenure and patterns of social organisation in an east Midlands village, 1252–1457* (Toronto, 1972); J. A. Raftis, *Warboys: two hundred years in the life of an English village* (Toronto, 1974); E. Britton, *The community of the vill: a study in the history of the family and village life in fourteenth-century England* (Toronto, 1977). For a criticism of aspects of their work, see Z. Razi, 'The Toronto School's reconstitution of medieval peasant society: a critical view', *Past and Present*, 85 (1978), pp. 141–57. See also Z. Razi, *Life, marriage and death in a medieval parish: economy, society and demography in Halesowen, 1280–1400* (Cambridge, 1980); and M. K. McIntosh, *Autonomy and community: the royal manor of Havering 1200–1550* (Cambridge, 1986).

INDEX

This is not intended to be a full index, but to improve the navigability of the book as a guide to the manor and its principal sources. It can be used to cross-reference subject matter as a supplement to the Contents and Glossary. The introductory sections to each chapter have been indexed comprehensively, including people and places. No attempt has been made to treat the original documents similarly, although an attempt has been made to direct the user towards those which provide either extensive coverage of the relevant subject matter, or some useful example of it: these documents (listed in the Contents) are indicated in **bold**.

Fawsley, 12
fealty, 27, 30, 169. **37, 39**
felony, 180. **41, 42, 46, 47**
field systems, 4, 13, 23, 40, 42, 43,
   113, 192. **12, 13, 29**
fines, 110, 170, 171, 176–7, 185. **36,
   37, 38, 39, 40**
fisheries, 3, 7, 108. **9, 10**
fishsilver, 30
foldcourses, 6, 32, 176
foreign receipts, 101. **19, 20**
Framwellgate, 7
frankpledge, 178–84, 191. **42, 43,
   44, 45**
free tenants, free tenure, 6, 7–9, 10,
   16, 24, 168, 169, 170, 176,
   179. **1, 4, 9, 11**
   definition of, 26–8
fugitives, 180
full-lands, 28

games, 1, 190–1
Gateshead, 7
Gedding, Nicholas de, 7
Glastonbury abbey, 3
glebe, 5
Golby, James, 40
grain, 30, 99, 101, 106, 107, 112–
   16. **19, 20, 28**
   measures of, 133n
Gressenhall, 169, 177, 190

Hanbury, 9
Harvey, Barbara, 2
Harvey, Paul, 21, 105
Havering, 9, 10, 173, 187
hayward, 171. **37**
   see also officers, manorial
Herefordshire, 180
heriot, 30, 34, 36, 169, 184. **8, 35,
   37**
Hertfordshire, 185
High Ercall, 4
Hinderclay, 170, 175
Holkham, 6, 10
Holne, 7

homage, 27. **37, 38**
   whole homage, 172, 174
homicide, 180. **46, 47**
Hornchurch priory, 9
hue and cry, 180, 183. **45, 46**
hundred, 179, 182
   see also courts
Hundred Rolls, 6–7
Hunstanton, 10
Hyams, Paul, 191

industry, 114, 189, 192
inheritance customs, 28–9, 35. **4, 8,
   37, 38**
Inquisitions Post Mortem (IPMs),
   25, 43. **9, 10**
inventories, 18, 102, 109. **7, 19**

juries, 24, 176, 180
   inquest juries, 173–6. **36**
   presentment juries, 104, 172,
      173–4, 176, 182, 187, 191. **38,
      39, 40, 43**
   see also presentments
Justices of the Peace (JPs), 188

Kempsey, 179
king, kingship, 8, 9, 11, 14, 18, 25
kinship, 192
Knight's fee, 14–15

labour services, 24, 25, 27, 28, 29,
   30–1, 34, 38, 99, 101, 106,
   109, 184. **3, 4, 9, 11, 20, 31,
   32**
Lancashire, 180, 189
land market, 2, 9, 10, 12–13, 28, 29,
   36–8, 169, 175, 186, 187, 192.
   38, 39, 40
land measurement, 23–4. **4**
landholding structure, 41–3, 187,
   192. **4, 11**
Lanfranc, archbishop, 14
lease of manors, 12, 17, 23, 88–95,
   97–8, 106, 108–10, 115, 184.
   17, 18, 21

leaseholds, 36–9, 110, 186, 187. **21, 22, 29**
Lestrange family, 10
leyrwite, 33, 34, 169. **46**
livestock, 99, 101, 106, 107, 109, 111, 113, 114. **20, 23, 24, 33, 40**
lordship, nature of, 8–10, 12–15, 20, 41, 43, 105, 109, 111–12, 191–2
love day, 172

McIntosh, Marjorie, 173, 188
maintenance clauses, 37, 109. **8, 17, 18, 40**
Maitland, F.W., 9, 11
majority, age of, 29
maltsilver, 30
manorialism, manorial structure, 5–10, 15–17, 27
manumission, 34
Marches, the, 182
markets, 6, 101, 189. **8, 9, 10, 50, 51**
memoranda, 101, 104. **25, 26, 27**
messuage, 28
merchet, 27, 32, 34, 169, 176, 184. **4, 35, 36**
midland England, 4, 7, 8, 27, 112, 179, 188
Mildenhall, 5
military service, 11–12, 14–15, 27
mill-suit, 30, 31, 34, 184. **4, 8, 37**
mills, 3, 6, 17, 24, 25, 31, 99, 108, 114. **1, 2, 3, 4**
mineral rights, 3, 114
Minister's accounts, 97
    see also accounts
multiple estates, 11–13
Municipal Incorporation Act, 189

Neel, Richard, 10
Newton Aycliffe, 1, 7
Newton Longville, 186
Norfolk, 10, 15, 112, 169, 177
Norman Conquest, 9, 14

Northamptonshire, 12
northern England, 4, 6, 7, 8, 112, 180, 182
Noy, Edward, 40

Oakington, 169
officers, manorial, 1, 31, 33, 34, 98–100, 107, 109–11, 168, 169, 171, 174. **20, 22, 25, 26, 27, 28, 38, 40**
Osset, 7

parcenars, 42
parish, 6–7, 18, 188–9
parks, 102. **9, 24, 30, 39**
Paston letters, 110
petitions, 104
pillory, 183
Plawsworth, 7
pleas, plaints, 168–9, 172, 173, 175, 177, 184, 187. **36, 37, 46, 51**
pledges, 172, 177, 185–6, 191. **38, 39, 51**
    capital pledges, 183. **44**
population, 41, 190, 192
Postles, David, 107
presentments, 171–2, 183, 184, 190. **40, 48**
    see also juries
profit and loss accounting, 102, 107–8
proof, 175
Property Act, 187

Quarter Sessions, 188

Razi, Zvi, 167, 177, 192
recognition fine, 32, 34, 184
rectory, 5. **23**
Redworth, Alicia de, 1
Redworth, John de, 1
reeve, 31, 98–100, 103–4, 106, 116, 171. **19, 20, 26**
relief, 27, 176
rent, 3, 27, 28, 29, 30, 34, 36, 38–9, 98, 99, 109, 110, 112, 114,